MUSICOPHILIA
IN MUMBAI

MUSICOPHILIA IN MUMBAI

PERFORMING SUBJECTS & THE METROPOLITAN UNCONSCIOUS

TEJASWINI NIRANJANA

Duke University Press   *Durham and London*   2020

© 2020 Tejaswini Niranjana
All rights reserved. Designed by Courtney Leigh Baker
and typeset in SangBleu and Knockout by Copperline Books

Library of Congress Cataloging-in-Publication Data
Names: Niranjana, Tejaswini, [date] author.
Title: Musicophilia in Mumbai : performing subjects and the
metropolitan unconscious / Tejaswini Niranjana.
Description: Durham : Duke University Press, 2020. | Includes
bibliographical references and index.
Identifiers: LCCN 2019032734 (print)
LCCN 2019032735 (ebook) |
ISBN 9781478006862 (hardcover)
ISBN 9781478008187 (paperback)
ISBN 9781478009191 (ebook)
Subjects: LCSH: Hindustani music—Social aspects—India—Mumbai. |
Hindustani music—India—Mumbai—History and criticism.
Classification: LCC ML3917.14 N57 2019 (print) | LCC ML3917.14 (ebook) |
DCC 780.954/792—dc23
LC record available at https://lccn.loc.gov/2019032734
LC ebook record available at https://lccn.loc.gov/2019032735

Cover art: Publicity poster for the exhibition *Making Music
Making Space*, Mumbai (2015). Courtesy: Jugal Mody.

For Seema, and for Ashish

Contents

Acknowledgments · ix

INTRODUCTION
On Not Being Able to Learn Music · 1

1
"YAA NAGARI MEIN LAKH DARWAZA"
Musicophilia and the Lingua Musica in Mumbai · 19

2
MEHFIL (PERFORMANCE)
The Spaces of Music · 46

3
DEEWAANA (THE MAD ONE)
The Lover of Music · 86

4
TALEEM
Pedagogy and the Performing Subject · 128

5
**NEARNESS AS DISTANCE,
OR DISTANCE AS NEARNESS** · 162

AFTERWORD · 181

Glossary · 199   Notes · 205
Selected Bibliography · 227   Index · 235

Acknowledgments

My greatest debt is to Neela Bhagwat, extraordinary feminist musician and scholar, who has guided me through the Hindustani music universe since 2003. With her, I got my first glimpse of *sina-basina* training. Amarendra (Nandu) Dhaneshwar, whom I will dare to call my *guru-bandhu*, has been more than generous in sharing his musical knowledge and his keen awareness of the social changes to do with cultural practice in Mumbai. Neela and Nandu welcomed me into their home, kitchen, neighborhood, and concert circuit—for all of this, I am truly grateful. I hope they will not be too unhappy with what I have made of this book.

In Bangalore, the musical doors Meghana Kulkarni opened for me eventually led me to Omkar Havaldar. His patience and generosity with my constant questioning and my unmusical concerns have been exemplary, as is his knowledge of Hindustani music. Rutuja Lad, who began by helping me translate Marathi writings on music, has become—through my current India-China project—a spirited collaborator and a touchstone for musical exuberance. Bindhumalini Narayanaswamy, who came into my musical life barely two years ago, is already a strongly engaged interlocutor, compelling me to confront complicated questions. My gratitude to these young vocalists for allowing me to accompany them at least part of the way on their twenty-first-century journeys.

Surabhi Sharma, longtime friend and collaborator, is director of *Returning to the First Beat* (2017), the docufilm that was interwoven with the research process of this book. Without her intrepid explorations of Girgaum and her fine sense of how to hold a shot, my understanding of musicophilia in Mumbai would have been the poorer. Kaiwan Mehta's Bhuleshwar walks were an early introduction to the wider native-town neighborhood. He and Sundararajan Rajan helped me understand the significance of motif and detailing in Mumbai's urban architecture. Farzan Dalal was an enthusiastic participant in the *Making Music Making Space* exhibition project, and his design skills showed what could be done with very little money but plenty of imagination. Sohnee Harshey, co-conspirator in adventures linguistic, has finessed my Hindi and Marathi usage into respectability. Tanveer Hasan bravely wielded the videocamera when there was no film crew at hand, and alerted me to the nuances of Urdu and Persian terms. Shaina Anand, Ashok Sukumaran, and Zinnia Ambapardiwala of CAMP helped the interview footage find a spacious home on pad.ma, and provided neighborly succor during my years in Chuim Village.

Grateful thanks are due to all those not mentioned elsewhere in these acknowledgments who agreed to be interviewed for the research: Aneesh Pradhan, Anjali Arondekar, Anmol Vellani, Arvind Parikh, Ashwini Bhide-Deshpande, the late Aslam Khan, the late Babanrao Haldankar, Balasaheb Tikekar, the late Chandrakant Ramjibhai Mewada, Shubhada and Shrikant Dadarkar, Dayalsingh Thakur, the late Dhondutai Kulkarni, Farida Sabnavis, the late Girish Karnad, Girish Sanzgiri, Kalyani Puranik, Kishor Merchant, Murli Manohar "Shukla," Namita Devidayal, Nayan Ghosh, Nilima Kilachand, Ramdas Bhatkal, Sangeeta Gogate, Satchit Dabholkar, the late Sharad Sathe, the late Sumathi Tikekar, and Sumitra Samant. Nitin Shirodkar's lively stories about Girgaum defined how we began to think about the spaces of music in Mumbai. Deepak Raja's kindness in supplying music, food, and stimulating conversation was unparalleled. A special thank you is due to Lalith Rao and Jayavanth Rao for indulging my requests for music, photographs, and contacts. The hours spent with them talking about Bombay/Mumbai have been truly memorable.

I am indebted to Prasad Shetty, whose insistence that we apply to the MMRDA's Heritage Conservation wing set Surabhi and myself on the path to discovering Girgaum's musicophilia. Surinder Jaswal at TISS was an enduring source of support; much of the exhibition work was enabled through her visionary ideas about what kind of challenges social sciences in India should take up. Arundhati Ghosh and Sumana Chandrashekhar at the India Foundation for the Arts saw the potential of the collaborative exploration of music in urban space. Rajeev Thakker of Studio X was a generous exhibition host. Satchit Dabholkar let us enter Laxmi Baug and fill it with Hindustani music once again.

My colleagues and students at the Centre for the Study of Culture and Society, Bangalore, offered critical comments on early versions of the ideas explored in this book. Over the years, my questions about music have been sharpened through conversations with Amlan Das Gupta, Ashwin Kumar AP, David Scott, Ding Naifei, Nisha Susan, Poorva Rajaram, Ritty Lukose, Samita Sen, and Urmila Bhirdikar. Anjeline De Dios and Steve Ferzacca of the "music group" in Singapore helped me think through questions of pedagogy in Hindustani music. M. Madhava Prasad offered comments on the manuscript at a crucial stage, inspiring me in finding the right peg on which to hang the afterword. I am grateful, as always, to Mary John and Satish Deshpande for their solidarity with my projects, and to Ila Ananya, my millennial reference point, for being on hand to organize the *ghar baithaks* and offer comments on my *riyaaz*.

Audiences in Mumbai, Bangalore, Hyderabad, Singapore, New Delhi, New York, Berlin, Kolkata, Ahmedabad, and Hong Kong have engaged with my work and asked far-reaching questions. I am grateful to the Wissenschafts Kolleg zu Berlin; the Institut Etudes de Avancees, Nantes; Chua Beng Huat and the Asia Research Institute, National University of Singapore; and Stephen Chan and the Department of Cultural Studies, Lingnan University, for finding me much-needed time and resources (including the wonderful librarians at all these institutions). The manuscript has benefited hugely from Kristine Reynaldo's keen eye for infelicities. Toto Eunsoo Lee's visit to Mumbai ensured that her spatial aesthetic was translated into the architecture of the website that accompanies this book: https://mumbaimusicophilia.wordpress.com. My thanks to the three anonymous reviewers whose suggestions were a joy to work with. I'm privileged to have as editor the amazing Ken Wissoker, and am grateful for that lunch invitation in New York that eventually resulted in our working together again.

This book is dedicated to two people who are central to my involvement in music, and to my formation as a social subject and an intellectual: Seemanthini Niranjana (1964–2008), gone too soon, who shared my childhood traumas and insisted on our reconnecting to music; I will always picture her riding a scooter after her surgery, singing aloud as she bade me "do." To be able to sing (at last), she used to say, is so marvelous. Ashish Rajadhyaksha has been my companion for over two decades, and he is as deeply invested in my musical training as he is in what sense I'm making of it. I count on him to keep offering me what we jokingly call "loving advice." Without his constant encouragement, I would have hesitated to take all those risks that are so important and so necessary.

I AM GRATEFUL to the Tata Institute of Social Sciences, Mumbai, and Lingnan University, Hong Kong, for their encouragement and support of the research on which this book is based. The Cultural Studies Cluster of the Asia Research Institute, National University of Singapore, provided a three-month fellowship in 2016, during which I did substantial library work. The manuscript was completed with support from the Research Grants Council of the University Grants Committee of Hong Kong, under the Hong Kong Humanities and Social Sciences Prestigious Fellowship Scheme [Project Code: LU 33000017 (131606)].

Earlier versions of chapters 1 and 2 have appeared in a different form in *Cultural Studies*: "Musicophilia and the Lingua Musica in Mumbai" (32, no. 2, 261–85), and "Deewana (the Mad One); the Lover of Music" (published online, August 19, 2018). A very early version of chapter 1 was published online as a working paper by the Tata Institute of Social Sciences, Mumbai (January 2015).

Introduction

ON NOT BEING ABLE TO LEARN MUSIC

I always characterize my engagement with music as having gone from singing Christmas carols in my English-medium primary school to learning Hindustani music in my forties. But when I think back on my tenuous connection to the Indian classical performing arts, I dredge up memories from a childhood filled with books, looking for moments when music came briefly into that space where R. L. Stevenson's *Treasure Island* jostled with Enid Blyton's *Famous Five* series and Alexandre Dumas's *The Count of Monte Cristo*.

Was I nine or ten years old when I was taken to the house of a woman called Radha, student of the great Ravi Shankar, who lived on Ninth Main Road in Jayanagar Third Block? I have a faint recollection that her husband was a pharmacist—perhaps they were new to the southern city of Bangalore of the late 1960s. I remember her fair, sulky, rather unhappy face—perhaps they had come down in the world? Was it perhaps because of her marriage that her social situation had changed for the worse and she had to give music lessons? A sitar was purchased by my parents, and I was taken—was it twice a week?—to the teacher's house for lessons. This lasted for three years. I don't remember the music meaning much to me or giving me much pleasure. When my school organized a radio program, I played "Jingle Bells" on my sitar, and the teacher was appalled when I told her what I had composed. Perhaps the lessons stopped because of my lack of interest—on the other hand, perhaps also because of a family crisis when my father had a paralytic stroke, an event that made us rearrange our daily lives to a considerable extent and practice small economies. For quite a few years, however, the deep indentation caused by pressing down on the sitar strings remained on my left index finger. Decades later, if I unconsciously touch the pad of that finger, I can still feel the ghostly presence of the hardened skin.

My parents are long gone, and I have no idea why they wanted me to learn the sitar. For my modernist father, it could have been Ravi Shankar's rise to international stardom in the 1960s that prompted an interest in the Indian instrument made world famous by Shankar and others in the age of the Beatles and Woodstock. I still have two LPs purchased by my father at the time: one by Ravi Shankar and the Beatles' *Abbey Road*. The family went to listen to Ravi Shankar and his accompanist Alla Rakha at the Ravindra Kalakshetra auditorium in Bangalore once, and I enjoyed the glamour and the lively music, but it seemed so distant from my own feeble strumming that it was no great loss when I stopped, and soon the sitar disappeared from the house.

Two or three years later, in the early 1970s, on my mother's insistence my little sister and I acquired a Carnatic vocal music teacher, who used to come to our house twice a week. I remember him as a bald, elderly man, a few teeth gone, dressed in a much-washed white dhoti and kurta, who must have gone around the city giving a number of lessons every day. We learned a few *padams* from him, and sang them with more vigor than enthusiasm. Every time he saw us, he would say sadly in Kannada, "Katcheri maadsi bidtheeni" (I'll get you ready to do a concert soon). The lessons lasted barely a year. Giving the excuse of my upcoming high school final examinations, I persuaded my mother to stop the lessons. In hindsight, I think we girls did not take to the intense Hindu devotionalism of Carnatic music, having grown up in a largely agnostic home.

By the 1960s and '70s, it was quite common for middle-class parents in southern India to have their daughters taught classical music and dance as part of the cultural competencies that would better their chances at making a suitable marriage.[1] My own parents, who had come from poor families and were thus first-generation middle class, were writers and also socialists. They maintained an ambivalent relationship to the classical arts, which they would have seen as not of the people. Additionally, they saw their daughters' futures not as tied to a "good marriage" alliance but to

Figure I.I. The author at age ten. Photo: T. S. Sathyanarayana Rao.

things they might choose to do by themselves. And given that there was no one on either side of our parentage who had any connection to music and dance, there was no context in which we grew up listening to music or watching Indian classical dance performances. Late in life, I remember being quite bemused when I started going to Hindustani music classes, and the teacher asked me to practice at home with a harmonium ("Surely there must be an old one lying around in your house?" she had said). It wasn't that kind of home, I said wryly to myself, wondering at the post-midcentury assumptions about class, caste, and cultural capital embedded in that question, which was actually a statement.[2]

Two things changed my connection to music forever. This happened in the 2000s. I had been doing research on the Caribbean and had become increasingly interested in the musical culture of Trinidad. Responding to the beat of calypso, soca, and chutney, I fashioned a book on women, music, and migration between India and Trinidad.³ While the manuscript was taking final shape, I took an Indian rock-pop singer, Remo Fernandes, to Jamaica and Trinidad, with a film crew documenting his journey and his collaborations. Ensconced in the music studios of southern Trinidad, listening to the singers who had dominated my academic research as they recorded with Remo lyrics that I had helped to write, I began to feel a different kind of immersion in the waves of sound during the production process than that experienced when I listened to already-recorded music or even a stage performance.

Although I am deeply envious of those who can do Caribbean-style wining, that fluidity of bodily movements is not something my limbs can emulate. So the physical response to music, and the feeding back of movement into voice production, is beyond my reach. By then I was two years into learning Hindustani music, first in a rather disorganized music school and then in one-on-one training. I knew that my breath control was poor, my Hindi accent atrocious, my voice loud and raw. I returned from the Caribbean tour determined to improve my musical practice. I also began to listen to more Hindustani musicians than I had ever done before.

One of the by-products of my Caribbean years was that I became increasingly skeptical about the distinctions between popular, folk, and classical music to which cultural studies scholars are accustomed. The influence of European and Anglophone music scholarship in India, converging with early twentieth-century nationalist efforts to assemble national traditions, had reinscribed these distinctions onto the diverse kinds of music in the subcontinent. So after the 1950s, the description "classical music" was attached to the North Indian (Hindustani) and the South Indian (Carnatic) strains of music that became the staple of radio broadcasts in newly independent India.⁴ The twentieth-century classicization of the Indian vocal and instrumental music coming out of imperial courtly culture involves its separation from the folk on the one hand and film music on the other. The efforts at separation also bear the impress of the debates musicians had with British enthusiasts such as Ernest Clements who looked for descriptors of classicism in India to match those that had emerged in Europe through the nineteenth century.⁵

Historicizing the emergence of notions of the classical had the advantage of encouraging someone like me, who had been involved for over a decade in contributing to the critique of how nationalist/national traditions were assembled, to engage more deeply with the practice itself, instead of merely thinking about classical music as an oppressive and discriminatory institution because of the mainstream nationalist framing of the classical as part of an exclusive elite culture.

Foregrounding the practice rather than the institution also allows one to acquire an embodied appreciation of musical meaning. So just as calypso and soca music pleasured and stimulated me, I now began to respond to Hindustani music in similar ways. But unlike calypso, which I could not figure out how to reproduce through my own voice, Hindustani voice production was closer to the Indian languages that I was familiar with from childhood as well as to film music and folk music. All of these kinds of music—so-called classical, film, and folk—are part of a sound spectrum that forms the ambient music of everyday life in India. This is a reflection in hindsight on routes taken and not taken, and deciding to learn Hindustani music rather than Carnatic in adult life may well have been prompted by the childhood memory of not being engaged with South Indian music. Likewise the choice to learn how to sing rather than to play an instrument could have been prompted by the indifferent training I was given on the sitar.

One of the problems with coming to music late in life is that teachers tend to treat me as a mere hobbyist, someone learning music just to pass the time. On the other hand, people who have been learning music since childhood are treated as those who have the *sanskaara* or traces of that cultivation, who understand the allusive references to what *taal* structure is and how rhythmic patterns work, who shake their heads appreciatively with the right gestures and give *daad* or praise at the correct moments. I felt like someone struggling to eat with knife and fork at a Western-style dinner, watching out of the corner of my eye to see what the person next to me was doing. To this day I'm overcome by this musical shyness while attending a concert performance, unable to reconcile my own deeply felt auditory response with the kind of gestures that the confident listener makes. As he marks time on his thigh, raises his right palm upward and shakes the fingers, moves his head from side to side, and exclaims, "Wah!" and "Kya baat hai!," I shrink further into my seat, all punctuations and murmurs frozen before they are formed.

I never faced any difficulty learning the melody of a composition or being able to sing it with the right pauses. But the idea of improvisation within a rigid rhythmic structure was hard to grasp. I spent an inordinate amount of time mastering the actual compositions, which I treated like songs, as well as the precomposed sound patterns of the *taans*. I felt compelled to write down taans in the hope of being able to memorize them. I was afraid to switch on the electronic tabla, let alone sing with a live accompanist. I acquired composition after composition from different teachers and developed a nodding acquaintance with the scales of a number of ragas. At the point at which one must jump off the precipice and skim along, held up only by the undulating music, I came to a standstill.

I refused to believe that this was simply a lack of dexterity or confidence. Seeing the problem in terms of a psychologized "real individual" would not help me understand the larger issues: issues to do with the shaping of modern postcolonial subjects through the tensions between the liberal idea of the enlightened subject that is part of both our political common sense and our legal system in India, and the excessive subject exemplified by musicophilia.[6] What I do in this book, then, is use my personal story of musical struggle as an entry point into framing the research, for thinking about how modern urban Indians were seized by musicophilia over the long twentieth century, how through this passion they gained a new sense of interiority as well as an idiom in which to express it, and how their love of music is an indicator of a subjectivity that emerges through its immersion in the social.

The questions that bothered me were: How does one study or practice music? How does one treat one's teacher? How does the teacher expect to be treated? Should one never question what the teacher is doing in the act of teaching or performing? Why did all the touching of feet and references to godliness and devotion bother me so much? Strangely, I was at once both inside and outside this connotative universe—inside, because of having grown up liminally aware of it as a horizon of understanding and daily life for most people I knew; and outside, because of having grown up with political vocabularies of socialism, communism, and feminism, with their trenchant belief in human equality and their critique of hierarchy. In my home it was unheard-of for us children to touch anyone's feet, let alone those of our parents. What does it mean, then, for a modern Indian woman to learn Hindustani music today? I propose two kinds of moves in order to address this question: looking back, to understand the historical context in which this music came into urban spaces; and looking sideways, at the experience of others—teachers, students, music lovers—over the long twentieth century. I look at the spectacular experience of Bombay/Mumbai from the mid-nineteenth century to the present to explore why and how modern Indians became obsessed with Hindustani music.

Looking back and looking sideways, then, I began to resolve my anxieties about cultures of learning. Finally, I did touch the feet of two people, since they would not have understood any other token of respect. Both were female, both preeminent singers, both born in the very early twentieth century: Gangubai Hangal was ninety-three when I met her, and Dhondutai Kulkarni was eighty-seven. Neither was my teacher, but I continue to learn from their exemplary and single-minded careers. I treat one of my earliest teachers, Neela Bhagwat, now seventy-five, quite differently. She is a self-professed leftist and feminist, and complains that she is so democratic that she cannot force her students to learn in the way she wants them to. Our relationship is a companionable one, our engagements infrequent. This lack of sustained contact tells on the learning process, as I'm all too aware, and the focus has been more on accumulating, or learning many compositions, rather than on deepening my understanding of the music.

Now I obtain my *taleem* or training from Omkar Havaldar, who is in his early thirties but has been learning music since he was four years old, most of his teachers having been in their late sixties or seventies. He is my teacher, but struggles to find a respectful term with which to address his oldest student, while I use the privilege of age to call him by his first name. These days most of our lessons are online, and imbued with what I call Skyptimacy—a new intimacy between teacher and student that is premised on geographical distance rather than closeness. Technology, instead of alienating me from the learning process, has actually strengthened aspects of it. I hear my teacher's soft voice more clearly because he uses a microphone. He holds up his iPhone, with the display of iTabla's percussive beats, and encourages me to follow the rhythmic cycle visually on the screen, while simultaneously listening to the sound of the tabla at his end. I improvise more and more and with greater ease these days, and I have begun to understand how to draw on a repertoire of musical phrases to create a sustained taan. Through my daily *riyaaz* or practice, I have begun to understand that knowing, and not remembering, is what propels the maker of music.

And so, finally, I am able to sing.

Musicophilia

In this book, I bring together the notions of sociality and subjectivity to throw light on the performance of modernity in the non-Western metropolis. My focus is on the port city of Bombay/Mumbai, where the centrality of Hindustani or North Indian classical music from the late nineteenth century onward helped form a distinctive kind of aural community. The aspirations of this community impacted the way in which urban spaces were organized, as the love for music created a culture of collective listening that brought together people of diverse social and linguistic backgrounds. The book suggests that this condition of collective listening enabled the formation of a new musical subject, the musicophiliac. The avid listener, the collector, the event organizer, the student, and the teacher—all came into Hindustani music as nontraditional musical subjects. I argue further that their attraction to a music that became publicly available by the late nineteenth century and their membership in a community of musicophiliacs are the factors that fed into the production of the musical interiority foregrounded in Hindustani music practice as it moved into the twentieth century.

The elephant in the room in debates about non-Western contexts is usually the issue of modernity. In a lucid summary of the key propositions of the debates, Lawrence Grossberg uses the term "euro-modernity" to refer to what is presented as normative, especially but not only in modernization theory from the 1950s on.[7] Then there have been the critiques: It's one thing, he says, to argue—as Timothy Mitchell does—that modernity is not created by the West but in interaction between the West and the non-West. It's another thing to say modernity was also invented elsewhere (other or alternate modernities), and yet another to say there are alternatives to modernity. Grossberg is of the view that to recognize either of these would require the near-impossible project of the decolonization of knowledge.[8] The problem with either, I propose, is the idea that there is indeed a norm (euro-modernity) against which, outside of Europe, we could aspire to have alternatives to modernity or alternate modernities. Cultural theorist Madhava Prasad, in a trenchant review of *Consuming Modernity*, drew attention to how, in spite of the different modernities signaled by the Public Modernity and Public Culture project, there always seemed to be beyond these a Modernity with a capital M.[9] This problem besets even that most nuanced of contemporary thinkers, Partha Chatterjee, to whom we are otherwise indebted for a host of insightful formulations about non-Western political formations. In a well-known essay titled "Our Modernity," Chatterjee describes the subjection of the colonized in India:

> Modernity for us is like a supermarket of foreign goods, displayed on the shelves; pay up and take away what you like. No one there believes that we could be producers of modernity. The bitter truth about our present is our subjection, our inability to be subjects in

our own right. And yet, it is because we want to be modern that our desire to be independent and creative is transposed onto our past. . . . Ours is the modernity of the once-colonized. The same historical process that has taught us the value of modernity has also made us the victims of modernity.[10]

In my account of musicophilia in Mumbai, I hope to persuade you that the modern subjects of that city have embarked on what Kwame Anthony Appiah in a different but related context called a "less anxious creativity."[11] I borrow Madhava Prasad's notion that while there is a concept called "modernity," it can only ever be realized in nationalized forms, since both "nation" and the "modernity" that requires political formations like "nation" and "nation-state" are of the same vintage. So there are truly different modernities, spatially divergent, albeit occupying the same time of the present. Once we stop invoking the Kantian enlightened subject, we can also stop conflating the concept of "modernity" with "the practical reality of modern social orders."[12] Referring to something as "our modernity," then, would mean we have in mind quite a different set of ideas about political formations, governance, relationships between institutions, and so on, than those obtaining in euro-modernity. Since there is no evidence that the reference is working in all these registers, calling something "our" may only mark a moment of elite postcolonial desire.[13]

But then we need another approach by which to understand the specific features of national modernity in India (which this book does not claim to address directly) or that of metropolitan modernity in Bombay/Mumbai (which is indeed the backdrop against which my arguments about musicophilia are mounted). The distinctiveness of Bombay's[14] modernity in certain domains has been the topic of significant scholarship in business and industrial history, associational history, and the history of education, of planning and architecture, and of entertainment—especially theater and film. None of these have dealt with the subject of this modernity, although we obtain glimpses of these in fiction and in memoirs.[15] By the early twentieth century, Bombay—as headquarters of the Bombay Presidency—displayed many of the features of other imperial cities of the time: a city planning and governing authority, a judiciary, a form of political representation through institutions like the municipal council, a local bourgeoisie, a major commercial and industrial sector, an entertainment industry, hospitals, professional schools, an elaborate education system ranging from primary to tertiary levels, and a multilanguage and vocal press. Peopling this large urban area were migrants from the immediate hinterland as well as from distant regions in the subcontinent.

Aspects of Mumbai's modernity could be seen in new structures of governance and new associational models, even those that brought people together on the basis of caste, place of origin, and language. There were platforms on which participants deliberated on issues of common good and spoke on behalf of constituencies they claimed to represent, or tried to exert pressure on the governors of the city by making civic concerns visible. But alongside these platforms, there were others, like those that brought musicophiliacs together, that did not necessarily function as a space of/for representation. In spite of the efforts of music critics to deploy classificatory systems and popularize standards of judgment, evidenced in sporadic debates in magazines, musicophiliacs were not bound to follow principles of rational discourse.[16] Instead, the space they occupied while listening to music was one of intense and vociferous expression of appreciation and devotion. Often it was a space in which people fell silent because they were so profoundly moved, and where head-shaking or swaying or weeping—marks of what we might call "bodies in affect"—were greatly in evidence. In order to be able to understand the musicophiliac as a subject embedded in colonial and postcolonial modernity, I propose that we grasp this subject as a social subject and not as an individual in the normative euro-modern sense.[17]

The Metropolitan Unconscious

This book provides an account of this social subject, the musicophiliac, by examining the kinds of spaces in and practices through which the love of music is manifested in Bombay/Mumbai. I claim that in this city obtains what I call a "metropolitan unconscious," a collectivized unconscious that includes the diverse pasts and experiences of the migrants who came to settle here under conditions of colonial modernity from the nineteenth century onward. The metropolitan unconscious draws on all these migrant histories but is not identical with any one of them. These would include, in the instance at hand, both the hereditary musicians who taught and performed here as well as the people who made up the musicophiliac audience. Internally fraught with divisions of caste, class, religion, gender, and language, the musicophiliacs—fixated on Hindustani music—could sidestep these distinctions to create a community of musical affect. It was not a matter of transcending the divisions but of negotiating them in ways that had to be performed and not laid out in contractual language. I suggest that while musicophilia represents some features of the excess of subject formation in the contingent historical conditions of urban Bombay, the metropolitan unconscious stands for the sedimented repertoire of ways of living and experiencing that people brought into Bombay and that underwent transformation in engaging with the conditions of the present, thus creating a unique mode of being for musical and other subjects. In the instance of Hindustani music in the city, we see what Anjali Arondekar calls the figure of repetition-rupture, as performers invoke the permanence of tradition in the very moment of its transformation.[18] How does this imbrication of past and present occur, and what can it tell us more generally about subject formation?

Through Pierre Bourdieu's concept of habitus we see how "habitual actions" may be understood as "embodiments of an external field of social forces which structure perception and experience."[19] The dispositions provided by the habitus, says Bourdieu, situate the subject in a web of structuring and structured experiences. The habitus "ensures the active presence of past experiences . . . deposited in each organism in the form of scheme of perception, thought and action."[20] For Bourdieu, the habitus offers a "conditioned and conditional freedom," the limits it sets on present action having been set by "historically and socially situated conditions." Where the idea of habitus helps me articulate the sociality of the subject is in its reference to "embodied history":

> The *habitus*—embodied history, internalized as a second nature and so forgotten as history—is the active presence of the whole past of which it is the product. As such, it is what gives practices their relative autonomy with respect to external determinations of the immediate present. This autonomy is that of the past, enacted and acting, which, functioning as accumulated capital, produces history on the basis of history and so ensures the permanence in change that makes the individual agent a world within the world. The *habitus* is a spontaneity without consciousness or will, opposed as much to the mechanical necessity of things without history in mechanistic theories as it is to the reflexive freedom of subjects "without inertia" in rationalist theories.[21]

Here Bourdieu usefully challenges the idea of the Cartesian-Kantian free-standing subject. But in his insistence that the dispositions determine the discourse of the subject, who then "goes along like a train laying its own rails," he tries to stuff the significatory excess that is the very condition of subject formation into a box, as it were.²²

Bourdieu's references to Durkheim's discussion of the collective unconscious and his own mention of the unconscious perhaps point to his, and our, dissatisfaction with the congealed histories in the "quasi-natures of *habitus*."²³ Mary Anne Rothenberg, in a perceptive comparative analysis of the concepts of habitus and the unconscious, argues, "The *habitus*, unlike the unconscious, is not itself transformed by the encounter with the present; neither are past and present transformed by their combination in practices. The *habitus* merely enables a variety of practices, each of which incorporates past and present in ways that do not alter their meanings."²⁴ Rothenberg contends that only a theory of the unconscious, with its retroversive mechanism (the *Nachträglichkeit* or *après-coup*) would help us grasp the fact that "the appropriation of the present by the past works a transformation on both past and present."²⁵ Without the retroversion, Bourdieu's effort to show the workings of history actually ends up in dehistoricization.²⁶

Performance of Modernity

I want to suggest that we modify the idea of habitus for the present project as follows: the coming together in the metropolitan space-time of colonial Bombay of multiple histories and their already determined limits on future action should be seen as creating not a sum of their parts but an altogether new entity, the metropolitan unconscious, the inhabiting of which affords new routes and new opportunities for the formation of social subjects. Under conditions of colonial modernity and the subsequent assembling of a national modern, subjects render their present livable by re-visioning the past, but they do so—as in the case of Hindustani music—by drawing on a shared archive, not an individuated one, even as they engage in personal quests for listening opportunities, in building a vocabulary of devotion around their favorite musician, or in attempting to learn to sing or play an instrument themselves. If, as I propose, the performance of modernity was an imperative of this metropolitan unconscious, the passion for music opened up an important route to the realization of this performance.

Although the word "performance" in contemporary English indicates the act of presenting a play or any other form of entertainment, or at the most may refer to doing a particular job or undertaking an activity, in Indian languages the word for performance, which is *pradarshan*, refers to enactment and exhibition on the one hand, and to demonstration or showing on the other. Drawing heavily on the connotations of *pradarshan* then, in this book I use its translation, "performance," to mean: render articulate, make visible, display, demonstrate. I hope to provide ample evidence of this kind of performance in the various chapters.

In the period I'm looking at, Hindustani music moved from being a courtly art to one firmly embedded in the urban marketplace. New structures of patronage for performers included musical theater companies, the emerging middle classes who set up music circles, gramophone companies, and state-owned radio. The new audiences for Hindustani music formed communities of listeners who often tried to learn music themselves, through the burgeoning music schools and through individual discipleship to great musicians. My research is based on archival and ethnographic work (participant observation of musical culture in Mumbai and in-depth interviews with performers). I also draw on a range of primary and secondary texts, which are referenced throughout the book: business history, accounts of the opium trade, community histories, autobiographies and biographies, architectural and town planning history, theater history, recording history, broadcasting, the history of education, of institutions, of railways, shipping, migration, and of publishing and print media. To a large extent, the effort has been not to produce new facts but to assemble an interpretive framework that may allow us to address anew the centrality of music as cultural practice in modern India and its role in creating the excessive subject of postcoloniality. By and large, the book focuses on vocal music, especially the *khayal* as well as semiclassical genres, and touches only occasionally on instrumental traditions. In this, I gesture toward the salience of the voice in the musical landscape of Mumbai in the long twentieth century about which I write.

I suggest that the musicophilia of Mumbai's inhabitants over the long twentieth century gives us new material with which to think through questions of urbanity, subjectivity, and culture. Although the study is a deeply localized one, I believe similar patterns can be traced elsewhere in the subcontinent, and the relationship between cultural practice and the formation of the social subject can speak to many other contexts, especially in the non-West.

It is hoped that this book will impact a number of scholarly domains, ranging from cultural history and urban studies to psychosocial studies broadly defined. The foregrounding of a set of research questions that draws upon these different fields and the showcasing of cultural practice as a site of engagement in turn could create ripple effects in the fields by bringing in new issues for them to deal with. These new issues, in particular those that discuss prominent cultural practices like music, will deepen our understanding of how urbanity has taken shape in our part of the world and how that process informs notions of sociality and subjectivity.

Throughout the book, I am in dialogue with the writings of those cultural theorists, ethnomusicologists, and historians who have made significant contributions to our understanding of the modern trajectories of art music in India. Early ethnomusicological accounts of North Indian music include those of Nazir Jairazbhoy and Daniel Neuman, the former providing an influential close reading of formal structures and the scalar evolution of Indian ragas, and the latter a finely detailed analysis of the social ecosystem of Hindustani music as he saw it in the 1960s and '70s.[27] Although appreciative of this scholarship, my book is not intended either as a contribution to music theory or as an anthropological account of Mumbai's Hindustani musicians and listeners.[28] Nor is it, like the impressive work of Aneesh Pradhan or Lakshmi Subramanian, a comprehensive history of music and its institutions in a colonial city.[29] Rather, it is closer in spirit and intellectual genealogy to Amanda Weidman's remarkable book on voice and subjectivity in Carnatic music or to Janaki Bakhle's pioneering scholarship on Hindustani music and nationalism in Maharashtra.[30] Like them, I focus not so much on the music but on questions that arise when music is foregrounded in a social and political context, questions to do with modernity and cultural practice. These are also questions about the continuous repositioning of what the past might mean in the present and, importantly, how that past comes to be assembled in the process of resignification.[31]

The Chapters

Chapter 1 is titled "*Yaa Nagari Mein Lakh Darwaaza*" (This city has a hundred thousand doors) and discusses the growth of Bombay's importance for the singers and other performers who began to seek a foothold in the metropolis in the late nineteenth century. As musicians from different *gayakis* or styles came to Bombay to perform and teach, and later to record their music, the passion for this music, what I call musicophilia, became an important facet of the metropolitan scene. I argue that in Bombay the centrality of music from the late nineteenth century onward helped form a distinctive urbanity, manifested in how urban spaces were organized and how they were experienced by musical subjects. In this chapter, I discuss the emergence of musicophilia and how it inspired modern forms of musical pedagogy in Bombay, and—drawing on existing work on nineteenth-century musical theater—I propose the notion of a *lingua musica* to describe the shared language of the musicophiliacs. Through the shared language, musical subjects found articulation for new notions of selfhood premised precisely on that which was shared.

In chapter 2, "*Mehfil* (Performance): The Spaces of Music," I look at the relationship between music and the organization of built space and of neighborhoods in Mumbai, trying to understand how this arrangement creates certain kinds of audiences and provides locations for the growth of musical practice through both performance and pedagogy. Hindustani music maps onto even as it helps reconfigure public space in Bombay. The journeys of performers, listeners, and students take them into different kinds of spaces in different neighborhoods, and over a century and a half these spaces resonate with the music over which the musicophiliac obsesses. These spaces of music are explored through the experiences of members of the city's audiences.

Through interviews, memoirs, and newspaper advertisements, I trace the presence of Hindustani music in Girgaum, the native town of Bombay, over a hundred-year period. The chapter takes the form of a photo essay referencing the buildings and locations that still survive and that mark the contours of the musicophiliac public from the late 1860s to the 1970s. Interview material used alongside the visuals speaks about the personal trajectories of the musicophiliacs and the significance of the topological circuits each created for their musical experiences.

The intensity of the condition of listening to Hindustani music in Bombay and the several ways in which it is manifested are the focus of chapter 3, titled "*Deewaana* (the Mad One): The Lover of Music." The characters who populate this chapter include the man with the cassette recorder hidden in his cloth bag who always sat under the big speakers at every concert; the man who died of a heart attack soon after a concert he had loved; the Hindu landlord who was won over by a Muslim singer's brilliance and turned a blind eye to the alcohol bottles littering the apartment; the fans who followed their favorite musicians from concert to concert, even cadging invitations to private homes to make sure they didn't miss a single performance. The chapter title is taken from one of my interviews, in which an instrument maker described taking his actor friend to the performances of courtesans so he could observe the audience to see how "really mad" people behaved—the *deewaane* who were mad about music. Love and madness come together in the metropolis as a condition of subjective excess, the condition of the musical subject's simultaneous psychic and social habitation of modern urban space.

In chapter 4, "*Taleem*: Pedagogy and the Performing Subject," I focus on musical pedagogy and the insertion into it of the musical subject. I explore the formation of the musical subject through in-depth interviews with musicians, discussing the nature of taleem (a concept that includes training as well as practice) imparted to them and how they themselves teach music today; what the taleem has meant to them; what the taleem process reveals about the relationship between guru and disciple and how that has been changing; and what the social circumstances were in which people underwent taleem at different times during the twentieth century. Chapter 5, "Nearness as Distance, or Distance as Nearness," supplements chapter 4. Here is a discussion of the increasing complexities of one-on-one training and what the modes of teaching and learning were, apart from the formal taleem process.

The figure of repetition-rupture I describe in chapter 1 is always present in the interviews that provide the material for chapters 4 and 5. One of the ways in which the figure is articulated in the performative and pedagogic space is through the creation of distinction, through describing and reinforcing differences between the *gharanas* or styles of music that emerged by the twentieth century. "Gharana" is derived from the Hindi/Urdu word *ghar* or home, referring here to the extended family of students who are not necessarily blood relations. The extended family is made up precisely of those nonhereditary musical subjects who have moved from music appreciation to performative discipleship and are attempting—as they see it—to forge a relationship with their cultural past. This is of course not only a collective relationship. At the same time, it is the individual performer—the new subject of music—who is forging a highly personal idiom of expression with its own interiority even while claiming musical modes passed down over a few hundred years. The two chapters on taleem focus on the experiences of eminent vocalists like Neela Bhagwat, Dhondutai Kulkarni, Lalith Rao, and Babanrao Haldankar while also drawing on the memoirs of

Vamanrao Deshpande and Govindrao Tembe, and the biographies of Bhaskarbuwa Bakhle, Abdul Karim Khan, and Khadim Husain Khan.

In the afterword, I talk about the film and curation project Making Music Making Space, in which I set up a collaboration with practitioners in film, architecture, and design that began in 2012 and lasted until 2015, when our exhibition was put up in Mumbai. In 2016, this exploration of Hindustani music, urban space, and the musical subject was displayed as *Riyaaz*, a video installation in the twelfth Shanghai Biennale. The conclusion reflects on the interdisciplinary engagements with practitioners that helped make visible the musical subject at the center of this book, and the idea of the metropolitan unconscious that constitutes and is constituted by this subject. The filmmaker, the designer, and the architects I worked with were not simply picking up my research findings in order to tag their practice onto them. On the contrary, the ways in which they approached the question of what I might now call the social subject often pushed me in directions I had not envisioned while doing the research. Exploring the neighborhood of Girgaum with an architect meant looking at facades or staircases or spatial organization in such a way as to ask again what it might have meant for musicophiliacs to move through that precinct and how it could have been an integral part of their musical memories. Through the film shooting and postproduction, we grappled with representational issues relating to sociality and subjectivity. Our challenge was to represent these in the contemporary moment, with voices that were embodied, with performing bodies that were live, and to represent them also as connected to the entire century of the rise of Bombay. It is through the slow visual exploration of historical built space on the one hand and the intense reaching after musical melodies on the other that we were able at last to make the cut.[32]

Finally, a word about the form of this book: the bulk of the chapters draw heavily on the interviews my collaborators and I conducted from 2012 to 2017, almost all in Mumbai, with musicians, music critics, instrument makers, organizers, and music students. My attempt has been to explore the formation of the psychosocial subject, the excessive subject, not just through analysis, but also by letting the material seep through—not just through describing the material but presenting it, often with all its mumbling, throat clearing, and repetitiveness. At one level, I showcase the tropes of devotion to one's teacher, the brilliance of the singer, and one's love of music, since these responses invoke a vocabulary of appreciation held in common by musicophiliacs. At another level, I want to emphasize that the stock phrases are not a gateway to understanding but a symptom of the workings of the psychosocial domain, where ruptured past and tangled present are sought to be continually unpicked even as they are continually sutured.

1

"YAA NAGARI MEIN LAKH DARWAZA"

MUSICOPHILIA AND THE LINGUA MUSICA IN MUMBAI

The title of this chapter, translated roughly from the Hindi original, means "This city has a hundred thousand doors." To any migrant who came to Mumbai in the nineteenth century looking to take up or create new opportunities, the *lakh darwaza* would have been an apt description of the metropolis, even if the phrase from Kabir's *doha* (verse) was not intended as a reference to the kind of city that only emerged a few hundred years after the saint-poet's time.

Bombay/Mumbai in the 1860s was a city that the trade in opium and cotton had already rendered immensely prosperous. Apart from the British who had made it the headquarters of the Bombay Presidency, the city's population included Indians drawn from the western part of the country as well as from several other regions. The growing entertainment industry, primarily centered on musical theater, provided audiences with exposure to Indian classical music in its lighter forms. I argue that in Bombay the passion for Indian music from the late nineteenth century onward helped shape a distinctive kind of performance of modernity, which also manifested itself in how urban spaces were organized and experienced by musical subjects. The love for music created a culture of collective listening, in turn bringing people of diverse social and linguistic backgrounds together. As I describe in other chapters, the diversity was also one of class background, a feature of musical publics not often mentioned by other writers. In this chapter, I discuss the emergence of musicophilia and propose the notion of lingua musica to describe the language of the musicophiliacs. Through this shared language, musical subjects found articulation for new notions of selfhood premised precisely on that which was shared. What follows is not a historical account of this process but an interpretive one. I draw attention to certain aspects of Hindustani music in Bombay/Mumbai in order to make an argument about the subjective and the social in the context of colonial modernity and its aftermath.

The fall of Awadh in northern India in 1857 during the British response to the so-called Sepoy Mutiny signified the dismantling and dispersal of the princely court that had, after the decline of the Mughal Empire, supported a large number of Hindustani music's practitioners.[1] After 1857, the singers, instrumentalists, and dancers began to migrate to other native states, big and small, seeking new patrons. Through the nineteenth century, as Bombay grew in importance as a major center of trade and commerce, connected to the hinterland as well as to overseas markets, it became a hub for musicians—both vocalists and instrumentalists—from different *gayakis* or musical styles who came there to perform, teach, and record their music.[2] Musicophilia became an important facet of the metropolitan scene, and although it was not Hindustani music alone that shaped this musicophilia, it formed a hugely significant part of it.

New kinds of listening experience were made possible in a growing number of public spaces—the Parsi theater and the Marathi *sangeet natak* or musical play, the music circle, the music school, the *baithak* or seated performance in a wealthy patron's home, the music conference, the concert stage in places like Laxmi Baug, Brahman Sabha, or Muzaffarabad Hall in the native town area of Girgaum, or the municipal gardens at Ranibaug and Malabar Hills, which also hosted radio performances relayed over wireless amplifiers. Not only did large numbers of people listen to live as well as recorded music, they also began to learn Hindustani music in the proliferating music schools and in discipleship to specific gurus or *ustads*. In aspiring to the status of a performer, a singer or instrumentalist under the public gaze, the nonhereditary musical subject attempted to perform a specific kind of modernity which was called into being—elusively and fleetingly—through performance itself. By the performance of modernity, I mean the ways by which people began to inhabit new structures of feeling, to use Raymond Williams's phrase, that were forged through the experience of living through accelerated social change, and the ways by which they began to find embodiment for their social and personal aspirations.³

The two women "exchanging notes" on the early twentieth-century postcard shown in figure 1.1 (photographed in Bombay and printed in Luxembourg), which was part of the colonial circulation of images of Indians—I imagine them to be a *devadasi/naikin* and a *tawaif*. I imagine also that they lived near Kennedy Bridge in the Grant Road–Lamington Road area where so many from their communities made a home in Bombay. The naikin from Goa in western India and the tawaif from northern India are part of the influx of performers into the city's entertainment industry from the 1860s on.⁴ Both had an intimate connection to Hindustani music; both were responsible for its being perpetuated in Bombay city; but very little public trace of either remains today.

Now look at figure 1.2, created by designer Jugal Mody for the 2015 exhibition, *Making Music Making Space*, which I curated.⁵ To use Anjali Arondekar's telling phrase from another context, Mody's design both "repeats and ruptures" the older image.

The new image has the women back to back, suspended in front of an old Girgaum house. The tawaif wears headphones and spins a disc. In this contemporary moment, what survives is the music sung by the women, coming through the headphones, but the figures of both naikin and tawaif have disappeared in the visual landscape of Hindustani music. The naikin learned Marathi, went into the sangeet natak and then into the film industry, married upward, acquired middle-class respectability. The tawaif also went into films and lingered as a ghostly presence in the Hindi courtesan movie that crops up from time to time, from *Pakeezah* (1968) to *Umrao Jaan* (1981) to *Dedh Ishqiya* (2014). The two women no longer look at each other in this image, but they remain joined at the hip. My two women are important early figures in the production of Mumbai's musicophilia, leaving traces of their musicianship in the long twentieth century as well.⁶

To understand the metropolitan unconscious in Mumbai, we need to pay attention to the specific historical conditions that mark the city's emergence and growth. Social historian David Willmer argues that the position of Bombay as the second most important city in the British Empire next to London is due to its unique history of indigenous trade, commerce, and seafaring that existed well before the consolidation of British forms of governance in the city. Instead of calling it a colonial city, and thus falling into the associated dichotomies of traditional-modern, Asian-Western, or preindustrial versus industrial, he proposes that we call

Figure I.I. Postcard from a private collection, London.

Figure I.2. Riff on old postcard, by Jugal Mody.

Bombay an imperial city in recognition of its specific form of urban development. This development was a process to which Indians actively contributed.[7] Indian aspirations about how to configure public space shaped their decisions about what to support financially and politically, and their aesthetic choices—whether manifested in architecture or cultural practices like Hindustani music—drew on the complex and socially diverse repertoire that became available in Bombay City through the in-migrations of the nineteenth century. Although Mumbai, or Bombaim (in Portuguese), came into British possession as part of the dowry of Catherine Braganza of Portugal, who was given in marriage to Charles II in 1662, it remained just a minor outpost rented out to the East India Company at ten pounds per annum. In 1800, however, the opium trade with China began to develop rapidly. The shipbuilders and merchants who moved to Bombay came from a heterogeneous group, including Parsis, Gujarati Banias, Marathi speakers, Marwaris, Bohras, Armenians, and Indo-Portuguese.[8] The East India Company, which administered the city, encouraged a variety of artisans to migrate from the Marathi-speaking hinterland as well as from the Konkan coast and from Gujarat, and with the numerous petty traders these became the inhabitants of the native town in the 1800s. Later in the century, this native town, known as Girgaum, also became home to the new middle-class professionals and to musicians and performers of different kinds.[9] The Census of 1891, which showed Bombay's population to be a little over eight lakhs (0.8 million), also indicated that only a quarter of these were born inside city limits, and that the population was overwhelmingly composed of migrants.[10] About thirty years later, we see in 1921 an even higher figure indicating that 84 percent of Bombay's population had been born outside the city.[11]

Significantly, there was no dominant community in this city, historically speaking, and no dominant language, since it was populated by speakers of Marathi, Gujarati (Hindu, Muslim, or Parsi by religious affiliation), Konkani, Hindustani-Urdu, Telugu, and other South Indian languages, as well as Christians (who spoke English and other languages) and Baghdadi Jews (who spoke a dialect of Arabic).[12] The linguistic diversity of Bombay's inhabitants is relevant to my argument about musicophilia in the city, as I demonstrate later.

What was the connection between music and migration as it was articulated in Bombay? I have already mentioned that after the dispersal of the court at Awadh in 1857, musicians and other performers began to seek new patrons.[13] The year 1857 is only a symbolic marker, though, since the dispersal process had begun much earlier through the period of the gradual decline of the Mughal Empire from the mid-eighteenth century onward, leading to the establishment of different styles of music in native states like Gwalior, Indore, Baroda, Jaipur, or Rampur, where leading musicians occupied the position of *asthan gayak* or court singer. Princely states in the Bombay Presidency region also patronized musicians, with Baroda, Kolhapur, and Sangli being important centers, and smaller states like Jamkhandi, Ichalkaranji, Miraj, and others also offering a measure of support to Hindustani music. As historian Ian Copland has pointed out, the strategy of indirect rule fashioned by the British Raj or empire diminished the authority of the native princes even as it gave them a seemingly separate cultural sphere in their *darbar* (court), where they held performances by singers, instrumentalists, and dancers.[14]

The city's growing population provided new markets for entertainment as well as new forms of patronage. Musicians and other performers started moving to Bombay from the princely states or from other parts of the Bombay Presidency, either to settle down in the city on a permanent basis or to maintain a connection of some sort with patrons, colleagues, and relatives that would enable their frequent visits. They came to Bombay for concerts and other kinds of performances, for recordings, to teach students, and to study with their own teachers. There are numerous references to these musical journeys in the memoirs and biographies of early to mid-twentieth-century musicians like Mallikarjun Mansur and Gangubai Hangal, who traveled frequently by train from Dharwad in the southern Bombay Presidency to Mumbai; Bhaskarbuwa Bakhle, who moved around—from Kolhapur to Mumbai to Dharwad to Mysore and back to Mumbai, learning from various ustads; or Abdul Karim Khan, who moved from Baroda to Mumbai (with Pune and Miraj as other stopping places), although he kept traveling through the Presidency region for his concerts.[15]

An early example of musical migrants into Mumbai is the Muslim musician brothers Nazir Khan, Chajju Khan, and Khadim Husain Khan, who came from Moradabad in what is today called Uttar Pradesh and settled down in the city around 1870. They had been trained by their father, Dilawar Hussain Khan, and also received instruction in the Rampur Sahaswan gharana and the Dagar gharana, but established their own gharana in Bombay by the 1890s—the Bhendibazar gharana, with its own distinctive features. Although the origin of the gharana concept cannot be accurately dated, it can almost certainly be linked to the migration of Hindustani musicians away from the Mughal court and their resettling in various princely states, some of which have given their names to the gharanas as they exist today, with the other gharanas being named after the birthplace of their founder. The strengthening of this concept through the twentieth century can also be attributed to the attempt to name certain stylistic features as distinctive to a family, a ghar, or a home, at a time when there was an increasing number of people from nonmusical backgrounds, such as my musicophiliacs, apprenticing themselves to the ustads, who in a previous generation taught only members of their own kinship network.[16] Most of these hereditary musicians formerly employed in royal courts in northern and then central and western India were Muslim, although a few were Hindu. The Hindus were mostly first-generation in Hindustani music, although their families may have been otherwise involved in music—usually as *kirtankars* singing devotional songs—and were likely to have received taleem or training from Muslim ustads in one of the princely states.[17]

Musicophilia and Modernity

Hindustani art music in its many forms, I suggest, provides a strong affective basis for the shared modernity taking shape in Mumbai in the late nineteenth and early to mid-twentieth centuries. This affect is created through listening together, and listening to each other, and through the culture of appreciation—the *wah wah mandali*—that develops in the city.[18] The affect is manifested in the linguistic zone that develops around Hindustani music, where people speaking many different Indian languages and coming from different social and religious backgrounds converged in singing—and listening to—a form of northern Indian music that presented its compositions primarily in Braj Bhasha and other dialects related to the Hindustani language.[19] I suggest that an investigation of the city's musicophiliac modernity would help us understand the formation of the metropolitan unconscious in Mumbai. Included in the practices of this modernity are a culture of discussion, debate, and argument around music; writing on music in newspapers and magazines; the habit of following certain favorite musicians to listen to them at different venues across the city; setting up or joining arts circles and music clubs; meeting and engaging with strangers over music; and the incitement to learn this music oneself. I suggest further that these practices should be seen not as externalized manifestations of urban Indian modernity but as integral to the development of the social subject of musicophilia.

Historian Janaki Bakhle has suggested that this modernity was tied to a particular vision of religion and nation. According to her, successful pedagogues like Vishnu Digambar Paluskar (1892–1931), who set up the Gandharva Mahavidyalaya (GMV) in Bombay in 1908, and who systematized the teaching of music, were instrumental in forging and popularizing a sacralized Hindu music that could be called properly Indian as well as Hindu.[20] While this argument has been forcefully made by Bakhle, it does not seem to offer an adequate account of the growth of Hindustani music in the twentieth century. Although there were indeed efforts afoot to codify and sanitize Hindustani music in accordance with new nationalist principles, I would argue that if we focus only on those efforts, we miss out on certain sedimented forms of musical persistence that both create the context for the psychic investments of the musical subjects and provide the archive for their listening and learning. I use "persistence" in tribute to the way in which the musical *swar* or note lingers on even when it is not actually being produced, as in this story about the legendary Abdul Karim Khan (1872–1937) told by Firoz Dastur, whose guru Sawai Gandharva was a disciple of Abdul Karim: Dastur says he once walked into a concert hall in Blavatsky Lodge in Girgaum, and saw that Abdul Karim Khan was sitting on the stage with his mouth open, but no sound could be heard. Dastur was mystified. But when the Khansaheb[21] then uttered the *nishad,* the seventh or final note, it became clear that he had sung an open "aa" or an open "sa," and that higher note had been completely assimilated into the atmosphere along with the sound of the strings of the accompanying drones or *tanpuras.*[22]

The point I'm making here is that the formation of Hindustani music across at least three to four hundred years, with its diverse content and modes of articulation, cannot simply be reduced to a key element in the Hindu nationalist discourse that interpellates a new Hindu subject in the early twentieth century, no matter how popular Vishnu Digambar Paluskar's classes were. Musicophiliacs obsessed with musical persistence of note and melody don't necessarily harness that to the expression of a religious identity, and even if they do, that expression doesn't exhaust the musicality. An important example of a Paluskar student who became an influential teacher is B. R. Deodhar (1901–90), whose musical platforms were widely appreciated for showcasing the talents of performers regardless of religious affiliation or political tendencies.

Instead of looking at the public utterances or writings of the music ideologues V. N. Bhatkhande and V. D. Paluskar, who are key protagonists of Bakhle's monograph, we should focus instead on how musicians and musicophiliacs talk about and engage in performance, practice, and teaching/learning—*mehfil*, *riyaaz*, and taleem. In these sites we will find plenty of evidence of persistence, of the note that lingers. Expressing his skepticism about Bakhle's privileging of the communal over other kinds of distinctions, such as those related to region or caste, ethnomusicologist Stephen Slawek comments that to not account for these multiple distinctions in modern Indian classical music would result in overlooking "the numerous instances of Muslim/Hindu, Hindustani/Karnataka [Karnatik or Carnatic], Indian/non-Indian, and other kinds of alliances and dyads that have contributed to the direction Indian music has taken."[23] Whereas Bakhle seems to suggest that Hindustani music took a devotional turn only in the nineteenth century, Slawek points out that in doing so she disregards "centuries-old traditions of devotional singing that set religious texts to melodies based in raga forms, traditions that have a continuous history up to the present."[24]

The point Slawek helps us make is that there is a devotional genre in Hindustani music, and that need not be only Hindu in its manifestations. For instance, as Amlan Das Gupta has argued, if we look at the *bandishes* or compositions sung by Hindu ideologues, we see a good deal of explicitly Islamic devotional content.[25] In my own experience of learning music, I can recall several of the bandishes in the Gwalior and the Kirana gharanas which seem similarly Islamic but have been sung and passed down by generations of Hindu singers. Similarly, it is an even better-known fact that not only did Muslim ustads routinely sing compositions about Hindu gods, they also sang in the Hindu temples; there is a strong collective memory of such singers among those who follow Hindustani music.[26]

The relationship between teacher and student is always complicated, even without the additional factor of religious difference. Look at some of the friendships and mentorships in the Hindustani music of Bombay involving both Hindus and Muslims. Paluskar's student B. R. Deodhar's most intimate interlocutors were two Muslim singers, Sinde Khan (a fakir), who became his revered teacher, and Bade Ghulam Ali Khan.[27] Deodhar's relationship with these musicians lasted nearly thirty years in each case. The prominent tabla player and music composer Nikhil Ghosh had Ustad Ahmed Jan Thirakwa living in his house for nearly ten years during the late 1950s and early '60s; sitar player Arvind Parikh and Ustad Vilayat Khan, apart from being student and teacher, had a deep friendship over half a century, until the latter's death in 2004. My favorite story, however, is the one about the circus manager V. M. Chhatre, whose checkered career included an initiation into Hindustani music by Haddu Khan, founder of the Gwalior gharana, when he went to Gwalior to learn horse training. Later in life, when he had a successful circus troupe, Chhatre came across a man begging in the streets of Banaras and recognized him as his guru's son Rahimat Khan (c. 1852–1922). Rescuing Rahimat Khan from opium addiction and bringing him into the performance space in Bombay was seen as Chhatre's enduring contribution to music.[28] These are just a few examples among dozens that abound in the stories told about friendships across religion between musicians in Bombay and elsewhere.[29] All this complicates the picture enormously, and the story of the assembling of a national music with Hindu features is probably neither unidirectional nor the kind of finished process Bakhle and others make it out to be. What these intimate relationships across religion and social class signify is how musicophiliacs strived to create the conditions that would allow them to perform modernity in the context of colonial society. Through new systems of patronage and cross-class relationships with musicians, they ensured that traditional music became an important part of the urban Indian collective experience.[30] The formation of the musical subject in modernity is to be understood thus as the formation of a social subject, a subject assembled through the workings of the metropolitan unconscious that brings past and present together, changing both in the process.

Theater and Hindustani Music

From the 1860s on, when the first proscenium theaters were built, the urban experience in Bombay included the entertainment afforded by the musical play.[31] The history of musical theater in Bombay is closely tied to the nineteenth-century emergence and growing popularity of Hindustani music. Whether it was in the Parsi theater (first in Gujarati, then in Hindustani/Urdu) or the Marathi-language sangeet natak, audiences encountered melodies from art music especially through lighter genres like the *dadra, hori, ghazal, qawwali,* and *thumri*.[32] While the Parsi theater or the sangeet natak did not usually provide a performance platform for classical music per se, the songs—often numbering more than sixty or seventy in each play—were raga-based, both Hindustani and Carnatic, and helped cultivate a taste for the melodic forms of such raga music among theater audiences. Several musicians were closely associated with the theater, as trainers, composers, actors, and even directors. Film scholar Ashish Rajadhyaksha points out that the theater industry was "the biggest, most visible, and most commercial of the cultural economies" of the time, and that "one might almost see it as the Bollywood of the late 19th–early 20th C."[33] Thus the significance of the theater's intimate connection to Hindustani raga music cannot be emphasized enough for our argument about musicophilia and the performance of modernity. In chapter 4, I present the experiences of several present-day musicophiliacs in Mumbai who themselves became musicians. Each of them speaks about their knowledge of and admiration for the sangeet natak, and emphasizes how that performative genre shaped their connection to Hindustani music from childhood on. In chapter 3, I share a description, from the actor Durga Khote's memoir, of the affective space of the musical theater and how the singing moved the audience to tears.

Early musicophiliacs connected to the Parsi theater included the founder of the Gayan Uttejak Mandali (GUM), Kaikhusro Navrojji Kabraji, social reformer and Gujarati journalist, who also wrote plays. V. N. Bhatkhande, who became the foremost Indian musicologist of the twentieth century, is another person from a modest social background (his father was a *munim* or clerk, and he himself went on to become a lawyer) who was obsessively drawn to Hindustani music. His exposure to this music in adult life came through membership in the GUM and taleem from ustads like Natthan Khan, Tanras Khan, and Inayat Husain Khan who taught there, and he later went on to establish his own school, Sharada Sangit Mandal, in the Fort area.[34]

Many singers who later became famous as classical musicians began their performing careers on the Marathi and Kannada stage, including Sawai Gandharva, his student Bhimsen Joshi, Mallikarjun Mansur, and others. A major singer of the early twentieth century, Bhaskarbuwa Bakhle, trained by three renowned ustads from three different gharanas (Faiz Mohammad Khan in Gwalior, Natthan Khan Agrawale in Agra, and Alladiya Khan in Jaipur-Atrauli), was not only famous as a concert performer but also, from 1916, as a composer for the Marathi theater and a mentor of leading theater singer-actors. Bal Gandharva, the stage phenomenon whose career spanned more than three decades and was perhaps the most popular actor in the history of the sangeet natak, benefited from Bakhle's rigorous classical training but chose to remain primarily in the theater. On the other hand, his contemporary and colleague Master Krishnarao had a career not only on the stage, but also as a performing concert musician and singer on the radio, and as a film actor and composer. Ashok Ranade details how these two singer-actors established the contemporary *khayal* form on the stage, thus making it possible for raga-based music to be widely appreciated among Marathi-speaking theatergoers. Two of the most famous Marathi plays, *Swayamvar* and *Draupadi*, provided between them exposure to about fifty ragas and over 110 songs, while *Manapaman* had fifty-four songs, thirty of them based on Hindustani music.[35]

Although in the 1860s directors like Vishnudas Bhave put up plays in both Marathi and Hindi, in later decades this form of theater confined itself to Marathi only, even as the melodic basis of the music it became famous for remained the Hindustani music originally taught by migrant Muslim ustads. When the talking films in Hindi and Marathi started being made in the 1930s, well-known musicians like Master Krishnarao composed for the films and also sang for them. The connection between Hindustani raga music and Hindi and Marathi film songs continued for nearly fifty years, well into the 1980s, when raga music receded as a result of newer musical influences coming into film composing. The popularity of the Parsi theater and the sangeet natak over nearly seven or eight decades helped cultivate a musical literacy not only in the theatergoing audience, but also in those who listened to stage songs over the radio after the 1930s, when the theater itself had begun to decline.

Kathryn Hansen has shown how the Parsi theater depended on Mumbai's emerging middle class for its content as well as for its audience, and the same could be said for Marathi-language plays. University graduates and journalists were among the playwrights and actors of the first phase of Parsi theater, although as it became professionalized, the actors were increasingly drawn from the city's lower classes, and the audience too became diversified by class. Although benefit shows at the Grant Road Theatre drew a more elite set of spectators, regular shows played to a wider audience, and "the middle class viewers came to include more Hindus, Muslims and non-Parsi spectators, an outcome in part of the Grant Road location but also related to the companies' attempts to diversify the thematic content of their dramas."[36]

The widespread appreciation of stage music was one of the key factors contributing to the clamor for learning Hindustani music that arose in Bombay in the late nineteenth and early twentieth centuries. The earliest students who came to Hindustani music in Mumbai consisted of Hindu and Parsi men from the new professional class—lawyers, accountants, doctors, and journalists; upper-caste Hindus from impoverished backgrounds with a familial connection to devotional music; and women from the devadasi or *kalavant* (performer) background.[37] These women had moved to Bombay from Goa and acquired patrons among Gujarati merchants, especially the upwardly mobile Bhatias, who often lived with the women and paid for their lessons from the ustad. The Goan women were a substantial presence among those who apprenticed themselves to Hindustani musicians. For example, the three Khan brothers from Moradabad mentioned earlier are said to have trained fifty to sixty Goan singers.[38] Not all of them became as famous as Anjanibai Malpekar, the star pupil of the Khan brothers, but they did perform publicly for a living.[39] There was a reputed Goan singer called Bablibai who was Natthan Khan Agrawale's disciple,[40] and then of course there were the most famous of them all: Alladiya Khan's disciples Mogubai Kurdikar and Kesarbai Kerkar, two of the most prominent names in twentieth-century Hindustani music.

There are apocryphal stories about actors from the Marathi theater who would accept invitations to perform with their companies in Bombay so as to get the opportunity to meet the great ustads and seek discipleship.[41] Yet another distinctive kind of singer was the tawaif—a woman performer from the courtly tradition—mentioned in the opening section of this chapter, who was likely to have been part of the same post-1857 set of migrations that brought the ustads to Bombay and other places. Tawaifs set up *kothas* or establishments in Bombay in and around the Grant Road–Lamington Road area where they sang, organized musical evenings, and played host to visiting male musicians. Two very famous Muslim singers who frequently stayed with the tawaif Gangabai in the compound opposite Congress House off Lamington Road in Girgaum were Bade Ghulam Ali Khan, who initially played the *sarangi* in the kotha to accompany the female singers, and Amir Khan. It has been remarked that not enough credit is given to the tawaifs for carrying forward—through their own learning and their support for practitioners—the musical lineages that found such welcome in Bombay.[42] Tawaifs were often not acknowledged by ustads as their real pupils—they were taught by *been* players and sarangi players who had assimilated the music of the great singers while accompanying them during their performances.[43] In the course of the twentieth century, with the rise of the film industry in Bombay, women performers from tawaif backgrounds found new employment in the Hindi-language cinema, and kalavant women singers from Goa and their descendants became important figures in the Marathi sangeet natak, while some also acted in Marathi films.

While naikins and tawaifs learned both classical and light forms of music from the ustads or from instrumental musicians, what about all those—

mostly middle-class and upper-caste men—who were drawn to the study of Hindustani music? Individual musicians who trained a select few in their own homes or those of their pupils, or in small schools, coexisted with large-scale new attempts to institutionalize the teaching of Hindustani music, such as V. N. Bhatkhande's Marris College in Lucknow— established in 1926, important for our story because its teachers and students included a number of Bombay musicians; Vishnu Digambar Paluskar's GMV (established in 1908 in Bombay); or B. R. Deodhar's School of Indian Music (1925). One of the earliest institutionalizing attempts, mentioned earlier, was that of the Parsi-dominated GUM, founded in 1870 by Kaikhusro Kabraji (Parsi journalist and editor of the leading newspaper *Rast Goftar*, social reformer, singer, actor, and municipal councilor). In terms of smaller schools, we have the example of Balakrishnabuwa Ichalkaranjikar (1849–1926), future teacher of Paluskar, who was in Bombay during 1882–84 and started a *gayan samaj*, or music society, in an area of Girgaum called Phanaswadi, with eminent public figures like Mahadev Apte, the scholar B. R. Bhandarkar, and the judge M. R. Telang among his students.[44] An important feature of this small school was that syllabic notation was used. This was nearly twenty years before Paluskar opened the first GMV school in Lahore in 1901, which is often credited with pedagogic innovations such as the notation of Indian music.[45]

A number of music-teaching institutions and associations that engaged with music formed in Bombay, starting in 1848 with the Students' Literary and Scientific Society (SLSS), which opened Marathi and Gujarati branches later that year. Dadabhai Naoroji, one of the four founders of the SLSS and a leading nationalist of his day, later became president of the Parsi-dominated GUM, founded by his protégé Kabraji. Music historian Michael Rosse lists thirty-four Mumbai institutions across seven decades until the late 1930s, including, in addition to those mentioned above, Bhatkhande's Sharada Sangeet Mandal (1917) and Abdul Karim Khan's Arya Sangeet Vidyalaya (1918).[46] Although the decline of the courts and the increased mobility of hereditary musicians had already made teaching outside the family prevalent by the mid-nineteenth century, and this phenomenon was quite visible in Mumbai, more and more listeners also had some exposure to Hindustani music in the schools, which began to teach men and women from a broader range of castes and classes than was hitherto possible. By the 1930s, women who were not from hereditary musical or performing families were beginning to take up the serious study of music, aided in their ambition by the proliferation of music schools.⁴⁷ At a later stage, well into the 1980s, middle-class and elite women were taught in their homes by teachers who came there to conduct "tuitions," giving the women the privilege of learning from any of the several eminent ustads, many from the Agra gharana, who lived in Bombay at the time.⁴⁸

Confronted by European knowledge in the modern education system, which was formalized after 1835, Indians responded in two ways, both of which are relevant for the discussion of music in Bombay: historians and theorists like Bhatkhande, for example, pulled together and codified Indian knowledge about music and attempted to represent it along the same parameters as Western knowledge, with an emphasis on rendering the music teachable to larger and larger numbers of people. Others connected strongly to conventions of performance (mehfil) and traditions of practice (riyaaz) coming out of a different way of training (taleem) based primarily on oral transmission. The schools built their pedagogy on older methods of teaching even as they developed elaborate notation systems to help build curriculum in a modern mode. And it was not unknown for a music school–trained singer to shift subsequently to a guru/ustad for individualized taleem. However, oppositions between the scholar of music and the performer emerged during the course of the twentieth century. For example, V. N. Bhatkhande (1860–1936), B. R. Deodhar (1901–90), or Ashok Ranade (1937–2011) were music scholars who could also sing on the public stage, but they did not see performance as their primary occupation. On the other hand, there were performers like Abdul Karim Khan (1872–1937), who contributed to discussions on notation systems, or performers who played an important role as teachers in a modern pedagogic setting, for example, Nikhil Ghosh (1919–95) in his Sangeet Mahabharathi school, but such musicians were rare. A more significant divide in the performative space existed between musicians who were part of a *gharanedaar* (often from a gharana with a Muslim founder) hereditary musical background and those who came from the more pedagogically oriented tradition of figures such as Srikrishna Ratanjankar, B. R. Deodhar, or Dinkar Kaikini, who headed music education institutions. Then there was a third category of musicians who did not come from hereditary musical families but had obtained taleem in such settings or from those who had learned from the great ustads. This kind of musician looked down on the "school trained" singer as someone who did not maintain the purity of a gayaki (style of singing, usually associated with a gharana) but learned bits of everything, often to obtain an academic degree or its equivalent.⁴⁹

I have already mentioned that the music schools that started functioning in Bombay and elsewhere in the subcontinent attracted a wider range of students than those who studied previously.[50] It is by now almost a commonplace of critical scholarship that the "revitalization of indigenous music" was driven by the attempt to rescue it from its traditional practitioners, to renarrate the story by showing how music was written about in ancient Sanskrit texts, and to "reform . . . the social context of music."[51] Writing about music schools and societies in Bombay, Michael Rosse suggests that the concerned individuals and groups held the view, expressed before their time as well, "that music had fallen into the hands of ignorant, mercenary people and needed to be rescued by educated men of selfless dedication and impeccable morality. The primary objects were to revamp theory so as to make it 'scientific,' to replace the offensive connotations found in some song texts with suitably moral or devotional ones, and to provide wholesome settings for listening to and learning music."[52] These could have been the stated or even inferred objectives of attempts to reform musical practice and pedagogy, but was the rendering respectable of music such an overwhelming concern for a number of diverse people, and was that the main reason for their engagement with Hindustani music? Is this by-now settled interpretation able to account for musicophilia in Mumbai?

The rationale for reform, as represented in the writings of music scholars like Bhatkhande, might well have been to save Hindustani music by removing it from the decadence of the older locations of performance and spreading the appreciation of the music among a wider public—to serve as the hallmark of a civilized country and be a fitting response to colonial criticisms of Indian society. The reform rationale also appeared to have a strong anti-Muslim bias. However, as Eriko Kobayashi argues in a pointed criticism of the critique-of-reform narrative evidenced in Rosse's and Bakhle's writings, the standard history of music reform focuses on the ideology of reform and not on actual engagements between musicians.[53] Hence the reform processes—which often involved long consultations and debate between hereditary musicians and their interlocutors, and sometimes engaged the energies of the former who started their own schools and wrote their own books—"did not necessarily tally with reformist *discourses*."[54] This is clearly in evidence in the debates in Marathi, compiled in *Vishrabdha Sharada*, which cover a number of topics to do with changes in performance and evaluation of musical worth in idioms that have very little to do with reformist concerns about morality, propriety, or social cleansing.[55] It is not self-evident that changes in musical pedagogy were

Musicophilia and the Lingua Musica · 35

directly related to the social reform impulse that pervaded a number of domains in early twentieth-century India. My point here is that to dwell on this is to de-emphasize the affective reasons that drew people to music, leaving us with a reductive understanding of the rapid growth of musicophilia in Mumbai. This growth was triggered by a number of factors, and a crucial one, I argue, was the linguistic diversity of the city from its inception. If, as I suggest, musical subjects were social subjects, what common language did they adopt to be able to inhabit that sociality?

Lingua Musica

As Kathryn Hansen points out in her insightful work on Parsi theater, Urdu and/or Hindustani

> was not the first language of many Bombay residents. In 1864, the first official census recorded that Muslims constituted 20% of the populace vs. 65% Hindus. The Muslims were divided between the mercantile communities (Bohras, Khojas, and Memons) all of whom spoke Gujarati, and industrial workers, artisans, and cultivators, who were primarily Konkani speakers. Among the Parsis, who made up 6% of the population, Hindustani may have been employed as a lingua franca in trade, but schooling was in Gujarati and English. In addition, many Parsi boys attended *madrasas* where they studied Persian and Arabic. Acquisition of Persian and the revival of historical ties to Iran could have assisted in fostering feelings for Urdu. As is made clear in the play prefaces, however, knowledge of Urdu was lacking among playwrights, actors, and spectators when the language was first introduced on stage.[56]

The number of native Hindustani speakers had not risen very much by 1881, when Mumbai's population was 773,196, out of which 50 percent spoke Marathi as their mother tongue, 28 percent Gujarati (including Kutchi), 12 percent Urdu, and 1 percent English.[57]

Hansen also details how initially the Parsi theater staged Gujarati-language plays, with Hindustani farces occupying a supplementary role. Very soon, as the ambition of the theater owners and managers grew and the companies began to travel in the Deccan and northward, it became necessary in the mid-nineteenth century to shift to Urdu, "the cosmopolitan version of Hindustani," to reach wider audiences. The move allowed Parsi theater to draw on the prestige of Urdu as a language with a strong heritage of "poetry, music, and narrative" and helped "legitimize [its] theatrical practice through the appropriation of valorized literary traditions."[58] Hansen's proposition is borne out by evidence from the advertisements of the time. A notice of January 12, 1871, in the *Times of India* mentions the opening of Kaikhusro Kabraji's new play, *Jamshed*, in Gujarati; advertisements for both Alfred Dramatic Company's *Jehanbux and Goolrookhsar* and Victoria Theatrical Company's *Bazon and Manizeh* ("for gentlemen") appeared on April 22, 1871; on May 4, 1872, we have an advertisement for a Parsi Gujarati play, *Shahzada Airuch*, accompanied by a "very amusing Hindoostanee farce," by the Bombay Amateurs. *Benazir Badremunir* (1872) was produced in Urdu by the Victoria Theatrical Company, followed by the popular *Hatim Tai* (advertisement, October 21, 1874).[59] In 1873 and 1874 there were competing shows by different Parsi-owned theatrical companies of *Indar Sabha*, Agha Hasan Amanat's Urdu play of 1853 transformed into an "opera."[60]

Writing about how the early Parsi theater helped renegotiate social boundaries, Hansen interrogates "the notion that the linguistic medium of popular culture is defined by a pre-existing group of speakers who are presumed to constitute its audience or public," arguing that "the circulation of linguistic forms through popular media itself articulates social boundaries and enables the configuration of linguistic identities."[61]

This is a brilliant insight, one which could be extended beyond the popular culture domain, whether it is nineteenth-century theater or twentieth-century Bombay cinema. However, if it is to be brought into our story of Hindustani music and the metropolitan unconscious, this insight about linguistic forms needs to be slightly modified. Instead of saying that the circulation of such forms enables linguistic identities to be configured, I would argue that it is precisely the circulation and normativization of Hindustani musical compositions that allow linguistic preferences to be layered, so that a person engaging with art music in Bombay—whether in the nineteenth century or the present—moves constantly between languages in daily interaction but privileges Hindustani (which includes all the dialects it subsumes) compositions. It was common in the music schools of Gwalior, Baroda, Lucknow, and Bombay in the early twentieth century to have instructors speaking in Marathi to get students to sing in Hindustani.[62] This could, of course, be an indication that most of the people who thronged the music schools were either native speakers of Marathi or were fluent in that language, like Konkani or Kannada speakers from the Bombay Presidency region. But I want to extend this idea—of moving between languages in the engagement with Hindustani music—to suggest that one reason why some form of Hindustani became the main mode of communication in Bombay and remains so to this day is precisely because it is underlaid with the lingua musica that had become part of the cultural vernacular of the city by the early twentieth century. Musicophiliacs encountered the expressive forms of the lingua musica through their experience as theatergoers, as concertgoers, and as students in music classes. It would be the same cultural idiom that they would meet in its refraction through the music of Hindi films. The significance of film music based on Hindustani ragas in mid-twentieth-century self-fashioning, however, is outside the scope of the present book.

The very performers who had brought Hindustani music into Bombay—Muslim ustads, the tawaifs from the north, and the naikins from western India—gradually diminished in numbers in the performative and pedagogic space in twentieth-century Bombay. Only a handful from this direct performative genealogy still survive into the twenty-first century. Muslim singers like Aslam Khan and Raja Miyan (cousins who had stopped speaking to one another but lived in the same building where generations of Agra gharana singers have lived—Ruby Mansion on Forjett Street) have taught a number of Hindu students and the occasional Parsi student. Some of the women with kalavant ancestry—like Kishori Amonkar, daughter of Alladiya Khan's student Mogubai Kurdikar and her Gujarati patron, or Hirabai Barodekar, whose maternal grandmother is said to have been a naikin from Goa, and whose father was Ustad Abdul Karim Khan—have managed to render themselves respectable in the eyes of middle-class audiences and have found a significant place on the concert stage; others married upward and gave up singing. Some of the descendants of tawaifs eke out a livelihood with difficulty in the *mujra* halls.[63]

The music schools, big and small, still flourish, partly aided by the huge number of reality TV shows dedicated to music and the young boys and girls who want to become Indian Idol or its regional equivalent. And individual singers continue to teach a small number of students each, through personal one-on-one instruction. It is no less difficult today, however, to become a concert singer of Hindustani music. The training and discipline required for this is not hugely different from what it was when its first Mumbai students emerged in the 1870s. The aesthetic principles of the music and the way people respond to it have undergone small changes but still bear a close resemblance to what took shape in the early twentieth century. So although the social background of the performers might have changed, the musical styles and pedagogic practices still draw on the musical archive assembled over a hundred years ago when the passion for Hindustani music began to spread in Mumbai city.

I end this chapter with a comment by the poet, artist, and nationalist thinker Rabindranath Tagore, who complained about Hindustani music, saying, "he want[s] to sing about his own individual sorrow; but the moment he breaks into Hindustani music, he finds himself singing about universal sorrow. Where, he asks, is the place for his personal joys and sorrows in Hindustani music? This is why he says that he wanted to write his own poetry, to compose his own music, and also to sing it."[64]

The idea of the Romantic individual striving for self-expression and freedom from social bonds was a recurring trope in modern Indian literature as it came into being in the late nineteenth century. This was a trope central to the English education that produced the new middle classes, and the features of the modern person to be brought into being by that education included rationality, autonomy, and freedom of choice. Through their musicophilia, the modern inhabitants of Bombay—a city where the visual and infrastructural aspects of India's public modernity were so strongly foregrounded—strained against the social and economic logic that informed their lives. Instead of writing about personal joys and sorrows, the musicophiliacs vocalized Hindustani music, where the melodic structures hint at the rigorous discipline of voice and body that enables expression. The private as well as public utterances of this community of musicophiliacs might have invoked the need to compile and codify Indian music to resemble modern forms of knowledge and thus contribute to the idea of a national tradition, but their lived experience of the music included affective obsessions that culminated in wanting to grasp the notes and the melody, not just through the ears but also in order to voice them. Coming from different religious, caste, and linguistic backgrounds, the musicophiliacs learned to speak to each other through the lingua musica. The history of Bombay/Mumbai gives us a clue as to how this lingua musica took shape, and how it was central to the experience of urbanity and the formation of the social subject in this *urbs prima in Indis*.

Mujra in Mumbai: 2017

Words like *thumri*, *tappa*, *kajri*, or *chaithi* are strange to the ears of today's mujra (song-dance) performers in Mumbai. When we make a *farmaish* or request for thumri, the musician says, "Woh puraane zamaane ka tha. Aaj toh sirf semi-classical hi chalta hain." (This is not like in the old times. Nowadays people only want semiclassical.) The reference to "puraane zamaane" (old times) is not precise, and it cannot be. It could be the time when tawaifs began to migrate to Mumbai in the late nineteenth century; or the time during which they were an established feature of the musical scene, well up until the 1960s; or the time until the Bollywood-themed bar dance more or less replaced the mujra in the 1980s (until its ban in 2006 and the return of some dancers to the mujra hall).[65] The term "semiclassical" is also interesting. Precisely the very genres like thumri that classical musicians refer to as semiclassical or light classical are being treated by the mujra-hall musicians as classical, with the qualifier "semi" reserved for pre-1980s Hindi film music, which is strongly raga based.

The spaces for mujra today are shrinking, and this form might well disappear in the next decade due to a number of factors, including diminished patronage and earnings. The mujra performers are licensed entertainers who work out of a kotha or larger establishment with several mujra rooms, each room headed by a senior performer. They pride themselves on performing to live music as opposed to the recorded music of the dance bars. Each mujra room has a harmonium, a *dholak* (upright drum), and a *dayan tabla*.[66] Two male musicians provide the singing as well as the accompaniment.

On the night of January 3, 2017, at the edge of Kamathipura, the red-light district of Bombay, I meet Varsha Kale, the indomitable honorary president of the Bhartiya Bargirls Union, who has been a vocal advocate of women's right to livelihood in the face of the Maharashtra government's ban on bar dancing. Varsha Kale is a familiar figure to both bar dancers and kotha performers, and she has made the necessary phone calls to allow us to enter areas where normally only male patrons go. With me are four young women and a young man, and Varsha shows up with a female friend as well as two middle-aged men who have driven down with her from Pune and who maintain a studied silence throughout the evening. We all try unsuccessfully to make ourselves unobtrusive as we slip into Bachuwadi behind Varsha, who greets a few of the inhabitants. Bachuwadi, which has the appearance of an early twentieth-century *wadi*—a cluster of homes with a central courtyard—is a ramshackle-looking structure with a number of small eateries on the outside, some of which are shut by the time we reach there, which is around 9:30 p.m. An entrance not more than two feet wide leads into the wadi courtyard, in which there are about twenty-five separate rectangular rooms, each about twelve feet by four feet. Each one is brightly lit, and each has drums and a harmonium. Some of the rooms have multicolored lights arranged in a cluster or chandelier.

We do not see many people around and wonder whether it is too early for patrons to show up. But it is still rather quiet two hours later as we leave, testifying perhaps to the mujra performers' assertion that business was down. One of the reasons for dwindling customers may have been the Modi government's November 2016 move to demonetize about 86 percent of the currency in use in India. We had been scrambling about all day trying to obtain change in smaller notes for the bright pink 2,000-rupee notes that were being issued in small quantities by the banks. But the mujra halls seemed to have this sorted out. In exchange for a pink note, from a box in the tiny back room would emerge fresh-from-the-mint bundles of ten- and twenty-rupee notes. We distribute these notes to each member of our group and sit on the snow-white *gaddi* or cushion, ready to express our appreciation.

Sonia, the chief performer or *deredar* (literally, owner of the tent), in her early forties, chats with Varsha about her children and about how she has begun to put on weight. So even if her face resembles that of the film star Urmila Matondkar, her body is no longer as slender as the actor's. She also mentions that she and her colleagues are Khans or Kanchan/Deredars, a performing caste or tribe from northern India who identify as Muslim by religion. Sonia is wearing a *churidar* and *anarkali* kurta in pale pink imitation georgette or chiffon with gold-colored trimmings. The sleeves are of translucent pink net. Her hair is simply secured with hairpins, and she is wearing some light foundation and blush, and lightly applied lipstick. Her eyes are enhanced with mascara. Another slightly younger woman dressed in a similarly styled black-and-red outfit is applying her makeup when we come in and continues doing so for a good twenty minutes without looking at us once. The four younger women, including the one who comes in last from her dance-bar job, are dressed in sleeveless strappy blouses and synthetic saris (bright red orange, dark green, bright blue). Two have *mangalsutra*s and one wears a big red bindi. The latter speaks about how she has just come back from her hometown after Moharram, the Muslim commemoration of the death of Husayn, the Prophet's grandson.

The musician with the drums starts singing in a loud and somewhat rough voice, a Jagjit Singh ghazal: "Honton se choo lo tum, mera geet amar kar do" (Touch with your lips, make my song immortal). The female performers sing this along with the male musicians, while Sonia, who has tied *ghunghroo*s to her feet, taps them to the rhythm too. There seems to be only one pair of ghunghroos that is being passed around to whichever dancer wants to wear them. (Our speculation: these were only for more old-style mujra dancing, performed by farmaish or request only, and not for the perhaps more popular contemporary Bollywood dance.) After one more song, Sonia asks whether we want to see some dancing too. After our enthusiastic yes, she proclaims that she will make us dance too. We all squirm a bit, unsure what it will involve. As if to reassure us, Sonia says, "Idhar kuch bhi nahin hota. Sirf dance" (Nothing at all happens here, except dance). She insists that there is no serving of alcohol on the premises, and "nothing else" happens apart from the mujra. The last assertion is perhaps aimed at public perception that associates these spaces with sex work.

The musicians start intoning, "Chandi jaisa rang hai tera, soni jaise baal" (Your complexion is like silver, your hair like gold). Sonia gets to her feet and breaks into a Kathak-inspired step. She keeps pulling out female members of our group to dance with her, twirling them around by the hand. She is followed by the dancer in red and black, who takes the ghunghroos from Sonia, and then by the younger dancers, who do faster numbers, often flinging their heads and long hair front to back and also shimmying, as in belly dancing. Sonia and the other woman in churidar kurta are adept at *adaakaari*—facial expressions and hand gestures—and make eye contact with their audience. The younger women, perhaps used to the different performative idiom of the bar dance as opposed to that of the kotha, are almost expressionless, and watch themselves in the mirror behind us as they dance. All of us take turns handing a sheaf of small bills to each dancer after a particularly vigorous sequence, and the money is handed to those dancers who are sitting. When we give money to the musicians, they tuck it away under the sheet on which they are seated. A tea supplier had come in earlier, and we are all served sweet milky tea in small glasses. At some point, a man comes dancing in, *gajras* or strings of jasmine flowers dangling from one arm, and holding a bunch of red roses in the other. Varsha's friend buys the roses, and we purchase the gajras, to be tied around each of our wrists.

One by one the dancers perform to film songs emphasizing the cruelty of the lover, the hopelessness of love, the sorrow of one who cannot reach the destination. One song begins with the line "Aasman se utara gaya, Zindagi deke mara gaya" (I was brought down from the sky with a promise of life, but I was killed instead), and goes on to say, "The one who dares to love should know that he will die an untimely death. If death does not kill you, love certainly will."[67]

Another fifteen songs later, each one lasting five to six minutes, we get up to take our leave. It is nearly 11:30 p.m., the official time by which the mujra halls have to close. Sonia and her girls pose with us for selfies, although the others are more reticent about being in the frame. On Varsha's advice, we have not taken any pictures or videos throughout the performance. Sonia wants us all to return for her birthday in early February.

Outside, we stand around giggling with the gajras on our wrists, until we hail *kaali-peeli* taxis to take us to Congress House, fifteen minutes away, off Grant Road. Once again, we follow Varsha Kale into the NB Compound, outside which I have lurked a dozen times in the daytime, trying to see what was inside. Here too the place is rather quiet, with the performers looking over the balconies or sitting on charpoys, chatting. We can see three buildings of three stories each, interconnected in a C shape. Varsha is asking about Dhanno, whom she had contacted. Three women are sitting on a charpoy to the right of the compound, and one of them—Ruby—recognizes Varsha and invites us into her kotha. Varsha tells us that Ruby is a fine dancer and that she, Varsha, had brought Shiamak Davar, the renowned Bollywood choreographer and dance instructor, to meet her. Davar had reportedly been enchanted with Ruby and had asked her to get in touch so they could work together, but Ruby never followed up.

As in Bachuwadi, we are offered *kuch thanda* (something cold, meaning cold soft drinks) or tea. We settle for water, which is handed to us in individual Bisleri bottles by the youngest woman. We are told the musicians have gone to perform at a wedding and are expected back any moment. When they finally arrive, it is well past midnight—two men in their late twenties, much younger and better dressed than the ones in Bachuwadi. The mujra room too is bigger and cleaner than the Foras Road place. One wall is painted a bright red, and another wall is completely covered with a mirror. There is a tiny curtained space at the back where the dancers go to change their costumes. White gaddis line both sides of the rectangular room, about fourteen feet by six feet, and we distribute ourselves on either side. The space in which the dancer performs is just three feet by six feet. As we wait for the musicians, we start talking to a sari-clad performer who tells us business is really bad. She considered employment as a bar dancer, but when she saw the audience there she decided not to go there again. Having always been in the Compound, she couldn't think of living another kind of life.

The musicians tune up, and Ruby begins to dance with fluid movements of feet and hands, to a song from the 2006 film *Umrao Jaan*, starring Rekha, about a tawaif in Lucknow: "In aankhon ki masti ke, mastaane hazaaron hai" (These eyes, with their intoxicating beauty, attract admirers by the thousands). Ruby's round, smoothly made-up face, however, is without much expression, and although she puts her green *dupatta* on her head, and winks at me from under it, it is a peculiarly de-eroticized wink. Unlike Sonia in Bachuwadi with her mobile face, all of Ruby's energy seems to go into whirling instead, her deep green patchwork anarkali kurta twirling around her, the *latkaan* (metal globes) tied to her dupatta flying in all directions. Occasionally she drops to the floor and glides toward her audience, gesturing with her hand.[68] Here we all take to throwing bills into the air, so that they also get under the dancers' feet. The performer who is sitting it out scoops the money into a plastic basket.

We ask the musicians for a thumri, and they want us to tell them which lyrics. "Mohe panghat par," I venture, adding "From *Mughal-e-Azam*." I am hoping that the 1960 film will be a more familiar reference point than the abstract mention of a genre that would have been performed in the NB Compound in the early to mid-twentieth century. After that, we start naming old Hindi films like *Anarkali* (1953) and *Pakeezah* (1972), which have tawaif characters. The kotha resounds with Ruby's ghunghroos and the melody of the *Anarkali* song, "Jab pyaar kiya toh daarna kya, jab pyaar kiya toh darna kya, Pyaar kiya koi chori nahi ki, chhup chhup aahein bharna kya." (Why be afraid if you have loved? You have been in love, not committed a crime. Why weep in secret?) The mirrored wall reflects Ruby's whirling figure, so it seems like there are two identically dressed green dancers moving at once.

The closest we come to a raunchy number is when the youngest dancer performs to "Laila main Laila, aisi hoon Laila / Har koi chahe mujhse milna akela" (I am Laila. I'm such a beauty that everyone wants to meet me alone), which had been performed in Bachuwadi also. What we couldn't determine on our short visit to the kothas is whether the repertoire we saw and heard was the common one, or whether the regular clients requested other songs. How much the mujra repertoire has changed over the twentieth century and in what ways the styles of performance have changed are hard to document, and much more needs to be understood about the transition from mujra to bar dancing and the way the latter affects the former.

The last item, by our farmaish or request, is a well-known ghazal: "Aaj jaane ki zid na karo" (Tonight don't insist on leaving). By the time we come out of Ruby's kotha, it is almost 1:30 a.m. The iron gate of the Bombay Sangeet Kalakaar Sangh is shut, with a smaller inset gate open in the center to let patrons out and residents in. Policemen from the nearby *chowki* are walking up and down. Taxis are readily available, especially because many have just arrived to drop off glamorously dressed young women returning home to the Compound, perhaps from their jobs as bar dancers or escorts.

We return to the hotel, but I am unable to sleep. We should have stayed longer in the kotha. We should have found more threads of conversation in which to engage, rather than experiencing an acute ethnographitis of the tongue.[69] "Kal ki kisko khabar jaan-e-jaan, rok lo aaj ki raat ko, aaj jaane ki zid na karo" (Who knows what tomorrow holds, but tonight—stop this night, tonight don't insist on leaving).

As we stood up to leave, Ruby had almost aggressively asked me to sing. It felt like a mocking challenge to the rank amateur from the professional performer. My reluctance as I feebly said "next time" could be read as my own difficulty in untangling the long history of how middle-class pleasures and subjectivities emerged and became entrenched precisely through the making invisible of figures such as the tawaif. This figure resurfaces in chapters 2 and 3, which discuss the spaces of music and the formation of Mumbai's musicophilia.

2

MEHFIL (PERFORMANCE)
THE SPACES OF MUSIC

When Surabhi Sharma and I began filming our documentary on Hindustani music in Mumbai, described in the afterword to this book, almost immediately we encountered a rather serious representational problem. All those spaces in Girgaum and elsewhere that people spoke about in connection with their memories of music were today empty and unused, or used for purposes other than music making, or lay in ruins. How then to shoot the spaces in such a way that despite their present state the past was also part of the frame? How to layer the visual image and the aural landscape of the present so that the past resonated through it? How to fill the space of the mehfil with voices from across the century without simply adding a soundtrack of musical masters? How, above all, to represent the deeply felt musicophilia invoked by each mehfil space? While the empty spaces of music in Girgaum posed one kind of problem for cinematic representation, they posed yet another for writing. Yet the provisional solution sought by both filmmaker and academic was similar. Each of us used a process of layering, of drawing attention to iterative histories of performance in the same area.

In this chapter, I pull together the discursive strands around the experience of music in specific spaces to create a sense of how the musicophiliac subject was formed. I look at the relationship between Hindustani music and the organization of built space and of neighborhoods in Mumbai, trying to understand how this arrangement constructs certain forms of sociality and provides locations for the growth of musical practice through both performance and pedagogy. Hindustani music, I suggest, maps onto even as it helps reconfigure urban space in Mumbai. The journeys of performers, listeners, and students take them into different kinds of spaces in different neighborhoods, and over a century and a half these spaces have resonated with the music over which the musicophiliac obsesses. While these are social spaces, in the sense of being occupied by several people at the same time who have come together for a specific purpose—to listen to a concert—I want to also present them here as spaces where the listener experiences music in an intensely intimate fashion. This is not to say that they are first one and then the other, but that the spaces of music listening are actually psychosocial spaces, and that the topology of the listening circuit is also a topology of the mind.

I focus here on the Girgaum area—the former native town (broadly defined to include Kalbadevi, Thakurdwar, Jagannath Shankarseth Road, Lamington Road, Grant Road, Foras Road, Kennedy Bridge, Phanaswadi, French Bridge, and stretching up to Forjett Street and Nana Chowk)— which was home to the Parsi theater, the Marathi sangeet natak, Hindustani art music, and light genres like thumri and qawwali. Girgaum was also the earliest location to have music schools, music clubs, concert halls, and wadis where musicians were invited to perform. The chapter takes the form of a photo essay referencing the buildings and locations that still survive and that help us mark the contours of the musicophiliac circuit from the late 1860s to the 1970s. The material from my interviews used alongside the visuals speaks about the personal trajectories of the musicophiliacs and the significance of the topological circuit each created for their musical experiences. Each space of music on the circuit is explored through the experiences of members of the city's audiences, gleaned from biographies, memoirs, and interviews. As Doreen Massey suggests, space is constituted through interaction and can itself be the unfolding of interaction.[1] Here in Mumbai, the significance of a space assembled through the interaction of musicophiliacs acquires density also through the iterative history of performativity in that space. Memory, more specifically the invocation of musical memory, is presented as the most significant topos—understood both as motif and place or site—for how a particular location is understood looking back. Through this looking back, the present space also acquires a different significance, just as the past too is reassembled. The metropolitan unconscious of the musicophiliac is palpable in this gesture.

USING MAP 2.1, which I put together, let's begin our walk through Girgaum at the Opera House crossroads, where turning left would take us to the Arabian Sea at Chowpatty Beach, turning right would lead us into the heart of Girgaum and eventually Bhuleshwar, and going straight would take us to Kennedy Bridge and Congress House.[2] As we stand at the intersection, the imposing baroque facade of the newly renovated Opera House looms up on our left. We are standing on Charni Road outside the Opera House, and behind us is the Fort area. The construction of the building was completed in 1912, in what architects describe as a blend of European and Indian architectural styles. The baroque elements were tempered in later years by art deco features that were also restored during the renovation project. The Opera House can be said to mark the boundary of the native town with the Fort area, and true to its liminal status it hosted performances of Western plays and variety shows as well as Bal Gandharva's Marathi sangeet natak and Prithviraj Kapoor's plays. Occasionally it hosted Hindustani music concerts, like the one described in a 1929 advertisement for "Miss Hirabai's Concerts." The "Bombay public" was promised the "rare opportunity to hear high class Indian music" at the Royal Opera House on Wednesday, April 7, at 9:30 p.m., and on Thursday at 9 p.m. Miss Hirabai was "reputed to be an accomplished artiste with a rich voice and well-versed in the scientific system of Indian singing."[3]

Through that decade and the next, such concerts were regularly held at the Opera House, which also screened films such as those from the Pathé company during that time. However, from 1935 on, with the rise of talking films, the Opera House became a major cinema as well.

If a musicophiliac had gone to listen to Miss Hirabai in 1929, he would have passed through the foyer under the crystal chandeliers donated by the David Sassoon family, Baghdadi Jews who made their fortune in Bombay and subsequently built a real estate empire in Shanghai.[4] He would have made himself comfortable in his cane chair in the stalls as the tanpuras were tuned, taken in the ornate carvings on the dome, and shook his head appreciatively as Hirabai began a slow *alaap*, her clear voice filling the hall without a microphone. He had heard her last perhaps in an impromptu performance at the Deodhar School across the road; in that school's annual *barsi* or death anniversary concert organized at Laxmi Baug in the

Map 2.1. Google Map of locations connected to music in the "native town," Mumbai.

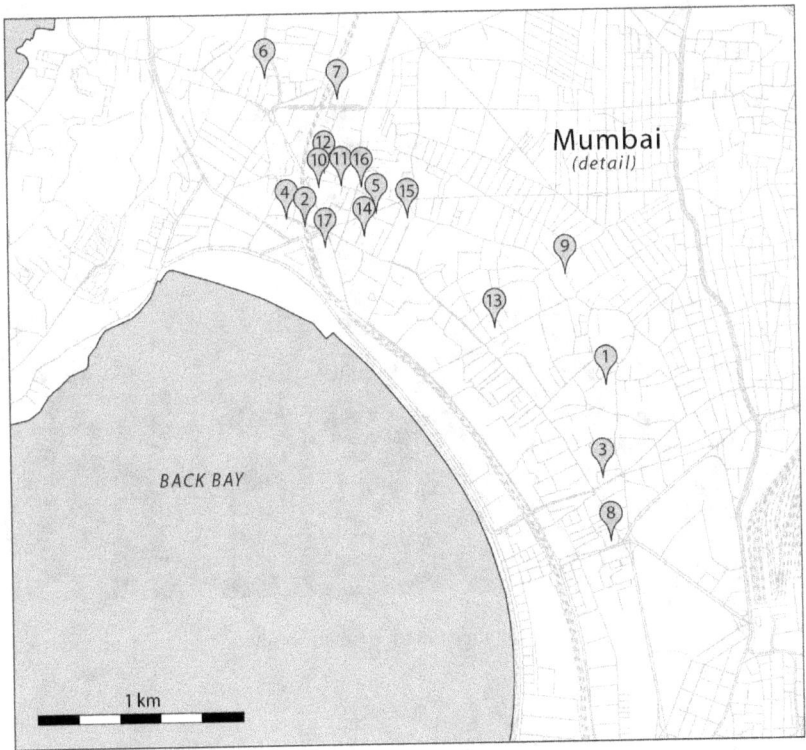

1. Gaiwadi, Kalbadevi
2. School of Indian Music, French Bridge
3. Bhangwadi, Kalbadevi
4. Blavatsky Lodge
5. Chaitsingh Gurbaxsingh Musical Instruments
6. Shastri Hall apartments
7. B. Merwan and Co., Irani Café
8. Framjee Cawasiee Institute
9. Madhav Baug Hall
10. Sangeet Kalakar Sangh – the kotha
11. Jinnah hall
12. Indian National Congress House
13. Bhaskarbuwa Bakhle Path, Mangalwadi, Girgaum
14. Laxmi Baug
15. Brahman Sabhagruha
16. Imperial Cinema
17. Royal Opera House Cinema

name of Deodhar's guru, Vishnu Digambar Paluskar, or in the Ganesh Utsav pandal at Chunam Lane off Lamington Road, close to the Saraswathi Sangeet Vidyalay music school founded by Hirabai's father, Abdul Karim Khan. Hirabai is a figure who straddled the dual worlds of the Marathi musical play, which was a major form of popular entertainment in Mumbai from the 1860s on, and the classical concert hall. It was well known in musical circles that despite her Hindu name she was the daughter of the Muslim Abdul Karim Khan, the Kirana gharana master, while her mother,

The Spaces of Music · 49

Figure 2.1. Royal Opera House, Mumbai. Photo: Hemangi Kadu.

Tarabai Mane, had been born to a naikin, a woman from a Goan performers' family.[5]

What would it mean to the listener to hear Hirabai at the Royal Opera House rather than at the Deodhar School or the Ganesh Utsav? Very often the performers and the listeners might be the same, and it is the venue that changes. I propose that the Western-style grandeur of the Opera House made for an experience of the social for Indians in Mumbai that was different from attending a music festival on the street or a wadi, and that the pleasure derived from Hirabai's voicing of the *pakad* or key phrases in Marwa, the hexatonic evening raga she may have presented in the concert, could not be separated from the pleasure of occupying a seat in such luxurious surroundings. Did the spectacular performance hall change the auditory experience? Or change the way members of the audience responded to the music? Did polite applause replace the enthusiastic "wah"? Did people shake their heads as they always did while listening to Indian music, and move their arms? Could performers make eye contact with their most dedicated followers? These are not questions that I can answer, but they are asked in the hope of generating answers from other texts, perhaps even those that are yet to be written.

At the other end of the spectrum from the Opera House would have been the kotha, a bare ten minutes' stroll away, in which tawaifs or courtesans organized performances. An early twentieth-century description of such performers in the Girgaum neighborhood is to be found in the *Gazetteer of Bombay City and Island* (1909):

> The trained Naikins, the Marwadi, Bene-Israel and Musalman dancing-girls who live in some style in the neighbourhood of Kalbadevi road and Grant road and are engaged to sing in private houses or at public native entertainments. Many of the latter have been well grounded in Urdu and Persian classics and freely spend the comparatively large incomes which they earn in singing and dancing in charity and on religious objects. They are formed into a regular *jamat* or sisterhood, presided over by one of the older members of the class, and in addition to participating in the ordinary festivals of the faith which they profess are wont to give entertainments known as *jalsa*. On these occasions a dancing-girl will invite all her personal friends in the *jamat* to her house and after feasting with them lavishly calls upon them to sing and dance. This latter portion of the entertainment is open to the public and the money received from those present is regarded as the private perquisite of the organiser of the *jalsa*, who subsequently divides the amount between herself and her *Ustads* (musicians) in the proportion of 10 annas and 6 annas respectively in the rupee. According to her means each dancing-girl supports 3 or 4 musicians, who accompany her songs on the *saringi* and the drum. They are given lodging and food and a certain fixed proportion of the earnings and in return perform various minor services for their patron.[6]

While the kothas of the native town have given way to what are now called mujra halls, even these started disappearing as the dance bar began to flourish in the 1990s. But Foras Road and the Congress House area still have active mujra halls where song-dance performances by women from hereditary performing backgrounds can be seen, as described at the end of chapter 1.[7]

The jalsas mentioned in the *Gazetteer* were held in kothas and were attended by predominantly male audiences, with the performers tending to be Muslim. Simultaneously coexisting with the kotha space we have the concert hall space, the music club space, the music school space, the private *wada* space, and the *sarvajanik* Ganesh Utsav (the festival for the Hindu god Ganesh was celebrated publicly in Bombay from 1894 onward as part of a nationalist strategy fashioned by Bal Gangadhar Tilak, with the first sarvajanik or public Ganesh being installed in Girgaum in the Keshavji Naik chawl[8]). This entire range of performance spaces was seen in Girgaum until about the mid-twentieth century, with some of the concert halls even functioning until the late 1980s.

But before we head toward Kennedy Bridge, Congress House, and the mujra halls, we have to visit a few other music spaces near Opera House. Turning the corner, we could stop in front of the impressive sandstone building of the Blavatsky Lodge, constructed in 1927–28. The two-story building houses the Theosophical Society Library of over seven thousand books, and a hall and meeting room that are rented out for seminars, lectures, music and dance classes, and concerts.

The Theosophical Society, devoted to occult religious and spiritual pursuits that aimed to bring together Eastern and Western approaches, was founded in New York in 1875 by Madame Blavatsky, descended from Russian nobility, and Col. H. S. Olcott.[9] In 1879 the founders settled in India, establishing the first headquarters of the society in Bombay. Annie Besant, an Irishwoman who became the spiritual heir of Madame Blavatsky, was active in Indian politics, becoming president of the Indian National Congress in 1917.[10] Under Besant's leadership, Theosophists took an interest in the struggle for independence, and Blavatsky Lodge became an important meeting place for nationalists. Interest in Indian cultural practice, including Hindustani music, was a corollary of the nationalist movement.[11] A newspaper advertisement of 1929 mentions that under the auspices of the Young Men's Parsee Association, the Framji Bharucha competition in Indian music would be held at Blavatsky Lodge on Saturday, October 5, at 5:30 p.m. B. R. Deodhar, the founder-principal of the School of Indian Music across the road, was often a judge at such competitions.

Blavatsky Lodge has been already mentioned in Firoz Dastur's story about going to listen to the founder of his gharana, Abdul Karim Khan, and entering a silent concert hall where the great singer had his mouth open, but the notes could no longer be heard because they had mingled with the sound of the tanpuras. Since Abdul Karim passed away in 1937, the incident narrated by Dastur must have taken place sometime before that. I have suggested, in relation to this story of the Khansaheb in Blavatsky

Figures 2.2 and 2.3. Blavatsky Lodge. Exterior photo: Tejaswini Niranjana. Interior: Ajay Noronha.

Figure 2.4. Entrance to the School of Indian Music. Photo: Hemangi Kadu.

Lodge, that the aesthetic experience of hearing something that cannot be heard is akin to referencing a past that cannot be articulated at a present moment still bearing its impress. There is no record of Hindustani musicians having been Theosophists, but Madame Blavatsky's effort to promote the teachings of the Indian mystics she had met found a good deal of resonance among the urban Indian middle classes, and the Theosophical Society's branches in Mumbai, Chennai, Bangalore, and other places continue to have a presence in Indian public life. Some of the members of this urban middle class in Mumbai would have overlapped with the musicophiliac public.

Across the road from Blavatsky Lodge, a few steps down from the main road next to French Bridge, on the eastern side of the railway line, is the School of Indian Music established by B. R. Deodhar in 1925.

Known in Marathi as the *soota-bootaache gavai* (the suit-boot singer) because of his Western-style clothing that set him apart from other Hindustani musicians, Deodhar was a student of Vishnu Digambar Paluskar, who set up the famous music school Gandharva Mahavidyalay in different cities including Mumbai—initially at Sandhurst Road in Girgaum. Paluskar had to close the Mumbai school in 1923 due to a series of organizational difficulties, but was keen that his student Deodhar set up a similar

Figure 2.5. Kathak class in progress. Photo: Tejaswini Niranjana.

institution. Starting off with holding music classes inside Rammohun Roy English School close by, an arrangement made possible with the help of officials of the religious and social reform organization the Prarthana Samaj, Deodhar was finally able to set up his School of Indian Music—said to have been named by nationalist leader and poet Sarojini Naidu—in 1925 at French Bridge. As of 2019, ninety-four years later, the school is still running, with Deodhar's granddaughter Sangeeta Gogate as principal. For a modest fee of Rs. 350 to 500 per month, the school offers classes in Indian dance fitness, singing, Western dance classes, Bollywood, aerobics, and power yoga.[12] However changed the curricular offerings may seem today, they still include classical music and dance, and still function as an affordable training ground for middle-class children.

During Deodhar's lifetime, however, the school was known only for its classes in Hindustani music and to some extent for kathak dance. Although, as Paluskar's student, Deodhar was affiliated to the Maharashtrian strand of the Gwalior gharana, he was well known for his openness to all styles of music. Not only did he bring exponents of all the gayakis or styles of singing to his school, he learned compositions from all of them. His friend Vamanrao Deshpande used to tease him by saying "that he changed his *gurus* every six months as one changed one's sandals."[13] Kirana, Agra, Gwalior, Jaipur—Deodhar absorbed aspects of all these gharanas, although according to Deshpande "the lasting influence on Deodhar was that of Khansaheb Bade Ghulam Ali Khan," to whom he was deeply devoted. I say more about this relationship in chapter 3.

Musician Vamanrao Deshpande writes about first meeting Deodhar at the Trinity Club in 1926 or 1927:

> I was surprised to see a person at the Club fully clad in Western dress. In those days one did not normally see a singer dressed like an Englishman. So I inquired in an undertone of a person sitting next to me, "Who is he?" He whispered back sarcastically, "Oh! He is Deodhar. A disciple of Pandit Vishnu Digambar. He also calls himself 'Professor'!" ... The man dressed in up-to-date Western clothes soon started singing and that gave me another shock. . . . His singing was pleasant and contained a spark of originality.[14]

For many decades, Deodhar held a concert every August for the barsi or death anniversary of his teacher, and the most renowned musicians of India sang at these concerts to large audiences, often without charging a fee.[15] Usually the anniversary concerts were organized at venues like Laxmi Baug, which we will visit in the latter half of our journey through Girgaum. Sitarist Arvind Parikh says, speaking of the 1950s, "As beginners, we looked forward to these *punya tithis* [death anniversaries], because they featured great masters like Gulam Ali Khan Saheb, Vilayat Hussain Khan, Azmat Hussain Khan, Latafat Hussain Khan, Khadim Husain Khan and many other well-known musicians."[16]

Every musicophiliac who remembers attending concerts at the Deodhar School speaks about the astonishing range of musicians who performed there. Some, of course, performed at the Paluskar anniversary function organized at Laxmi Baug or other popular concert venues. But it appears that dozens of impromptu mehfils took place in the school itself, with its entrance very much like that of a suburban home and its nondescript smallish rooms. Even today, when visitors walk into the school, they can hear the sound of anklets from the hall where little girls from the vicinity are learning kathak dance, while through closed doors the sounds of tabla, tanpura, violin, and harmonium mingle with young male and female voices at their singing classes.

So in the space of the School of Indian Music itself, musicians were constantly passing through and constantly performing in front of their peers, appreciative students, and musicophiliacs. As Deodhar's granddaughter

Sangeeta Gogate says, pointing to a part of the room in which we sat as the interview was conducted,

> Actually Bade Ghulam Ali Khansaab, Ravi Shankar, Ali Akbar, all renowned people, they have performed here. And *sarod* and sitar *ki jugalbandi* [two instruments responding to one another] they used to do *na*, Ali Akbar and Pandit Ravi Shankar, *woh* first time *yahaan pe* perform *kiya tha* [they performed here for the first time]. And Bade Ghulam Ali Khan was in love with my Dadaji, always used to come to him, they used to have those *sangeetik charchas joh hum log bolte hain* [musical debates or discussions as we call them], they always used to have that. *Dadaji kuch bandishe unse seekthe thae, woh Dadaji se kuch seekthe thae. Toh is prakar, yahin pe hota tha.* [Dadaji used to learn some compositions from him, and he used to learn some from Dadaji. And this used to happen right here.] And we used to have a private concert kind of thing, many people used to come here, and they used to perform.[17]

Legendary vocalist Kumar Gandharva (1924–92) was one of the most famous alumni of the Deodhar School, having spent his formative years as a singer there, and he performed frequently at this venue. I have more to say about him in the discussion of Jinnah Hall below.

Coming up the steps from the Deodhar School and back onto the narrow road running alongside French Bridge, if we walk a few meters further we can turn right into Haji Kasam Wadi.

Haji Kasam Wadi, also known as Raghavwadi, is on the western side of the railway line, and you can see the suburban trains clattering past if you stand at the outer edge of the wadi, which was home to the family of the Jaipur-Atrauli gharana's founder, Alladiya Khan, in the 1930s. In his memoirs, Mallikarjun Mansur mentions that in 1935 he started learning music from Ustad Manji Khan (Alladiya Khan's son and musical heir) in Haji Kasam Wadi.[18] His taleem would last from eight in the morning to one in the afternoon every day. This went on for one and a half years, until Manji Khan's untimely death. Mansur's description of his *gandabandh* or initiation ceremony draws on a memory that is over fifty years old but is still vividly expressed because it draws on an intense transformative moment. Manji Khan taught him Raag Bhimpalas as part of the ceremony.

> The grace and beauty of his style was inexplicable. The distinct nuances of the raga came out through every *swararekha* [line of sound,

Figure 2.6. Facade of Haji Kasam Wadi. Photo: Tejaswini Niranjana.

of a note]. I realized for the first time that something more than a mere rendition of the note is necessary to bring forth the essence of the raga. In his singing, I saw the raga blossoming in all its splendour and glory. I almost went into a frenzy when I heard the rebellious union of the *shadja* [first note] with the *nishad* [seventh note]. The *meend* or the glide from *madhyam* [fourth note] to *shadja* was breathtakingly sonorous. . . . Breath and music merged until there was no distinction between the two.[19]

Mansur compares his guru's rendition with the precision of a goldsmith drawing out strings of gold. "Each *boltaan* [melodic elaboration of the words of the composition]," he says, "throbbed with melody," and the "landing on the *sam* [the beginning and end note of a rhythmic cycle] was light, perfect and smooth." On that day in 1935, Mansur says he felt like he had been reborn.[20]

Retracing our steps to the Opera House junction, we now turn left and approach Kennedy Bridge. If you walk on the side of the bridge, keeping the actual bridge to your left, with large old chawls to the right where my male friends recall being solicited by sex workers on the street, you emerge onto Grant Road, or VP Road as it is now named, with Queen

Figure 2.7. Congress House Restaurant and NB Compound. Photo: Hemangi Kadu.

Mary's School on the left and the restaurant called Congress House opposite it, which itself faces the NB Compound pictured in figure 2.7, where I visited the mujra hall described in chapter 1. Next to the restaurant is the real Congress House, an unremarkable brick-and-concrete building dating back to the 1920s, a center of nationalist activity during the freedom struggle. It is well known that pans for making salt were kept on the terrace during Mahatma Gandhi's Dandi March and the Salt Satyagraha in 1930. Jinnah Hall, named after Muslim League leader and founder of Pakistan Mohammed Ali Jinnah, is part of Congress House and is still in use today. It was built partly through funds donated by Jinnah, then a congressman, and became an important performance space for Hindustani musicians from the 1930s on.[21]

Vamanrao Deshpande gives us a description of the debut performance of Kumar Gandharva at the age of eleven at the music conference organized in 1936 at Jinnah Hall by Vamanrao, Deodhar, and Motiram Pai. Deshpande says that "the excellence of the quality of artists" in that mehfil was "reflected in the unbounded enthusiasm of the audience."[22] Enter the child Kumar, looking even younger than his real age:

He cast his spell on the audience by his extraordinarily melodious

The Spaces of Music · 59

voice and captivated [everyone] instantly. Every tonal play and ornamental phrase of his was appreciated.... Every listener present there was convinced that every note uttered by Kumar was for that listener alone. Kumar sang only for a short while, but there was astonishment etched on every face. Every knowledgeable listener and artist present was overflowing with admiration and there were showers of praises and presents. Some gave cash presents, others medals. The donors included Khan Sahebs, renowned Hindu vocalists and female singers.[23]

The only reference we have to what Kumar sang that day is provided by Vamanrao himself. The boy presented, among other compositions, Abdul Karim Khan's famous "Jamuna ke teer" with complete accuracy. Kumar gained a reputation as a young boy for being able to correctly imitate a number of fine singers from different gharanas. In doing so, he was said to not reproduce the recording but in some sense represent the "entire music of that musician."[24] Perhaps some of those he imitated were in the audience in Jinnah Hall, including the "female singers" from Goa whom the author mentions separately from the male vocalists he has classified as Muslim or Hindu. We know that Hirabai, neither Hindu nor Muslim, who sang nearly a decade before in the Royal Opera House and who asked the organizers to "announce her present" for the prodigy, was there.[25] Perhaps she was charmed by the boy's rendering of her father Abdul Karim's "Jamuna ke teer." Perhaps he again sang Hirabai's *maand* in Jhinjhoti ("Tum bin meri kaun khabar ley govardhan giridhari"), which he had presented in a Wadia Movietones film the previous year.[26] Kumar Gandharva's extraordinary musical performance ability was formed in his early childhood by his capacity to imitate whatever recordings he listened to, rather than by any singular discipleship. His teacher from 1937 to 1949, B. R. Deodhar, offered him training that did not entangle him in any one gharana but exposed him to the range of musicians who frequented the School of Indian Music and to thoroughgoing analyses of each style so that Kumar could pick the most attractive qualities of each and steer clear of what Deodhar saw as their defects.

Figure 2.9 shows the entrance to the NB Compound, opposite Congress House. This used to be a kotha where tawaifs or courtesans performed, and was one of the places where musicians who came to Mumbai stayed.[27] From about the 1930s until well into the 1960s, it was a major center of entertainment in the city, according to Thatra, who also points out the interesting codevelopment in that era of the actual Congress House build-

Figure 2.8. The People's Jinnah Hall—the auditorium today. Photo: Ajay Noronha.

Figure 2.9. NB Compound entrance. Photo: Tejaswini Niranjana.

ing, purchased through collecting public funds—to which the tawaifs also contributed—as in the Tilak Swaraj Fund of 1921 and the Jinnah Fund of 1918. Opposite the kotha is the Congress Restaurant, its name alluding to the building next door, the office of the Indian National Congress from 1925 and throughout the freedom struggle. The NB Compound had rooms in which deredar tawaifs hosted music and dance sessions. These included the *jumme ki baithak* or Friday afternoon postprayer sessions in which veteran musicians showcased their disciples and offered advice and criticism to the students of their colleagues. Sitar and tabla player Nayan Ghosh, son of musician Nikhil Ghosh, speaks of his father's visits with his guru to the compound and to Foras Road, where other courtesans had their kothas. Nikhil Ghosh's teacher, Amir Hussain Khan, lived at the NB Compound and was the *chaudhury* or chief of the musicians.[28] The courtesans not only offered financial support to the musicians they learned from, they also looked after young apprentice musicians. In chapter 1, I discussed the sessions that still take place at the compound.

Music critic Batuk Diwanji, in his book *Sangeetkaro ane Sangeetagno*, describes Gangabai, a prominent tawaif of the 1940s and 1950s:

> Gangabai lived at Kennedy Bridge [in the NB Compound], which was also called Pavanpul. She was known to be the "chaudharani" of all the women singers in the area because if any new singer from out of town came to live there, they would first have to offer her a present (called *nazar*). She would also resolve disputes among the singers. Her second daughter was a very good dancer. Ustad Bade Ghulam Ali Khan and Ustad Ahmadjan Thirakva, in the early days, would stay at Gangabai's place whenever they visited Mumbai. The women singers of Pavanpul would start singing at around eight in the evening and go on till late in the night. The word "tem" [local pronunciation of the English word "time"] was used for these mehfils.[29]

While the jumme ki baithak usually had khayal and *dhrupad* music, the "time" or mehfil in the evenings tended to have more semiclassical forms, like ghazal, qawwali, dadra, and thumri. These were performed by the tawaif, often in a sitting position, with the required *ada* and *nazakat*, using conventions of facial expression and hand movement that conveyed erotic longing. As the last section of chapter 1 conveys, today the tawaif's descendants perform only the Hindi-cinema–derived ghazals and thumris, and are unfamiliar with the older repertoire.

So the musicophiliac in Girgaum—perhaps a wealthy merchant, perhaps a middle-class accountant or lawyer—going to a mehfil in the compound in the 1940s would have entered a room with mirrors, chandeliers, and divans with bolsters. As tabla maker Chandrakant Mewada, who grew up in the neighborhood, told us, "All these rich people would come with their horse carriages. They could come leaving their wives behind.... They would come here to listen to music."[30] Thus the audience would be all male, and the performers—with the exception of the sarangi, tabla, and harmonium accompanists—all female, the mehfil replicating in its arrangements a courtly setting from at least a hundred years before. The question of the new musical subject in the kotha setting might be tied, in terms of content, to other mehfils, other concerts in Girgaum, where the audience was becoming slowly more mixed in terms of gender by this time. But the idea of standing in for the courtly listener could, I suggest, stir up imagined pasts glimpsed by Indians only in theatrical or textual fictions (influential cinematic Mughal stories like *Anarkali* or *Mughal-e-Azam* were yet to be made). Through the bandish thumri, itself a nineteenth-century invention reputedly from the court of Nawab Wajid Ali Shah of Lucknow, the listener in Gangabai's mehfil would fashion a new musical aesthetic that connected at once to the intimate subjective space where the tawaif performed just for the senses of the man who felt interpellated as her beloved, and to the world of the social where this music was being publicly taught and recognized.

For musicians both Hindu and Muslim, the compound was a significant place on the circuit, whether it was B. R. Deodhar the musicologist, Pandharinath Mangeshkar the tabla player, Naushad the film music composer, or several Muslim musicians (Bade Ghulam Ali Khan in particular, who lived there for several years, and also vocalist Amir Khan, tabla player Amir Hussain Khan, and many others who needed a place to stay in Mumbai). Under Gangabai's benevolence, the compound was a place providing tea, snacks, and musical conversation and exchange for everyone who came by. Frequent visitors included the film stars Raj Kapoor and Dilip Kumar, Gangabai's grandson recalls.[31]

As our tour continues, after glimpsing the NB Compound from the outside, we can walk ahead to Paper Mill Galli, where legendary early twentieth-century composer and vocalist Bhaskarbuwa Bakhle lived, and finally reach the lane named after him, off Mughbat Galli.[32] The first building on the narrow road is the chawl that houses the Trinity Club.

Figure 2.10 is a picture of the chawl to the right of Kennedy Bridge, which we passed on our way to Congress House. In structure, it is very

Figure 2.10. Chawl adjacent to Kennedy Bridge. Photo: Tejaswini Niranjana.

similar to the one housing the Trinity Club, or the one in which Mallikarjun Mansur stayed when he was getting taleem from Manji Khan. Mansur could not afford to rent a place by himself, so he stayed with his friend Taikar, who was a clerk for the HMV gramophone company.

The chawl where Taikar lived was in Zaobawadi, and his *kholi* or room was so small that when Mansur wanted to do his riyaaz or practice at night, the accompanists had to sit outside in the corridor. Musicophiliacs like the Marathi poet Pu La Deshpande sought out their favorite singers in the chawls and came often to listen to them practicing.

The chawl is a style of building that originated in colonial India, becoming a prominent feature of a rapidly industrializing metropolis like Mumbai in the late nineteenth century. It became a standard housing structure in the twentieth century, in particular in Girgaum, the heart of the native town, and should be read, says architecture theorist Kaiwan Mehta, along with the codes of citizenship and nationalism in addition to colonialism and industrialization. Mehta suggests that "the *chawl* then becomes a site where these codes can be read and described; the building then becomes a historical crucible itself of these concepts and ideas."[33]

In chapter 1, I discussed how migration was the most important reason for the growth of the population in Bombay, and this is true as much now as it was in the nineteenth century. As Mehta notes, the emergence of chawls and wadis is simultaneous with the influx of new migrant populations who sought to reproduce some semblance of kinship and social coherence in the bewildering urban metropolitan landscape, which had an economic as well as spatial organization very different from the areas from which the migrants came. We get a sense from the Gujarati short stories of Saroj Pathak, quoted by Mehta, as to the occupants of the new chawls: primary school teachers, compounders, shop assistants, bus conductors, pushcart vendors—up to fifteen families living on a floor and sharing a toilet at the far end. Architect Arvind Adarkar's memories of chawl life indicate that Girgaum chawls had mostly middle-class occupants, although this is a definition of middle-class that includes office peons too. In terms of caste background, there was a wider spread across the spectrum, although some upper-caste chawls were single-caste buildings. Adarkar also remembers that until about the 1950s the chawls were predominantly occupied by Marathi speakers.[34]

An important insight of Mehta's is that the chawl is "a building and a neighbourhood at the same time."[35] This idea is helpful in understanding the historical space of musical performance in the Girgaum area. For example, if we look at the Trinity Club on Pandit Bhaskarbuwa Bakhle Path, which we come to after passing the famous Bedekar pickle factory, it is on the upper floor of a chawl. The kholi was dedicated to the use of musicians by one Bodas, who worked for the Shaw Wallace Company and was a fan of Hindustani music, and requested that the famous singer Bhaskarbuwa Bakhle initiate musical activities in the chawl, probably in 1907.[36] So we can infer that the building, which still exists, is well over a hundred years old. When musicians would perform in the club, which is housed in a room approximately ten by fifteen feet, the audience used to spill over into the chawl corridor outside, and people lined the staircase as well as the street outside listening for hours on end.[37] Thus the performance space was not limited just to one room but expanded to include the neighborhood itself.

Balasaheb Tikekar, president of the committee presently running the Trinity Club, described how it all began under the patronage of preeminent singer Bhaskarbuwa Bakhle. Speaking in Marathi, he said, "So someone brought the harmonium, the tabla, and they started singing in that space

Figure 2.11. The door of Trinity Club, seen at the end of the corridor. Photo: Tejaswini Niranjana.

and people would come and chat [Tar koni tari peti aanli, tabla aanla, aani tya zaage madhaye gaana gana suruvat zhaali, gappa marne aata]."

Balasaheb was not even born at the time, so he is passing on a memory acquired through being a musicophiliac in Girgaum.

> What was Bhaskarbua's aim in establishing Trinity Club? His aim was to provide a space for musicians who would travel to Mumbai and did not have a space to stay. [Aata Trinity Club cha uddesha kai hota hi jaga sthapana maage Bhaskarbuancha? Ki je bahergaon je kalakar yetat gaanare mhana, vaajavnare mhana tya lokana jaaga rahala ashi navti kutech.] Even if it was just for their programs they would come and stay here for their business and leave. [Te ek karyakramapurti ka hoi na te aapla jaaget ithe yaayche aani rahaiche tithe aapla vyaysay pan karaiche sangeetacha aani jaiche parat.] A lot of famous artists would come and stay here. [Ase moth mothe kalakar jithe yet asat rahat asat.]³⁸

Along the walls of the little room that houses the Trinity Club are large black-and-white photographs of the entire pantheon of Hindustani vocalists from the long twentieth century, all of whom have performed here. The photographs have not been dusted in a while, and some are falling off the wall. But one can imagine what it must have been like for a relatively young singer to perform in the club surrounded by these pictures. The act of listening, just as much as the act of performing under the gaze of these preeminent musicians, who are not simply wall decorations but have actually sung in this space—what do these acts signify? By listening, by performing at the Trinity Club, one gathers in all the notes that have been articulated there, all the compositions that have soared through the night, all the alaapi that has heralded each raga as it unfolds. This gathering in of notes transforms the actual moment of listening in the present, so that it resonates both with past performances and with the repertoires of the gharana from which the performer comes. Every new performance becomes the perspective from which the archive is heard as well as transformed in memory. Here, in the act of listening, we can observe the workings of the metropolitan unconscious and glimpse the ways in which musicophilia forms the social subject.

Coming back onto the street after descending the stairs of the Trinity Club chawl, if you turn right and walk a couple of meters you will see the signboard of Azad Avanadh Vadyalaya, a tabla maker's shop, where Chandrakant Ramjibhai Mewada (d. 2014), known as Chandubhai, worked in the shop his father established in 1945. We still find a few small artisanal shops like this one in Girgaum, where the worker-proprietor and his family live, work, cook, and eat in the same tiny space.

Chandrakant Mewada's name evokes yet another community, Meghwal, an artisanal subcaste that migrated from Rajasthan via Gujarat to Girgaum in Mumbai. The shop was established just before Independence by his nationalist father, hence the name Azad, referring to freedom. This tiny space has seen informal baithak performances by a number of Hindustani musicians, and the tabla maker's family was closely associated with many of them, including Alla Rakha, Ravi Shankar's tabla accompanist. When the British took Chandu's father into custody for naming his shop Azad, eminent citizens of Mumbai came to vouch for him and get him released. Help also came from Gangabai, the singer from Pavanpul or Kennedy Bridge-Congress House. "This shop, Gangabai's kotha, and the Bhangwadi theatre were places where the nationalists met," said Chandubhai. "Gangabai often passed information to the Swatantra Sena or freedom brigade."

"Singers like Behrebua and then Bhimsen Joshi would come and sit in this shop and sing," said Chandubhai. He narrated the story of a music ses-

Figure 2.12. Inside Trinity Club. Photo: Hemangi Kadu.

Figure 2.13. Azad Avanadh Vadyalay entrance. Photo: Tejaswini Niranjana.

Figure 2.14. Chandubhai at work. Photo: Tejaswini Niranjana.

sion that took place in the shop space when he was a teenager, the narrative building up to the point where the intensity of the performance produces a godly vision:

> TN: Singers came here, right? So did they also sing here? At the shop? [Idhar toh log toh aate thae na gaanewale toh idhar bhi gaate thae kya? Dukaan pe?]
>
> CR: Yes … don't ask! Sometimes we would have programs the whole night. We would put the work aside at eight o'clock; the shop used to shut. Then my father would go to the corner sweetshop and would bring a two-kilo box of sweets. Now I'm talking about [the singer] Abid Hussain from Janjira. He was sitting inside our place at around 9 to 10 p.m. and said, "Ramjibhai, give me a new towel and a new dhoti." Father asked what happened? What is it? "Get a new dhoti, new towel." Father quickly opened the cupboard—gave him a new dhoti, new towel. "Do you have perfume?" "Yes, I do." At that time in the night [musician] Azim Khan was also here. [Ha … Arre wah poocho mat! Kabhi kabhi raat bhar chalu rahta programme. Kaam

baaju mein, 8 baje dukaan bandh. Phir baba naake pe jaye mithai ka, do kilo ka pede ka mithai le aave. Yeh Abid Hussain wale ki baat karta hoon, Janjira waale. Woh andar baithe raat ko 9–10 baje aur (bole), "Ramji naya towel nava dhoti nikaalo." Baba (bole) kem? Su thaiyu? Su che? "Naya dhoti nikalo naya towel nikalo." Baba ne phat se kapaat khola—nayi dhoti, naya towel. "Attar ki batli hai kya?" "Haan hai." Woh time pe raat ko Azim Khan aake baith gaye idhar.]

Everyone was sitting and waiting. Jaikishan [the film music composer] was standing there. "Ramjibhai, what's happening?" he asked me. Nothing, I said. The Khansaabs are sitting here and I'm going to listen to them. He told his driver to take his car away. Jaikishan was sitting on the ledge here. Then Khansaab came out after his bath, lit an incense stick to God. Inside he lit a lamp, he prayed, and then he sat down here suddenly. [Sab log baithe hai Jaikishan khada reh gaya udhar, "Ramjibhai kya hai?" Bole kuch nahi sab Khansaab log baithe hai main sunta hoon. Usne driver ko gaadi bhej diya, chalo bhaago yahan se. Woh yahan ote pe baitha Jaikishan. Phir aaya naah dhoke agarbatti lagayi bhagwaan ko, diya lagaya, andar diya lagaya, Khansaab ne prarthana ki aur yahan baith gaye ekdum.]

TN: And there were tanpuras too? [Aur Tanpure bhi thae?]

CR: We got them from Madhubhai, who runs his music classes in Fanaswadi. We got two tanpuras. He started with Raag Bhatiyar at two, two thirty. Like black *sheesham* wood standing, and there's Lord Shankara here. The lamp was on and he was standing here. Azim Khan said, "Son, don't open your eyes. Now that Raag Bhatiyar is being sung at the right time [according to the timetable] for this raag, something of beauty will appear. Chandu, you don't open your eyes." [Madhubhai se mangwa liya baju mein, Fanaswadi mein unki class. Do taanpure aa gaye. Baithe . . . Bhatiyar chalu kiya do-adhai baje. Kaala sheesham jaise yahan khada reh gaya Bhatiyar, idhar yahaan Shankarji hai. Diya chalu woh yahaan khada hai. Yeh bole, Azim Khan bole, "Beta koi aankh ko kholna mat yeh jo abhi isne timetable dekh ke raag chheda hai Bhatiyar do ke baad mein, abhi yahaan uski kuch na kuch khoobsoorti aayegi beta. Chandu tu aankhein mat kholna."]

I was sitting next to him. He was standing here very comfortably; a dark man—he was wearing a lot of jewelry, and he was holding a mace in his hand. [Main unke baju main baitha tha. Yahan aaram se khada ho gaya kaala Sheesham jaisa aadmi dagina bhara hua aur haath mein gadha aisi.]

The ones who work with a good heart sing and call on the gods, like we do during a *hom*. By making . . . oblation or offering during the hom, the one who does it, he gets the fruit of his efforts. Khansaab showed it to us here. That time I must have been seventeen to eighteen years old or maybe I was fifteen years old. I was sitting next to Azim Khan Saab. I opened my eyes a little. Azim Khan said, "See, there's a dark man standing there wearing jewelry." He was there for ten minutes. When Khansaab stopped singing, the man left. [Woh achhe dil se kaam karte hai, gaana gaate hai uske avhaan karte hai apan hom mein nahi karte avhaan dete hai. Yeh karke . . . ahuti dete hai hom ke andar accha jo yeh hove hawan dene wala woh aadmi usko fal milta hi uska. Khansaab ne woh humko dikha diya yahan. Tabhi umar humari hogi kuch 17–18 saal ya aisa 15 saal ke umar mein Azim Khansaab ke baaju mein thoda aankh khola Khansaab bole, "dekh le kaala admi khada hai udhar daagina pehna hua," Dus minute gaya sab kuch darshan usne diya. Khansaab ne band kar diya woh chale gaye.]

The perfume that Khansaab was wearing . . . my father too was fond of perfume—rose, jasmine, and he had kept henna, everything was mixed—and he put some on Azim Khan and he was wearing it too. He put some perfume on the images of the gods as well, and then Abid Hussain started singing. The Nom Tom that he started—don't even ask me about it. Even though I'm illiterate about music, I was just sitting, stunned. We couldn't move. Our minds were shut down. [Woh attar aisa lagaaya na Khansaab ne. Pitaji bhi attar ke bahut shaukeen—gulaab, mogra, aur henna bhi rakha tha. Sab sab mix kar ke Azim Khan ko lagaaya aur khud ko bhi laga liya. Aur wahaan bhagwaan ko attar laga diya usne. Phir jo apna chalu kiya usne gaana. Nom Tom jo chalu kiya ke poocho mat! Apun angootha chaap isliye kya sangeet ke andar main bhi aisa baith gaya ek dum. Yaane apne ko hilne, yeh sab mind band kar diya humaara sab ka.]

There were at least fifteen to twenty people here, and fifteen to twenty people were sitting inside; no one even went to the washroom. Everyone was just sitting. [Yahan kareeban 15–20 aadmi yahan baithe thae 15–20 ander baithe thae ko yahan bhi bahi gaya sab aise ke aise hi baithe sab log.]³⁹

Figure 2.15. Brahman Sabha entrance. Photo: Tejaswini Niranjana.

This long story of a spellbound audience listening to a singer and hardly noticing a godly figure who has appeared among them presents through its repetitive phrases an incantatory sense of musicophilia, in which the god too is a fellow musicophiliac. It is a vivid memory for the loquacious Chandubhai and forms an important part of his narrative of musical Girgaum, tied as it is to the audience of connoisseurs like the ones who frequented the Trinity Club next door.[40] The idea of a Hindu god coming in to listen to a Muslim ustad singing recurs in my account of Saraswati Sangeet Vidyalaya below.

Close to the Trinity Club is the Brahman Sabha, off Lamington Road on Raja Ram Mohun Roy Marg in Bhatwadi, which was a major venue for Hindustani music in the mid-twentieth century. The Sabha was established in 1888, but the building in figure 2.15 looks as though it dates from the 1920s or 1930s. An important architectural feature of Mumbai buildings at this time was specifically Indian elements; here they include the stepped arch and the deep *chajjiyas* or eaves, possibly derived from Gujarati styles. Today the custodians of the place deny that Hindustani music was ever performed there, saying that only devotional music like *bhajans* is permitted. But every

Figure 2.16. Laxmi Baug facade. Photo: Hemangi Kadu.

Figure 2.17. Laxmi Baug interior. Photo: Nikhil Arolkar.

musicophiliac we spoke to remembered fondly that his or her favorite vocalists performed at Brahman Sabha, and that there were often three concerts going on at the same time in three different halls in the building.

Not far from Brahman Sabha is Laxmi Baug, a key performance space in Girgaum by the 1920s, situated off Lamington Road on Avantikabai Gokhale Road. It is built in a Venetian villa or palazzo style, with a central door and a triangular pediment above. The building, including the interior space, is very well preserved, with a central performance area and carved wooden balconies above. Above the performance space hangs a huge chandelier.

Satchit Dabholkar, the current owner/trustee of Laxmi Baug, told us that his great-grandmother Laxmibai Narayan Dabholkar had left money in her will for a building to be built for charitable purposes. Even to this day the hall is rented out for a very modest amount (approximately Rs. 2,000) for weddings and other functions. Dabholkar recalls that up until the 1960s, Laxmi Baug regularly hosted a large number of Hindustani music concerts. Nearly three hundred people would sit on the ground baithak-style in the main hall, and many more on chairs on the balcony. The concerts would go on until 2 a.m., and audience members who had missed the last train to the suburbs tipped the servants so they could catch some sleep in the hall until 5 a.m. or so, and then get on a train to go home.[41] Nitin Shirodkar, a longtime Girgaum resident, said, "Laxmi Baug in those days was acoustically suited for baithaks. It was like having a baithak in your own house because of those vintage windows and that wooden stage."[42]

At that time, Laxmi Baug also functioned as a popular wedding hall, as it still is today, although concerts were no longer held after the 1980s. Sitarist Arvind Parikh writes about the hall:

> I vividly remember a concert of Wahid Khan Saheb in Laxmi Baug, one evening. He played raga Puriya. Believe it or not, he played the raga for over two hours, and it was all the old traditional *baj*—lots of pre-composed phrases and step-by-step development—all *dhrupad*-based. He was fairly old at that time, but played extraordinarily well. [Wahid Khan played the *surbahar* and had taught his nephews Vilayat Khan and his brother Imrat Khan to play it too.][43]

Writing about the mid- to late 1940s, Parikh reminisces:

> In the evenings, unlike today, great masters used to come to Laxmi Baug, and sit in an adjoining room or verandah for a cup of tea/

coffee, gossip, and listen to music. Kishori's first ever concert [Kishori Jhaveri, who married Parikh in 1949] ... was in Laxmi Baug, which Master Navrang had organized. I recollect vividly that she sang raga Chandrakauns. Bade Ghulam Ali Khan Saheb, Ameer Khan Saheb, Azmat Hussain Khan Saheb, Vilayat Hussain Khan Saheb all the great vocalists, were present. Allarakha Khan Saheb was there, too. They were sitting outside and were intrigued by this new girl with a powerful voice, singing effortlessly in the *tar saptak* (higher octave), going up to the *ati tar sa* (the peak of the higher octave). . . . These concerts were a kind of test for musicians, where new talent was discovered and endorsed by the stalwarts.[44]

All these performance spaces, from Trinity Club to Laxmi Baug to Brahman Sabha, as well as other venues I have not described—such as the Marwadi Vidyalaya or school, or Wagle Hall in Gaiwadi—combine into a musical precinct, where the wider neighborhood becomes unified through the audiences who go from one performance to the next, especially during the Ganesh Utsav (festival for the god Ganesh). One of the biggest Ganesh festivals was held off Lamington Road in Chunam Lane, where the Lamington *cha raja* (king of Lamington) presided, and where all the major musicians performed during the festival every year. In chapter 3, I describe how the Ganesh Utsav functioned as a major occasion for musicophiliac discussion.

Experiencing the Musical Precinct

The to-and-fro movement of audiences helps us trace the circumference of the musical neighborhood. There are stories of how runners were employed to go between Laxmi Baug and Brahman Sabha, for example, carrying information about which singer was still tuning his tanpuras, which one had already started his or her alaap, and so on. This allowed the audiences to rush en masse from one venue to the other as the performances progressed.[45] This story was told by Kirana maestro Firoz Dastur to his disciples Girish Sanzgiri and Nitin Shirodkar, both Girgaum residents, and has become part of their collective memory of the neighborhood. Speaking in a mixture of Marathi and English, Shirodkar said:

> NS: That is what Dasturji has told *ke* this thing that he told me, *ki* [that] his guru Sawai Gandharva apparently before a performance would take a lot of time for his, you know, *gala taapaila* [to warm up

his throat] and the *kharaj mehnat* [exercising the voice in the lowest octave]. He used to prefer to do it in the washroom . . . and then when Sawai Gandharva would start, then there would be some other artiste in Brahman Sabha, and then there were these runners who would come and give *ke aata tikade* that *artistcha Pancham laglela aahe* [that artist is now singing the Pancham or fifth note] and *ikade aata* [now here] Sawai Gandharva is about to take off, so all of them would come to Laxmi Baug and vice versa. *Asa sagla hoiche* [this is what used to happen] *aani sakali doodhwalya barobar aamhi ghari jaiche* [and we would go home with the milkman].[46]

The Hindustani music audience was largely drawn from the middle and lower-middle classes, with the occasional appearance of wealthy merchants and in later years even film stars. The first three categories lived in Girgaum itself, in chawls, apartments, or independent houses depending on the social stratum of the resident. While Girgaum was largely populated at its core by Marathi- and Gujarati-speaking Hindus, there were also specific areas where Parsis lived (Firoz Dastur, the Parsi disciple of Sawai Gandharva, lived on Grant Road), and Goan or north Karnataka kalavant families in Thakurdwar, Konkani-speaking Saraswat Brahmins in Talmakiwadi on the northern side of Girgaum, as well as courtesans or tawaifs of different religious backgrounds on Grant Road and Kalbadevi Road. The diversity of the Girgaum population is to some extent reflected in the architectural styles and ornamental details, where colonial architectural repertoires meet motifs and spatial arrangements drawn from communities migrating into the city. As I discussed in chapter 1, a linguistically diverse audience was drawn to a mode of singing that was done almost entirely in Hindustani. The geography of Girgaum's musical neighborhood was rendered coherent through the repetitive invocation of the lingua musica. In the coming together of these new audiences for Hindustani music, spaces for the performance of modernity took shape.

Pila House, a corruption of the word "playhouse," refers to the Foras Road (RS Nimkar Marg today)–Falkland Road–Grant Road area, where there were several theaters dating from the 1850s, one of the oldest being the Grant Road Theatre, built in 1846 with the support of leading Mumbai merchants Jagannath Shankarsheth and Jamsetjee Jeejeebhoy. The neoclassical Edward Theatre, built in the 1880s, is still running, now as a film theater.

Newspaper advertisements from the 1880s indicate that apart from

Figure 2.18. Edward Theatre entrance. Photo: Tejaswini Niranjana.

staging plays, these theaters were also used for variety and magic shows. Grant Road was at the heart of the mid- to late-nineteenth-century entertainment industry, showcasing the Parsi theater (initially in Gujarati and then in Urdu/Hindustani) and the sangeet natak (in Marathi), both of which drew on the melodic structure of Hindustani ragas for their musical scores. Major plays often had up to seventy songs each. As I discussed in chapter 1, the theater was perhaps the most significant site for people's exposure to Hindustani music from the 1860s well into the 1930s. Even those who grew up in the 1950s and 1960s have strong memories of the Marathi sangeet natak, although by then the plays were staged only intermittently, and of its songs, which were composed according to the melodic patterns of Hindustani music.

The music school was established in 1914 by Abdul Karim Khan with the help of his disciple Balkrishnabuwa Kapileshwari, who shifted it to Swastik House in 1939, where it is still located, having first started it in Kalbadevi. Kalyani Puranik, daughter of Kapileshwari and herself a singer, spoke of the lectures on music that used to take place in Abdul Karim's school, where scientists and musicians came together to discuss *shrutis*

Figure 2.19. Saraswati Sangeet Vidyalay. Photo: Hemangi Kadu.

Figure 2.20. Inside Saraswati Sangeet Vidyalay—daughters of Balakrishnabuwa Kapileshwari, disciple of Abdul Karim Khan. Photo: Ajay Noronha.

or lyrics and their place in Indian music. Kalyani Puranik showed us a 120-year-old "female" tanpura, which had been used by the major women singers who had performed in the school—Gangubai Hangal, Hirabai Barodekar, Mogubai Kurdikar, Kishori Amonkar, and others. She also told us the story of an evening performance by Abdul Karim Khan.

> KP: The credit for this actually goes to Abdul Karim Khansaab. When he came to Maharashtra, he opened this institution. He was never greedy for money. He would happily accept whatever was offered. He was satisfied and content with it. Once there was a mehfil with about ten to twelve people. Khansaab's performance was ending. [Iska shray toh Abdul Karim Khansaab ji ko hi jaata hai actually. Kyunki jab yeh Maharashtra mein aaye toh inhone yeh sanstha kholi. Ek hai ki Khansaab dhan ke lobhi bilkul nahi thae. Saamne waala jo deve, woh lete thae. Santusht thae usme, trupt thae. Ek din aise hi hua sab poori mehfil thi, 10–12 log thae. Khansaab ji ka jalsa ho gaya.]
>
> He sang *"karuna meri kyun nahi aave."* He would close his eyes and immerse himself completely in the song. The mehfil ended and everyone had left. A man came forward, and with folded hands asked him, "Miyan, have you stopped singing?" They had already stopped sounding the tanpura by then. [Khansaab ne "karuna meri kyun nahi aave" . . . aankh band karke talleen ho ke gaate thae. Mehfil khatam ho gayi, sab log jaa nikal gaye. Ek aadmi aage aa gaya Khansaab ji ko bola pranaam karke, "Miyan, gaana khatam hua?" Unhone tanpure bhi band kar diye thae.]
>
> "I would like to make a request to you," the man said. Khansaab said, "Why request? You should command me! Command." "I want to listen to you singing *gopala meri karuna* once more." He was a very old man, a *grihast* [this term for householder probably suggests that his clothing was not that of a saint, sage, or beggar]. Khansaab sang once again, just for this man. ["Main ek aapko araj karna chahta hoon." Khansaab bole, "Araj kyun, tum hukum karo! Hukum." "Mujhe aur ek baar aapka Gopala meri karuna . . . gaana sunna hai." Bahut hi vriddhh grihast thae. Ek hi aadmi ko unhone gaana sunaya.]
>
> The tanpuras were strummed again. My father and other *shagirds* [disciples] were sitting right there. He sang this one song. Then the man said, "I have been blessed," and touched Khansaab's feet. He walked away singing to himself. Khansaab felt deep down that this man may be an *auliya* or saint. . . . He had such liking for his music,

for this song. He sent his shagird to look outside, but by then he had disappeared. Then Khansaab said he must have been an auliya or else an incarnation of lord Shri Krishna. [Phir tanpure chhede. Humare pitashri wagareh saath mein baithe thae shagird. Ek hi gaana unhone sunaaya. Phir usne kaha "main dhanya ho gaya hoon," charan chhooke. Aur woh bhi aise gaate gaate nikal gaya bahar. Unko phir antaratma boli Khansaab ji ki yeh koi auliya hai . . . itna woh chahte hai yeh gaana. Isliye inhone apne shagird ko bahar dekhne . . . tab tak woh anta. Phir Khansaab bole ya toh koi auliya hai ya shri Krishna bhagwan ka roop prakat hua hai.][47]

Just across the road from Abdul Karim Khan's school is Chunam Lane, home of the Lamington cha Raja, one of the biggest Ganesh pandals in Girgaum.[48] In June 2015, in the company of journalist Reema Gehi of the *Times of India*, my colleague Kaiwan Mehta and I took a walk around the neighborhood in preparation for our exhibition, *Making Music Making Space*. In Chunam Lane, we met some longtime residents who appeared to be in their sixties, and who said they remembered listening to Bhimsen Joshi, Gangubai Hangal, and Kumar Gandharva at their Ganesh pandal. One of them recalled, "Speakers had to be stationed right along the road, because the entire lane would be packed."[49]

Moving southward, we come to Bhangwadi, where professional Gujarati theater flourished as it tried to carve out an identity separate from the Parsi-Gujarati theater. The Deshi Natak Samaj's performances, which began in 1874, attracted audiences from as far as Surat, Baroda, and Ahmedabad, who came on special trains for the performances. Large ornate cement elephants, represented as in Gujarati and Rajasthani art and architecture, perch over the entrance, with the balconies looking like howdahs carried by the elephants. The intricate facade, carved by Kathiawari craftsmen, is now dulled, although there are traces of carved windows and galleries invoking the visual memories of the migrants. The courtyard is surrounded by chawl-like rooms, which is a typical wadi structure. It was called Bhangwadi, because one could buy bowls of *bhang* (a brew prepared from the leaves and flowers of cannabis) here. The theater inside was called the Princess Theatre, operational from 1905 to 1979. There was also a Shiv Mandir, which has now become a Jain Derasar or temple.[50] Gujarati theater, like its Marathi and Parsi theater counterparts, would have featured dozens of songs based on Gujarati *bhavai* folk tunes and the melodies of Hindustani music. It is said that the singing and dancing women from

Figure 2.21. Bhangwadi. Photo: Hemangi Kadu.

the kothas of Foras Road took down the notation of the Bhangwadi songs to practice and perform during their mehfils. The Girgaum musicophiliac would have sampled the range of the different sites where Hindustani music appeared in Mumbai—from the musical theater to the Ganesh Utsav to the concert hall to the private baithak. Each presentation format and genre sharpened the audience's musical senses, so that the music flowed along a spectrum, now emerging as a thumri in a kotha or a private baithak, as a khayal in the concert, or as *natya sangeet* in Bhangwadi or the Pila House theaters.

Further south, we come to the edge of Girgaum, to the Framjee Cowasjee Institute. Situated in Kalbadevi opposite Metro Cinema in Dhobitalao on the southern edge of Girgaum, this building replaced the tank built in 1831 by the philanthropist Framji Cowasjee.[51] The Gayan Uttejak Mandali (GUM), established in 1870 and which I discussed in chapter 1, regularly held its functions in the Framjee Cowasjee Institute. It was also a popular venue for lectures and talks, including those given by the Dnyan Prasarak Mandali (Propagation of Knowledge Organisation), established by Kaikhushro Kabraji, also the founder of the GUM. The hall today is of-

Figure 2.22. Framjee Cowasjee Institute. Photo: Hemangi Kadu.

ten rented out for sales of various kinds. The building is of a large neoclassical villa type; its size, layout, and design—including a large portico and a pediment—indicate that it was meant to be a symbolically important building for colonial Bombay. The fact that it has both a public hall and a library space indicates the metropolitan ambition of the elite to construct places where citizens could meet. The institute library and reading room is still functional, occupied mostly by retired men reading the daily newspaper or students preparing for examinations.

A *Times of India* advertisement for March 9, 1886, offers—at Framjee Cowasjee Institute on Saturday, March 13—"An Entertainment of Native Music" by the "celebrated ustads from Agra," Natthan Khan and Hussain Bux. Reserved seats cost two rupees, and front seats, one. Although the GUM is not mentioned, its founder, K. N. Kabraji, is listed as one of the people who can be contacted for tickets. Presumably the GUM's members attended such concerts regularly, since a number of Parsis—including Kaikhushro Kabraji, playwrights Framji Bharucha and Dhanjibhai Patel, and theater company owner Dadabhai Thunthi—took to learning Hindustani music during the 1870s and 1880s. We don't know what the ustads sang on March 13, 1886, but we can speculate that Natthan Khan may have performed Raag Nand, of which he is said to have been quite fond, and perhaps the *vilambit* teentaal composition by "Daras Piya" (pen name of his brother-in-law Mehboob Khan): *Dhoondo baar saiyyan tohe sakal ban dhoondo* (I search again and again for you, my beloved, I look for you in the whole forest).[52] As Natthan Khan returned to the samm on the first part of the word *saiyyan*, and pulled the *meend* from the stability of the *ga* (*saiy-*) to the upbeat *ma* (*-yan*), his audience would perhaps have applauded themselves and their efforts through the GUM to establish an institution of Indian music. As I mention in chapter 1, the doctors, lawyers, and journalists of Mumbai, both Parsi and Hindu, were among the earliest nonhereditary students of Hindustani music.

And so we have circumnavigated Girgaum, walking from the Opera House to Bhuleshwar where Bhangwadi is, and then to the Framjee Cowasjee Institute in Kalbadevi. If you don't fancy walking back all the way to Grant Road, you can simply board a local train at Marine Lines station and go two stops north. As you come out of the station you will see B. Merwan Irani restaurant, haunt of musicophiliacs, which reappears in chapter 3. If you go around instead, having climbed the stairs from the platform, and get onto the bridge on the eastern side of the tracks, between Grant Road Hotel and the Grant Road Masjid, you will see Muzaffarabad Hall, which is today a magnificent ruin of a mansion. Once you're on the bridge leading to Lamington Road, you can glimpse the ruin, almost like a tangible whisper, on the right. Find the steps to take you down to where there are a bunch of small shops, mostly selling automotive parts, and if you go into the *galli* on the left, you will see the arch of the hall's gateway to your left. It is now supposedly up for redevelopment (the security guard told us at least three towers would be built).

In 1899, at the age of sixteen, Anjanibai Malpekar—brilliant disciple of Nazir Khan of the Bhendi Bazar gharana mentioned in chapter 1—had her debut performance at Muzaffarabad Hall. No one remembers who owned this palatial bungalow where private baithaks took place in the early twentieth century.[53] Because the Muslim family split during Partition, and one part of it chose to go to Pakistan, the property is allegedly under disputed ownership today. The residents of the neighborhood have no memory, individual or collective, of the musical history of Muzaffarabad Hall. Anjanibai, however, is part of musicophiliac history, although she stopped performing in 1923 at the age of forty a short time after the death of her guru, Nazir Khan. She continued to support musicians of all kinds and

Figures 2.23 and 2.24. Muzaffarabad Hall ruins.

also taught occasionally, her students including Kumar Gandharva, Kishori Amonkar, and the renowned ghazal singer Begum Akhtar.[54] The figure of Anjanibai brings together the trajectory of the Goan naikin who moved to Bombay and acquired a Gujarati patron who would pay for her music lessons, the seasoned performer at mehfils at Laxmi Baug and private baithaks such as those in Muzaffarabad Hall, and the beloved teacher of great musicians, a woman who stopped performing in public but who experimented with creating a blend of thumri and khayal in later life ("mein ek nayi cheez bana rahi hoon" [I'm making something]).

Persuading the security guard to let us into the enclosure of the ruined mansion, camera hidden in a backpack, we walk in the footsteps of musicophiliacs of a hundred years ago. As we pass through the arch that marked the entrance to the mansion, we hear through the dull traffic noise from Grant Road Bridge the full-throated voice of Anjanibai singing Raag Hameer: *ga ma dha, re ni dha pa, ga ma dha,* wave upon wave of notes, cascading from meend to meend, climbing up smoothly from *ma* to *ni*, hitting the *re* in the upper octave and gliding down to the nishad, producing a sheer musical curtain through which the pale blue of the mansion's crumbling back wall can be glimpsed.

3

DEEWAANA (THE MAD ONE)
THE LOVER OF MUSIC

The intensity of the practice of listening to Hindustani music in Mumbai and the structuring of the social subject through the passion for music can be explored through the listening experiences of the city's inhabitants. The characters you will meet here share an emotion called *deewaanapan* (a Persian-derived Hindi/Urdu word for madness, insanity, being madly in love), an emotion directed not toward a person but toward a cultural practice. As I argue in chapter 1, this condition of collective listening enabled the formation of a new musical subject, the musicophiliac. The avid listener, the collector, the event organizer, the student, and the teacher—all of these figures came into Hindustani music as nontraditional musical subjects. Their attraction to a music that emerged from court and temple to become publicly available by the late nineteenth century, and their membership in the community of musicophiliacs, are among the factors that fed into the production and privileging of the musical interiority that began to prevail in Hindustani music as it moved into the twentieth century. I try to convey the musicophiliacs' responses through their own words wherever possible, and avoid mere summaries of what they said, since how they said it is also something to which we should pay attention. I heard the word "deewaane" in relation to music from Chandubhai the tabla maker, proprietor of Azad Avanadh Vadyalay. He was telling me about taking his actor friend to witness tawaif performances in the kothas of Foras Road so he could see how "really mad" people behaved, the deewaane who were mad about music. Deewaanapan is a condition of subjective excess, the condition of the musical subject's simultaneous psychic and social habitation of modern urban space.

The theory of *rasa* has been redeployed by some recent writers on Indian music, following in the wake of Sanskrit theorists like Abhinavagupta (c. 950–1060 CE), to refer to what the musician intends to evoke or achieve as well as to what the audience experiences while listening.[1] According to this theory, the musician through presentation of a raga activates a *sthayi bhava*, one of the stable emotions of a human being, and the experience of this activation produces "rasa" (juice, sap, essence) in the listener, a transitory emotion that invokes the bhava in question.[2] While I find it interesting to see what this tries to capture about audience response, I have some reservations about having recourse to ancient Indian aesthetics in order to explain contemporary experience. In spite of the venerable legacy of such a theoretical move, I worry that it could well rest on the idea of an essential and unvarying Indian cultural response, without taking into account possible transformations over time in musical perception and enjoyment because of changes in form as well as context. There is also a curious intentionalism in the invocation of rasa theory, which focuses on what effect the musician intends to achieve, as though that is enough to ensure a particular emotion in the listener. In contrast, continuing my preoccupation in this book with actual musical practice and the ways in which an emerging musicophiliac community engaged with it, I attempt to bring out music's significance for its Mumbai audiences through a recontextualization of their responses.

For the most part, this chapter discusses people's responses to Hindustani music as based on learning new ways of listening through the long twentieth century. Of course to some extent there is a relay of effect and affect here: newer members of the audience begin to imitate the responses of the regular concertgoers, and over time cultivate a recognizable repertoire of exclamations and gestures that contribute to producing the *mahaul*, atmosphere or ambience, within which a performance takes place. As discussed in chapter 1, the lingua musica acquired by Mumbai's audiences ensures that the vocalized responses are in Hindi, even if the audience members are native speakers of such diverse languages as Marathi, Konkani, Gujarati, or Kannada. One aspect of learning to listen is thus the acquisition of the repertoire of response. The other crucial aspect is acquiring a familiarity with the different ragas or melodic structures. An experienced listener can, by listening to the opening phrases of the melody, differentiate one raga from another, and one variant of a raga from the others. But there are also listeners, equally devoted to Hindustani music, who may not be able to tell one raga from another, or know only some ragas, but claim that they know good music when they hear it.

Again, I'm not claiming here that the acquisition of familiarity is a task only for Mumbai's audiences, since it can be generalized to any form of music in any part of India or the world. Instead, I'm drawing attention to the contexts and locations in which Hindustani music was made familiar in Mumbai over the twentieth century, whether it was the Ganesh Utsav concerts described below by writer Pu La Deshpande, or the private baithaks described by Nilima Kilachand of the Sajan Milap forum, or the concerts in Laxmi Baug and Brahman Sabha, or the kotha of NB Compound near Congress House in Dayalsingh Thakur's account. Earlier in the twentieth century, a primary site for hearing Hindustani melodies was the Marathi musical play, sangeet natak, as I mention in chapter 1. Singer-actors such as Bal Gandharva had strong training in Hindustani music, and the songs were composed by leading musicians such as vocalist Bhaskarbuwa Bakhle or harmonium player Govindrao Tembe, who had parallel careers as concert performers.

Bodies in Affect

An evocative passage from the film actor Durga Khote's autobiography describes the sangeet natak audience of the first decade of the twentieth century: "Even today when I hear Narayanrao's—Bal Gandharva's—recorded songs, the sounds and sights of that era of theatre return to me in every detail. Elphinstone Theatre, its broken, slithery wooden chairs, the enraptured audience, swaying in sheer bliss for hours on end to the sound of music, spellbound by the flow of emotions, grown one with the stage ... they seduce me yet again with their magic."[3] Khote also mentions how the famous Jaipur gharana vocalist Alladiya Khan, one of the gurus of Bhaskarbuwa Bakhle who had in turn trained Bal Gandharva, often visited the Elphinstone Theatre:

> That solemn imposing figure in a pink turban and blue-tinted glasses, with his pure white hair, beard, moustache, and side whiskers, swayed for hours to Bal Gandharva's music. ... He would sit completely absorbed, for ten hours at a time, carried away by the flow

of the music. When Bal Gandharva hit a particularly fine note, or a rapid *taan* burbled by in a spontaneous stream of crystal drops, Khansaheb's fingers would gently wipe away the tears flowing from his eyes.[4]

Interestingly, although sangeet natak theatergoers have spoken about the beauty of the costumes, the splendid acting and backdrops, and the thrilling stories, in Khote's memories they seem to recede in importance compared to the music. The enrapturement, the bliss, and the tears of happiness not only were experienced in the theater, but also appeared in accounts of private baithaks and public concerts, where the music also visibly moved the listener.

When musicophiliac Vamanrao Deshpande, who later became a chartered accountant by profession, first heard the Kirana gharana singer and Abdul Karim Khan's son Sureshbabu Mane, he "found his music so utterly entrancing and captivating that [he] was instantly enslaved by him. It was not just music but pure hypnotism."[5] When musician Murli Manohar Shukla first listened to Laxmi Prasad Jaipurwaale, the man who later became one of his gurus, he was singing the Raag Malkauns, with *"Tero hi naam dayaghar"* as the opening line, so wonderfully—"itna badhiyan Malkauns gaaya ki maine zindagi mein phir kabhi nahi suna" (he never heard anything like that for the rest of his life).[6] "Aap vishwaas nahi karenge mere rongte aaj bhi khade ho rahe hain" (You won't believe me if I say that even as I am telling this to you today, I'm getting goosebumps).

Shukla went on to say that there was not a sound from the audience—"Koi ek shabd nahi bola." And he says he almost forgot to play the tanpura with which he was accompanying the singer—"Aur mera tanpure ka haath beech mein band ho raha tha." The musician sang for an hour. No one stirred, and no one spoke—"Na koi utha, na kisi ne poocha." Everyone's eyes were closed. The silence and stillness in this instance were for Shukla real marks of enjoyment—"Toh bada mazaa aaya." In both these instances, the listener who was captivated was sitting amid many others—it is the context and setting of the mehfil that provides the individuated listening experience that leaves people spellbound. *Mehfil maarna*—literally, to kill the mehfil, meaning to capture the concert, is a term that musicians use to describe what a performer should aspire to.

We don't have empirical data about the social composition of Mumbai's music audiences, and whenever I made an attempt to find out who was listening to a particular performance, the answer was usually something like,

"Oh, everyone, but everyone, was there. Everyone liked to listen to music." This response was given by Dayalsingh Thakur, grandson of the famous Gangabai who was the chaudharayin or chief courtesan of the NB Compound near Congress House in Girgaum from before the days of Independence. Dayalsingh also told us this story of an ardent musicophiliac, which indicates that the passion for music did extend beyond the middle class:

> Whoever was in Mumbai at the time, they would come to the mehfil or concert in NB Compound. Usually my mother—Gangabai's daughter—would sing at the end, which would be about 4 or 5 a.m. in the morning. [Aur jo bhi uss waqt Bombay mein ho, woh aa jaate thae uss mehfil mein. Aur zyaadatar last mein meri mother ka gaana hota tha. Kuch uss waqt subah ke 4–5 baj rahe hote thae.]
>
> I remember that once Naseer Khan of Delhi was sitting in the audience, and so was Amir Khan saab. So my mother was singing, and outside—you know there was a milk booth outside—an Aarey Milk van drove up. The driver of the van came straight inside the compound. My mother was singing. I don't know what happened to the man—perhaps he was someone who understood music—but he fell at her feet and burst out crying. He was so . . . It was early morning. She was singing a thumri in Bhairavi, and when I looked at the others, they too had their handkerchiefs out. It was such that everyone had tears in their eyes. [Ek baar yaad hai mehfil mein Dilli ke Naseer Khan saab baithe hue thae. Aur Amir Khan saab bhi baithe hue thae wahaan pe. Aur woh gaa raheen thi aur baahar woh doodh ka booth tha . . . kya kehte hain. Aarey Milk ki gaadi aati thi. Uska joh driver tha woh seedha chalaa aaya. Woh gaa rahi thi wahaan pe. Pataa nahi kya hua, shayad woh sangeet samajhta tha, woh ekdum unke pairon mein gir ke rone laga. Itna usko . . . Kyunki subah ka waqt tha, Bhairavi mein Thumri gaa rahi thi woh aur yeh log ko bhi dekha toh inke bhi rumaal nikal aaye thae. Aisa hua tha ki aankhon mein aansu aa gaye thae.][7]

It is possible that the mehfils held in the NB Compound, which has a *dargah* (a shrine or tomb of a Sufi saint), attracted a more mixed audience, and that concert halls like Laxmi Baug or Brahman Sabha drew a predominantly Marathi, Gujarati, or Konkani middle-class musicophiliac.[8] Sitarist Arvind Parikh speaks about the concert hall audience as 90–95 percent Maharashtrian in Girgaum, although he mentioned that many of the great

Muslim musicians used to attend the concerts too. Here he speaks about the *punyatithi* or death anniversary of Vishnu Digambar Paluskar, which the Deodhar Music School used to commemorate by hosting all-day and all-night performances: "Morning, whole night—and the musicians used to come and listen—Amir Khan and [Bade] Ghulam Ali Khan and all people were sitting . . . Ghulam Ali Khan-saab, Latafat Khan, Khadim Husain Khan."[9]

Another story about the general appreciation of music in Mumbai is set in a working-class chawl in Girgaum. Sawai Gandharva, the disciple of Abdul Karim Khan who performed with Hirabai in the musical plays put up by her company, had a parallel career as a concert musician. While living in Khetwadi in Girgaum, he taught a young Parsi called Firoz Dastur, who went on to become an important Kirana gharana singer, alongside Gangubai Hangal and Bhimsen Joshi from Dharwad in Karnataka, who also owed a significant part of their fame to the opportunities that Mumbai audiences gave them. Once when Dastur was preparing for a radio program, he wanted to sing Raag Gujari Todi, but realized he did not have the *drut* or fast-paced composition for that raga.[10] He went to his guru, Sawai Gandharva, and asked to learn the drut. "Why don't you get it from the recording of the Khansaab (Abdul Karim Khan, the guru of Sawai Gandharva)?" asked the guru. "But it would be better if you taught me directly," pleaded Dastur. Sawai Gandharva made him sit down right there in the courtyard of the chawl and began to teach him the composition. When they finished, they realized that over a hundred people, probably people who lived in that chawl, were surrounding them, listening in absolute silence. Perhaps the setting of the music lesson ensured the silence, since if it were an actual performance the listeners might have been more ready to express their appreciation at different moments in the execution of the raga. Perhaps these working-class listeners did not possess the repertoire of appreciative exclamations that regular concertgoers had acquired and therefore stood in silence.[11]

A vivid description of the sweet misery of the musicophiliac suffering from too much choice during the Ganesh Utsav is to be found in the Marathi writer Pu La Deshpande's writings:

> For music lovers, the ten days of the festival were somewhat difficult. In one little location, Girgaum, numerous singers would sing in different *vada*s (private homes). One Saturday night and so many music performances! In Ambevadi [there was] Mallikarjun Mansur, in an-

Figure 3.1. B. Merwan: Irani café opposite Grant Road Station. Photo: Tejaswini Niranjana.

other [there was] Kagalkarbua, in Brahman Sabha [there was] Master Krishnarao (Phulambrikar), in Shastri Hall [there was] Rambhau Savai Gandharva, in Tara Temple Lane [there was] Gangubai [known in Maharashtra as Gandhari Hangal], in Chunam Lane [there was] Hirabai Badodekar—one would get completely torn and anxious! Who should one listen to? . . . Until about 3:30 in the morning, we ran from place to place and eventually wound up in front of Goodman, Persian-Indian, Merwaan, Viceroy of India, or some other Irani restaurant and wait for their doors to open to have *brun-maska* [hard-crusted bread with fresh butter]. Staying awake all night listening to music, we needed a nightcap, [which had to be] tea from an Irani restaurant without which the evening was not complete. And at that hotel, an impromptu music round table conference would come together. . . . Some would say Rambhau's voice had reached new heights that night, some would praise Gangubai's *miyan malhar*.[12]

What is common to all these accounts of being spellbound by Hindustani music, even to the point of being driven to emotional excess, is that the musical response is produced in a space of sociality, not in solitude. A short discussion of the khayal should help contextualize this response of the social subject.

The long twentieth century is also the period of the rise and domination of the Hindustani musical scene by the khayal form, which almost entirely replaced the dhrupad, which had contributed to the early training of the musicians mentioned both in Parikh's account of Laxmi Baug and in Deshpande's account of the Ganesh Utsav season. The khayal foregrounds, as the name derived from Urdu/Arabic suggests, the play of imagination, providing, according to musicians and scholars, more room for improvisation than the more structured dhrupad which gave birth to it. While the khayal singers of the first part of the twentieth century sang by projecting their voices and without any technological enhancement, by the 1950s the microphone was everywhere. Vocalists' techniques of voice production and modulation changed to accommodate this, and eventually listeners' tastes changed too, now privileging the softer voice or the one that sounded better with a microphone. Thus the technology-enhanced khayal strengthened the production of interiority that the genre had inaugurated, but which required a sense of listening together. Intimacy and interiority as represented in the khayal performance and in the setting of musciophiliac listening is social and public as well.

The Gender of Deewaanapan

How did distance and intimacy work across genders? And across class-caste? Again, it is not possible to find empirical evidence of how many women in Mumbai attended musical events through the twentieth century, but we can make a guess by extrapolating from other public events. Available documentation of the struggle for Indian independence in the first part of the century suggests that large numbers of women were involved in mass civil disobedience and other forms of political action. Music, however, may have borne a different set of connotations, some illicit, connected to courtesans and Muslim musicians, that would have kept middle-class Hindu women out of audiences like the one described by Dayalsingh Thakur above. The timing of mehfils would have been another important consideration: the performance would begin around 11 p.m. and go on until 5 a.m. in the early decades of the twentieth century, as musician Govindrao Tembe testifies in his memoirs.[13] Again, as we can see from these memoirs, going to listen to music was a form of male socializing, and while it might have provided a link between rich patrons and not-so-wealthy musicophiliacs who were also perhaps performers, it seems to have left women out of the picture. The only women mentioned in such autobiographies are female performers, who at that time were clearly not from a middle-class background.

Thus it appears from these accounts that women in the musicophiliac context, at least before the 1940s, would have been those from performing and courtesan backgrounds who had become proficient in art music, or sang the so-called light classical forms like thumri and ghazal. There are references to Anjanibai Malpekar hosting other musicians in her house to take part in musical exchange and discussion. They included well-known women singers from Benares and Kolkata, like Gauharjan, Vidyadhari Devi, Rasoolanbai, and Siddheshwari Devi.[14] Tarabai Velingkar, known as Baputara because she functioned like a male head of household (*bapu* meaning father), regularly organized baithaks in her house and patronized a number of musicians.[15] Gangabai, the chaudhurayin of the NB Compound near Congress House, took part in musical exchanges that she hosted. The lack of references to noncourtesan women in relation to music is puzzling if we recall that from the 1870s on, Kaikhusro Kabraji, founder of the Gayan Uttejak Mandali, wanted Parsi women to learn Hindustani music so that men would hear them singing at home and stop patronizing entertainers outside. Although Kabraji's ideas were not popular among the Parsis, the Mandali did enable a number of Parsi women to become familiar with Indian music. And when Paluskar started the Bombay branch of the Gandharva Mahavidyalay (GMV) in 1908, he was able to attract both Hindu and Parsi women to his school. As Janaki Bakhle says, the Bombay GMV in 1911 "had a total of 792 students on its roster, of whom eighty-eight were women."[16] We don't know about the class background of these women, but some of them were probably training to be music teachers. Paluskar himself, according to Bakhle, did not encourage women to become performers. Given Paluskar's focus on what he thought of as Hindu music, there was a good deal of emphasis on learning devotional songs like bhajans and kirtans that women could sing at home during Hindu religious fesivals.[17]

When Paluskar's student B. R. Deodhar started his School of Indian Music in 1925, he was able to bring in even larger numbers of students, both men and women. Ramdas Bhatkal, a musicophiliac whose profile I discuss at length later in this chapter, mentions that his sister was learning music at the Deodhar School in the early 1940s, and that the syllabus consisted only of Hindustani raga music, even if the compositions included traditional as well as more recently composed devotional ragas.[18] We hear about schoolgirls learning music from Deodhar at the Prarthana Samaj in the 1920s. In the words of Deodhar's granddaughter Sangeeta Gogate:

Mr. Kore of the Prarthana Samaj used to meet Deodhar regularly, and when Deodhar told him he wanted to teach music classes, Kore gave him the books published by Prarthana Samaj which had prayers in them, and asked him to put them to music and teach them to the schoolgirls. [Prarthana Samaj ke Mr. Kore, he used to meet him regularly, toh unhe aise bataaye ke mujhe aise aise karna hai, aur unhone kya kiya tha ki Prarthana Samaj ki jo book thi, is mein sab prarthanaye thi, woh sab books inke diyi thi ke unko tune kar ke aap hamare Prarthana Samaj-wale ladkiyaan ko sikhaana.]

Deodhar then asked Mr. Kore whether he could have space to conduct Hindustani music classes, and was given a couple of rooms in Rammohun School. From four or five girls in 1925, Deodhar's school grew to thirty female pupils, and then boys also started coming.[19]

It is possible that new platforms of dissemination, like the radio, were acceptable for middle-class women who were being trained in Hindustani music. A Bombay Radio Club listing of April 17, 1925, from the *Times of India*, for example, announces a "special programme of Indian music" by Mr. S. H. Sukthankar, along with his pupils "Miss Kusum S. Dhurandhar and Miss Mirabai S. Kerkar," from 9 to 10:30 p.m. While famous singers from a courtesan background like Bai Sunderabai are listed with just the prefix "Bai," the prefix "Miss" and the women's surnames in this announcement suggest that they probably come from respectable Hindu families.

The fact that so many young women were learning Hindustani music by the 1920s did not necessarily translate into their presence at public musical events, but as the long twentieth century wore on, women became part of the concert audiences: Trinity Club photos from the 1960s show some women listening intently, although they are fewer than the men in the room. At the Ganesh Utsavs, which are huge public events, there would certainly have been large numbers of women. The musical play, through which many people learned to follow Hindustani music, also had many female fans. In the public concerts or for amplified radio broadcasts at Ranibaug (Victoria Garden) and Malabar Hill, we may speculate that the audiences included many women, perhaps on an outing with their families.[20] But whether these women with their multiple responsibilities could afford to be crazy about music is another matter.

I asked Nilima Kilachand, from a wealthy music-loving Jain family, who spoke about growing up in the 1960s, whether she had many opportunities to listen to music in public settings:

> You know for me, very few, because my mother was interested but my father wasn't. He was a diamond merchant. He would travel to Antwerp and all. Really not into music, but my mother was. She had learnt the sitar and vocal music. But there was no opportunity or I think it wasn't the culture in those days to buy tickets and go and listen to late night. . . . We sort of did what everyone else did in the family. By the time I got into college and had my own music-loving friends, I was almost seventeen–eighteen. At twenty I got married. So yes, I did go to concerts after I got married—my husband and I [in the 1970s].[21]

We know very little about Mumbai's women musicophiliacs who were not themselves singers. But one piece of information catches the eye. A wealthy widow named Dhaklibai Sukthankar or Bai lived in a three-story house by the sea in Walkeshwar. She had inherited a great deal of property from her father, being the only surviving child. Being "passionately fond of music" and, as a woman of the upper classes, not being able to learn music herself (this would have been in the 1910s or early 1920s), she supported the work of Vishnu Narayan Bhatkhande, the famous codifier of Hindustani music discussed in chapter 1. Almost an entire floor of Bai's house was dedicated to Bhatkhande's Hindustani Music Research Project. In her actor-granddaughter Durga Khote's account, "Bai spent thousands of rupees to help him [Bhatkhande] in his project of evolving a notation system to teach Hindustani music. She paid honoraria to all the musicians who assisted him in his work, and housed them. She enabled him to travel all over India to collect the information he required. The teaching methodology for Hindustani music that he evolved was built on the strength of her support. Yet, the house where this was happening was itself musically mute."[22]

Another woman, identified only as the mother of a music student, is vividly presented in this story told by Girgaum resident Nitin Shirodkar about his guru Firoz Dastur and the guru's guru:

> Firoz Dastur's mother was a sacrificing woman. That entire Grant Road, Khetwadi area during the monsoons, even today you have knee-deep water—one spell of rain and there is knee-deep water. Savai Gandharva used to come to teach Panditji at his house because they had a very big house; his father, Dasturji's father, had a billiards table on the first floor. Dasturji's mother doted on her son a lot and she was the one who was encouraging him to learn from Savai Gand-

harva. It so happened that one day Savai Gandharvaji said that I'm coming and it was raining cats and dogs. One hour passed, two hours passed—she was all the time going into the balcony to see whether from Khetwadi she can see Savai Gandharva coming, and after about two hours she saw a man wading through knee-deep water trying to protect his dhoti from the rain with his umbrella. Finally, he reached his pupil's house. The mother offered him a towel to dry himself and the taleem started right in earnest. Panditiji says, "I went into the kitchen to see what my mother was doing and Savai Gandharva's wet leather slippers were being dried on the pan."

"The pan that my mother used to make rotis, that same pan was being used to dry guruji's slippers." She felt if guruji's slippers remained wet he would get a fever and I would miss my training the next day; this is what my mother did for me. I can never forget this sacrifice that my mother made for me, especially when it came to Guruji. [Jya tavyavar ti chapatya karaichi majhi aai tya tavyavar ti guruji chya chappala ti sukhvat hoti. Karan tila vatat hota ki gurujinchya chappla jar olya rahilya tar tyana taap beep aala tar udya majhi taaleem chukel, hey majhya aaine majhya saathi keleli sacrifice te me visru shakat nahi te guruji chya babtit keleli.][23]

Dastur's mother and other female members of the family stood behind the curtain dividing the taleem room from the rest of the house to listen to the singing. This was in the late 1930s when Sawai Gandharva was teaching the young Firoz. Why drying out the guru's footwear is seen as a sacrifice is interesting. Is it because the slippers were being dried on a cooking pan? Or because touching someone else's footwear is seen as polluting in a Hindu context? Does the Parsi Dastur use the word "sacrifice" because he is embedding his experience in a majoritarian understanding of purity and pollution? Is this the word Dastur used, or is it the word his acolyte Nitin remembers him using?[24]

As my interviews show, by the 1960s it was a common practice for Hindu women in wealthy business families to learn Hindustani music at home, usually from a Muslim ustad. However, by the 1940s, large numbers of middle-class women were attending music schools like the School of Indian Music in Girgaum or any of the numerous classes that were on offer. In the early twenty-first century, when I conducted my interviews with musicians and musicophiliacs in Mumbai, it was impossible to think of middle-class (and especially Hindu) women as not having a place among students, practitioners, and audiences of Hindustani music. Over nearly eighty years, they have come to achieve a centrality in how the music is both represented and perpetuated. While the achievement has something to do with the de-eroticization and sacralization of Indian music through nationalist efforts, it was also spurred on by the growing opportunities for women to learn music through music schools as well as through individual discipleship.[25]

The Indian Broadcasting Company started using a high-powered transmitter in 1927, and Indian music formed an important part of its programming, just as it was for the Bombay Presidency Radio Club from the early 1920s. Now that Hindustani raga music was coming directly into the home, it is likely that more and more people, women as well as men, were exposed to it. While in the earlier decades of Hindustani music's emergence in Mumbai, the only way in which musicophiliacs could listen to their favorite singers was by attending concerts or private baithaks, or going to the Ganesh Utsav festivities, the habit of listening was additionally cultivated through radio broadcasts from the mid-1930s on. These broadcasts often provided the earliest initiation into classical music for middle-class families. As Murli Manohar Shukla puts it:

> Including my father, there were four brothers [in the family]. Although all four were music lovers, my father fancied music the most, maybe because he was the eldest. Every night All India Radio used to be on, and from 10 p.m. to midnight he would take me into his lap to listen.... I was four years old at the time. I would listen to the radio, and sometimes I would fall asleep, even as my father kept asking, "You're listening, right?" [Yeh chaar bhai thae mere pitaji ko milaakar. Aur yeh chaaron sangeet-premi thae, lekin keval pitaji bade thae toh sangeet ke zyaada shaukeen thae. Humesha raat ko jab woh All India Radio on hota tha, toh raat ko 10 se 12 baje tak mujhe goad mein leke ... main tab 4 baras ka tha. Mujhe radio sunaate thae aur main so bhi jaun toh bolte thae, sun rahe ho na.][26]

Another musicophiliac, Ramdas Bhatkal, speaks about the importance of the radio in offering *shravan shiksha* or musical instruction through listening:

> At the time there were really good programs on the radio at night and actually even during the day. *Tya velela radio var ratri chaan karyakram asaiche kimbhavna diwas bhar suddha,* what they called

marathon—somebody would sing in the morning, in the afternoon and evening, and mind you those days were not days of recording so the singer had to actually wait there throughout the day and sing live. But anyway, for us as listeners everyday there was a feast. To add to that, post-Independence some of the greats started singing regularly, even Faiyaz Khan, Bade Ghulam Ali Khan—they would be fairly regular. And the best thing was Dr. [B. V.] Keskar [minister of information and broadcasting from 1952] and his idea of National Program (of Music), with that *deed taas* (one and a half hours) every Saturday, we would really listen to somebody really great, some of whom we couldn't [otherwise] have listened to at all. . . . So we learnt a great deal through listening.[27]

Musical Transgression

While the radio was creating a community of listeners that would tune in at the same time to listen to Hindustani music and semiclassical forms such as the natya sangeet, it was merely complementary to the varied physical settings in which the musicophiliac encountered music. Social transgressions—spatially understood—were sometimes inspired by the act of listening. At the same time as the radio was introducing a larger public to singers like Amir Khan, who performed regularly in Mumbai mehfils, his fans would disregard conventional notions of respectability and enter spaces like Gangabai's kotha where he stayed. Thus the musicophiliac would without hesitation cross social boundaries to have the privilege of being with a musician he loved. As a young student of music, Murli Manohar Shukla went to the NB Compound to see Amir Khan: "I was free, and since I was little I had the habit of making my way into places, like a mouse. And every kind of place would accept me. [Main free tha . . . chhota tha na, ghusne ki aadat thi . . . choohe ki tarah. Toh mujhe sab jagah accept karte thae.]"

> TN: [Have you ever gone near Congress House?] Aap kabhi Congress House ke paas gaye hain?
>
> MS: Yes, I've gone to his house. I shut my eyes and went in. I went to meet him there. I went in the morning, reaching there at ten o'clock. Amir Khan says to me, *"Arrey,* why have you come so early in the morning?" I said, "How can anyone call ten o'clock early morning? It's going to be noon soon!" He was brushing his teeth at 10 a.m.

[Haan, main unke ghar pe gaya hoon. Aankh band kar ke chala gaya. Mila wahaan unse. Arrey, subah subah . . . Main 10 baje pahuncha hoon, aur Amir Khan saab bole subah subah kahaan aa gaye?! Maine kaha 10 baje koi subah kehta hai? Thodi der mein dopahar hone waali hai! Brush kar rahe the woh 10 baje.]

Shukla's recalling that he shut his eyes and went into the compound suggests that as a middle-class Brahmin he was not really supposed to be at a kotha. He also makes a bemused comment about Amir Khan brushing his teeth at 10 a.m., which seemed very late to the youngster of regular habits, suggesting perhaps a decadent lifestyle of the people who lived in the kotha, who would not be up too early in the morning. The contrast is with nonhereditary musician Shukla himself, who as a youth also stayed up until the early hours listening to music or accompanying performers, but became accustomed to sleeping very little.

However, the option of going into a kotha to meet singers was, unsurprisingly, not available to middle-class women. Musician Lalith Rao, who trained under Khadim Husain Khan in the 1960s and '70s, said she knew that her accompanists—who played the sarangi, the tabla, or the harmonium—lived in the NB Compound, but it would have been impossible for her to obtain a glimpse of that world, even though she lived practically next door in the Grant Road area. Her community of Chitrapur Saraswats, all music lovers, would have been scandalized, she says, at a woman of her class being seen in a place like the compound.[28] Incidentally, this is the same Brahmin subcaste to which Murli Manohar Shukla belongs.[29]

Nayan Ghosh, a well-known sitar and tabla player and principal of Sangit Mahabharati, spoke about his father, the musician Nikhil Ghosh, going to a kotha on the summons of his guru Amir Hussain Khan. Nayan Ghosh referred to it as the "forbidden area" and called the tawaif's house, where the musicians gathered, the dangal (wrestling arena):

NG: The tawaif would sponsor one particular evening. This was on *jummas* . . . on Fridays. My father, initially when his guru took him there the first time, he was shocked with the whole atmosphere . . . the whole area . . . as you walk through the gullies and streets.[30] His guru used to tell him, "Come with me—let's go there, to that bai's house, to the other bai's house." ["Chalo aaj mere saath wahaan . . . so and so bai ke ghar mein, so and so bai ke ghar mein."] And then he saw some of the greatest musicians. Young musicians would perform first. And seniors would all sit around and listen to him. And if somewhere a young musician went wrong or faltered—it could be vocal, it could be sarangi, sitar, tabla, anything—they would be stopped by the senior musicians. "Stop, son, play this again. Who's your teacher?" ["Ruko beta, yeh fir se bajao. Kaun hain . . . tumhare ustad kaun hain?"] Then they come to know that the ustad is sitting there in that corner. ["Pataa chala kone mein baithe hain."] *Toh* they would tell that ustad that please correct this so-and-so thing. Quality control was there! Correct this thing and bring him back. "You come back after six Fridays, and you come back after ten Fridays. And play again." ["Tum cheh jumme ke baad aa jao, tum dus jumme ke baad aa jaana. Phir se bajao."] So they used to give time to repair that, make the correction, and come and perform again. So it would go from junior to senior musicians and often, there would be challenges by some senior musician. He would play something and another would challenge or take objections, saying, "I don't agree with this thing." Either they would come to an understanding, or often there were fights. And very serious fights!

TN: And these musicians were Muslims, Hindus, or Parsis?

NG: Mostly all musicians were Muslims. So, my father felt all the more kind of out of place there [Nikhil Ghosh was Hindu]. Umm, however, he saw that all that happened in these places was music and nothing else. And quality music, you know! And the senior ustads would sit there, and the tawaifs had such etiquette, you know! They used to have this kind of a cane curtain. And all the ladies would sit behind, and they listen to these mehfils. They would arrange for the tea, and the *paan*, and the snacks and all that. So, it would start at about four in the afternoon and go on till about twelve or one in the night. And one by one, musicians would perform and some . . . when they entered into challenges or fights, it happened for the good of the music. Like somebody would say, "The other composition in this pair is missing." ["Iska joda nahi hai. Iss cheez ka joda nahi hai."] Another musician would say, "I'll bring the other one in the pair next Friday." ["Agle jumme ko main joda le aata hoon."] And he would compose something and come and give an answer to that, you know. Make another composition. Our music grew primarily in such areas. Generally, we know about nawabs and maharajahs and temples. But this was a big contribution . . . this place where tawaifs helped a lot, you know!

Once, Nikhil Ghosh had to defend his teacher's reputation by playing in front of the senior musicians, and he was commended for his performance. The tawaifs also praised him.

> And they very much were fond of him. They were all like mother figures, you know. He went to the extent of saying that these were the real devis, you know, the real goddesses. These were the real devis who saved our music and kept it alive. So when we were young... he said, "Grow up a little more. I'll take you to these areas and you must touch the feet of these ladies," he said. "They are the people who kept our music alive."

In spite of the elder Ghosh's obvious fascination for the kotha where he had defended his guru's reputation, he never went back to see it, although—according to his son—he often asked Muslim musicians that he met at concerts whether certain tawaifs that he had known were still alive.

The learned "Professor" Deodhar had a close friendship with Bade Gulam Ali Khan ("they were in love with each other," says Sangeeta Gogate, Deodhar's granddaughter, referring to their lengthy musical conversations), who was always to be found at the Deodhar School at French Bridge, a short walk from Chowpatty Beach.[31] The students used to spend as much time as they could with the Khansaheb and get him to sing to them. Not being content with seeing him at their school, they often went to his residence in the NB Compound to listen to him. What little we know about the demographics of music students in the 1940s when Bade Ghulam Ali began to spend sustained periods in Mumbai suggests that they were middle class and mostly Hindu. By going to the compound where Gangabai's kotha was, they were, like Shukla, and like Nikhil Ghosh, giving into a musicophilia that enabled social transgression.

Music-Mad in the Kotha

Chandrakant (Chandu) Ramjibhai speaks about the time he took his childhood friend Hari, later to become famous as the film star Sanjeev Kumar, to see "really crazy people" or deewaane:

> I got training for Foras Road since my childhood. [His father would send him to the kothas to return repaired tablas.] My mother would always say, "Why are you sending him there? The boy will be spoiled." With me was Hari, Sanjeev Kumar. He would tell me, "Chandubhai,

I want to see crazy people." He used to work in minor plays at the time. "I want to see how crazy people behave," he said. [Woh bachpan se mujhe training mile hai, woh Foras Road ki. Jao, ma hamesha. "Kya tame, kyan moklocho? Kyun bhejte ho udhar, ladka kharab ho jayega." Mere saath Hari, Sanjeev Kumar woh bhi. Mujhe woh bolta hai mereko, "Chandubhai mujhe ganda dekhna ka hai, yaane deewani mujhe dekhne ka hai" Woh time mein chote chote natak mein kaam kar raha tha, woh time pe deewana dekhne ka mereko, kaise deewane rehte hai.]

I told him to wear a torn shirt. He used to live in Bhuleshwar. We also lived there earlier and from that time the two of us were friends, Hari being six months or a year older than me. He carried two tablas and we went walking to Foras Road. At that time my father would give me one rupee for the tram. The tram would cost ten paise one anna . . . one anna for the tram from Colaba to Mahim and you could go up to Dadar for one anna. [Baba dekh ek kaam kar uska fata hua shirt pehen le tu. Woh Bhuleshwar mein rahta hai, hum bhi pehle Bhuleshwar mein rehte the wahan se hum dono dost log aur Hari mere se 6 mahine-saal bada tha. Woh bhi do tabla uthave chalte chalte Foras road jaave. Tabhi woh time pe baba Pitaji mere ek rupaiya dete thae tram ka. Dus paise ki tram thi ek anna . . . ek anna ki tram Colaba se leke Mahim tak, Dadar tak jaave ek aane mein.]

But we would save that one rupee [by walking]. We would go and give back the [repaired] tablas. I said, "Hari, look, these are all the crazy people who sit here." He said, "Yes, Chandubhai." Allarakhibai recognized us, and said, "Chandubhai, who is this? Artist?" I said, "Yes, he acts a little in plays. . . ." "He looks like he does," she said. Then she said, "Son, you come here. You want to see crazy people? You will find them all here." They would come at one or two in the night to listen, all these rich people. Even without drinking alcohol, they would be intoxicated [because of the music]. The act of being a crazy person, he [Sanjeev Kumar] used it in [the film] *Khilona*. [Magar hum ek rupaiya bachate thae woh time pe. Phir wahan jaake tabley dete thae. Main bola "Hari dekh le yeh sab deewane baithe hai." Bole, "haan Chandubhai." Allarakhi bai pehchante hai, "Chandubhai kaun hai yeh? Kalakar?" "Haan, hai woh natak mein thoda sa kaam . . ." "Dikhta hi aisa." Phir baad mein bole, "Beta tu yahan aa ja tereko deewani dekhne hai na milega sab." Raat ek ek do do baje aate the Foras road sab sunne ko yeh seth log. Pe ke begair peeye huye sab masti mein rehte thae, woh hi kaam usko Khilona mein kaam laga usko. Woh kaam usne deewane ka kaam usne Khilona mein banaya usne.][32]

The kotha was frequented by popular Hindi film music composers like Naushad and Madan Mohan, into whose tunes the thumri, the ghazal, and the khayal often entered. One day, Chandhubhai, wearing a bamboo silk coat and a tie, went to give a repaired tabla to the tawaif Punjabi Jodharan in her kotha and saw Naushad sitting there.

> I said, "Mother, I have kept the tabla over there." She said, "Yes, son, come sit here"; I said, "Ammaji, I want to hear 'Ka karoon sajani aye na baalam' in your voice." Naushad pricked up his ears. "Barkat Ali Khan Saab's 'Ka karoon sajani aye na baalam,' I want to hear that, and then I'll leave in two minutes." [Bola Ammaji tabla rakha udhar peeche wahan pe bole, ha beta aao baith baith idhar, main kaho Ammaji, mujhe "Ka karoon sajani aye na baalam" itna sunna tha aapke gale se. Naushad ke kaan tight ho gaye aarey kahan ka Barkat Ali Khan Saab ka, Ka karoon sajani aye na baalam woh mujhe sunao ek main jata hoon abhi do minute ke andar.]
>
> Naushad said, "Punjaban, who is this boy? He must be just about seventeen, and he requested a song from you? Who is this boy?" Madan Mohan [the film composer] was sitting nearby. Punjaban said, "This boy is like my son. Sometimes when he gets into the mood he wants to hear me sing a ghazal, so I have to sing for him ... and I sing for him with love." [Naushad bole, "Punjaban yeh kaun ladka hai? Umar uski 17 saal ki hai woh aapko farmaish kar liya? Kya hai ladka kaun hai?" Madan Mohan baju mein baitha tha ghazal mereko sunne ki thi bole, "yeh ladka hai apne ladke ke barabar hai magar kabhi mood mein aaye toh bol deta hai mujko mujhe gaana sunana padta hai, woh ghazal sunane padti hai mereko usko ek pyaar se main suna dete hoon suko."]
>
> And then the songs she presented ... Punjaban Jodhan ... all these singers and musicians, they would come there to listen, because they would get something from it. They didn't come there to pass time. They would get something from there. [Phir jo unhone ek cheez batayi hai ... wah wah Punjaban Jodhan ne yeh sab gaanewale jo sangeetkar bhi hai woh wahan aate thae sunne ke liye, unhe uske andar

kuch milta tha unlog ko. Aise hi wahan aate nahi the timepass karne ke liye. Jara bhi usko bhi kuch cheez milti thi usko.]

Chandubhai is a figure who doesn't identify his action of going to the kotha as socially transgressive, because his father owns a tabla-making shop, and he runs errands for him, taking the instruments wherever they are required, whether it's the music conference, the concert hall, or the kotha. For his friend Hari, it was clearly the first time he was entering such a space, although he was from the world of theater; for Chandubhai's mother, a craftsman's wife, her teenage son would be "spoiled" if he frequented the Foras Road establishments, even though the same male musicians and composers who went there also came to the tabla shop. In the kotha, the young tabla maker occupies a position of equality with famous film composers since they are all deewaane together, all mad about music.

Listening as Seva or Service

The idea of "serving music" comes up in stories told by those who were regular listeners at different kinds of music events. Chandubhai, for example, was fond of attending music conferences:

> This is a hobby. Music is very good. Music is my strength. All illness goes away when you listen to music; all the diseases will go away. Cancer, diabetes, everything will go away—that's what I have heard. I'm seventy-three now, and I haven't had any illness. I used to be there in the [music] conference for ten days. I would never get tired. . . . I would have a bath and eat my *bajra roti* and have some milk and I would go to the Sangeet Sabha. That was my duty. That was the only thing in my head. I wanted to serve everyone; I didn't want money. [Yeh shauk hai apne ko, kya? Yeh sangeet bahut hi accha hai. Sangeet bole toh tandaroosti hai apni. Tandaroosti bole jo apne andar rog hota hai na woh sab nikal jaata hai sangeet ke andar jab sunenge na aap yeh iske andar woh sab rog nikal jaate hai cancer bole, diabetes bole sab kuch nikal jate uske andar maine aisa suna hai. Woh mere abhi tak 73 umar hai abhi mujhe ek bhi rog nahi malum nahi. Conference mein dus dus din rahta tha magar thakaan kuch nahi mereko. . . . Naha dhoke khana bajri ki roti aur doodh peeke main jaata tha Sangeet Sabha ke andar. Woh apni duty thi

apna woh hi dimaag bas Seva kare apun sab ki paise ki apun kuch jaroorat nahi thi.]

Although Chandubhai did not explicitly say so, his last sentence implies that he used to offer his services for free in case the instruments needed a bit of tinkering or emergency attention during the performances.

The idea of serving music can also be found in those who belonged to the music circles. As Nilima Kilachand described those who frequented the circle she helped to establish: "You know, we had the true *rasikas* and by that I don't mean in a snobbish way. But they were listeners who were looking for gharanedaar taleem. So they did not necessarily go [because of] the artistes. Of course the artiste had to represent the taleem and gharana well. But they went because it was a particular guru's shagird. If it was a Sharad Sathe shagird, or a Dinkar Kaikini shagird, you got to listen because you will learn something about the stylistic elements and you will really enrich your musical knowledge."[33]

With this strong interest in gharanedaar music, the music circle members who had heard a singer perform on another platform would recommend names to Kilachand and her co-organizers. She said, "They were really involved with the circle, the featuring of the artist, and there may have been artists whom we as a committee may not have heard of, so they would source them for us." The service to music did not end with sourcing performers, however.

> Then after a particular concert was over, they would talk to the performer. This was not a formal talk. They would say, "I had heard this particular Ustaad sing this particular bandish in a different way. *Woh samm alag tha, woh lay alag thi.* [The starting note was arrived at differently; the rhythm was different.]" So they discussed it with the musician, "*ki isme dhaivat lagta nahi tha* [in this raga the sixth note—*dhaivat*—was not touched at all]." They were people who knew and understood music, so they would share their experiences. It was not really a counseling which they gave them; it was a sharing of their experience. Whether the performer was interested in that or not, there was that kind of intimacy and informality.

The baithak audience, says Kilachand, was never more than seventy or eighty people, with the number going up to 150 if a particularly well-known musician was performing.[34]

It was also common for musicophiliacs who hosted their favorite singer to hold a small musical event in their houses. Kilachand speaks of "a gentleman called Mr. Bengeri. He was a great fan of Mallikarjun Mansur. In fact, Pandit-ji used to stay in his house."

TN: Where was that?

NK: Somewhere in Parle. It was a sort of small nondescript kholi with two or three rooms, but Pandit-ji was happy there. They [the musicians] were not even demanding in their expectations. Whenever Pandit-ji came here [to Mumbai] for a concert, Bengeri would organize a small mehfil in his house the next day or the day before the concert. And unbelievable music we've heard there. There were barely twenty to thirty people sitting there. He used to have a ground-floor flat, and the windows had these bars. There were people on the road who would stop and look [through] the bars and listen to the concerts. There was that kind of enthusiasm.

TN: When would this be, approximately?

NK: 1980s, very early '80s. And Bhimsen-ji for instance, until he passed away, was staying with a friend of ours called Kakubhai Khimji. And Kakubhai took advantage of that, not in a bad way. We have been to Kakubhai's house at four in the morning. The concert would begin at four. Why? Because we don't get to hear ragas of that *prahar* at that time. So there was no light. He lived all the way in Matunga. Bhimsen-ji agreed to do that sort of thing and he wanted to really sing these ragas. Then there were concerts that started at one thirty after lunch, so everyone got there at one thirty. There were concerts that started at nine at night. They were all-night concerts but got over at two to two thirty.

TN: These are all private baithaks?

NK: All private.

Musicophiliac as Organizer: Nilima Kilachand

Now in her late sixties or early seventies, Nilima comes from a family of Jain traders who migrated from Lucknow to Bombay. After she married into the Kilachand business family in her twenties, Kilachand and her husband used to attend public classical music concerts regularly. There was also a tradition of hosting mehfils in their own home, which is an enormous mansion, almost a palace, built as a town house by the maharaja of Patiala, who eventually sold it to the Kilachand family. Nilima Kilachand's interview was conducted in English, although she used key Hindustani phrases when she talked about certain aspects of the music.

Nilima never performed on the concert stage, but has stayed connected to music all her life.[35] In the 1970s, she was a well-known co-organizer of small baithaks on the Bharatiya Vidya Bhavan premises, an activity that was part of the Sajan Milap forum she cofounded. This was apart from hosting private baithaks at her own mansion. She continues her music involvement as a member of various cultural policy-making bodies in Mumbai.

> NK: In this house, they are all very interested in classical music. We've had Faiyyaz Khan Sahib perform here; we've had Vilayat Hussain perform here; and all the big Agra gharana people—Sharafat Khan Sahib, Khadim Husain Khan Sahib, Lalith [Rao] have performed here. But the earlier maestros like Anwar Hussain Khan Sahib, Raja Miyan's father, they have all performed here. Bhimsen-ji has performed here several times. Siddheshwari Bai has performed. Birju Maharaj has performed. We had dance also. In this house, we were really patrons of the arts. Every concert festival we would go ... and gharana *sammelans* ... we were still continuing with Sajan Milap. We would attend every monthly baithak. We would go to private mehfils, which was a big thing. We would give up everything for private concerts in people's homes.

> TN: Did you host your baithaks once a month? When did you have all these major singers perform?

> NK: Usually at home, usually in the winter season because it was more convenient. But I have had some guru *poornimas* [annual get-together of a musician's students to pay their respects through performing] over here also. I've just hosted them for Khan Sahib. So that was in the monsoon, usually it is July. But mostly in the winters. Summer it becomes a little hot. From about November to early March or mid-March we would have Holi concerts. We have had a lot of concerts here. We've had [Alarmel] Valli dance here, Malavika Sarukkai dance here. Birju Maharaj has danced ten or eleven times.

> TN: Do you have an auditorium space?

NK: I'll show you. It is not an auditorium. This house was a palace which belonged to the maharaja of Patiala, and we bought it from him. It has got all elements of a palace. We have—it's not a darbar hall, but it's a large hall where we would have performances. But not without PA systems. The hall is too large.

TN: And you'd invite about a hundred people?

NK: No, no, it can accommodate many more.

Apart from organizing the house baithaks, Kilachand also helped form a music circle called Sajan Milap along with some of the musicians and music lovers she knew. The name came from the pseudonym of her teacher Khadim Husain Khan, who signed himself as Sajan Piya in his compositions and who was the guru of Lalith Rao and Babanrao Haldankar. Lalith Rao's husband, Jayavanth Rao, became an important figure in Sajan Milap, contributing time and effort to raising funds and organizing concerts. Says Kilachand, "There were so many music circles like us who were really rendering human service, but never bothered about the profitability angle or about promoting any one gharana or one artist. That's what our Khan Sahib really was all about—listen, not to be entertained, but to learn. And that's how you grow musically."

Referring to the practitioner as distinct from the performer, Kilachand speaks of those who lived their lives in music.

NK: So they would become members of music circles. They would also initiate themselves as practitioners of music, not necessarily performers. There is a slight difference. You are sort of practicing music, you may be teaching, you may not be good for a concert stage, you may not have the ability to draw audiences, etc., but they still were practitioners. I would call them practitioners. So they were quite well informed. We valued their contribution to the circle and the selection and funding sometimes. They would use their good offices to get funds. All this became a very large ecosystem which all helped us to survive and classical music to survive. That was really very nice. Everyone thought it was almost their moral duty to see that classical music survives in Sajan Milaap. They were sort of doing it for that reason. So there was a great intimacy and there was a great involvement.[36]

TN: So you see this phase of organizing around music as really a high point in your own investment in music?

NK: Absolutely. In fact, I really owe Khan Sahib [Khadim Husain Khan] a cultural heritage that he has given me. I owe it to Khan Sahib. I'll never be able to repay that. Though I looked after Khan Sahib a lot, as much as I could, when he was not well and finally passed away. And still the family and all mean a lot to me. I'll never be able to repay the heritage he has given me, the legacy he has given me. Whether I understand that music, at what level I understand it, it is not the issue. The issue is that he has sensitized me to music.

But because we had this group which was very . . . they were all performers, Lalith, Baban, all of them. We got into this whole thing and then we wanted to do it for Khan Sahib's sake. That's how I got into it, really. Yes, my knowledge of music, whatever level and stage it may be, it is enough to make me passionate about music . . . which again I owe to Khan Sahib. He was able to really bring out a kind of passion for the art form. The way he taught, the way he . . . it was not just about teaching music. It was a lot more than music he taught us. He taught us to listen well. He taught us to be good listeners.[37]

Balasaheb Tikekar, Trinity Club Trustee

The Trinity Club or Trimurti Mandal was established around 1907 with vocalist Bhaskarbuwa Bakhle as patron. Chapter 2 discusses the space of the club and the neighborhood in which it still exists. Here I bring in Balasaheb Tikekar, a musicophiliac who spent decades as an organizer of this music circle and is still its trustee even as it has become almost unknown. He and his wife live in an apartment in Shastri Hall near Nana Chowk, in an old dwelling complex that has housed many musicians over the century. Balasaheb spoke mostly in Marathi.

Balasaheb's association with the club began in 1955, nearly fifty years after it was established. He spoke of the days when he first got involved:

After a few days some people decided we should have weekly music sessions on the weekends, and they decided to have it on Sunday mornings at ten. [Pan kahi divasani kahi lokani tharavla ki aapan apla weekly basat jauya gaayala Shanivar kinva Ravivar asa kahi tari tharavuya. Tya pramane Ravivar tharla asa sakali 10 vajta gayala basaicha.]

And we would find someone who had instruments—someone would offer their harmonium, some other would bring the tabla. Somebody would say, "I have a tanpura." We would go and bring them. This is how the programs started. Someone used to sing and we would ask, "Can you play the tabla? Come play for [us] sometime. And then is there anyone who can play the harmonium? Do you sing? Come and sit here in the center. The harmonium and tabla will be right next to you." [Aani peti tabla koni tari bhetaiche arre majhi peti aahe, majha tabla aahe. Mhajya kade tanpura aahe mag tanpure jamuya aapan tanpure aanaiche. Asa karun aamche karkyakram suru karaiche kon gaayla mhanaiche. "Ha tumhi tabla vajavta ka? thoda basa tabla vajva koni peti aahe ka peti wala? ki chala ya. Tumhi gaata ka chala basa madhye basa bajula tabla aani peti aahe."]

This is how the music sessions started and soon the word spread and more people came. They said this was good. There was a space to sing and there were instruments, and people started attending. [Asa karun gayala suruvat jhali te majha aiklyanantar aankhi lok aale te mhanale ki chala bara ithe aaplyala jaga aahe ganya saathi and sagle loka aahet aani sagli instruments vagare aahet mhanun ase lok jamaila laagli.]

Balasaheb's memories are of a musicophiliac public in which the members are themselves students of music and willing to perform occasionally in front of other music lovers. The reputation of the Trinity Club, however, from the time that it was established, was that of a platform where musicians sang to and performed before other musicians.

Someone would take the lead and sponsor tea for everyone, or paan. People would eat paan in those days—betelnut with tobacco, areca nut, and so on. There would be a plate full of paan. People ate paan. If it was someone's birthday or something they offered sweets, food, and drinks. [Koni tari lead ghyaycha ki chala me baba yeto aaj chaha majhya kadun tumhala saglyana chaha. Saglyana chaha dyaycha . . . konala paan aani. Paan khayche tyavelela tambaku paan, supari vagere paancha tabak asayche. Lok pan bin khayche aani konacha vaadh divas asel kahi asel tar kai pedehe, khaana peena.]

Now you may ask me who was paying the rent for this place. But there were many generous music lovers, and we had the permission of the owner of the space to run the Trinity Club in that space. So there was no question about the giving and taking of money or charging people for tickets. It was open to all to come, and all to sing.

[Aata tumhi prashna vicharaal hya jaagecha bhada bida kon det hota? Pan ashech kone tari denekan ganyache shaukin mandali. Aani te je mukhya te he hote te baghatach hote, tyancha laksha hota, aani tyanchi parvangi ghetleli ki amhi. Trinity Club hya jaage saathi aamhi hi jaga dileli aahe, tyamule paise denya ghenacha, bara ticket lavnacha asa kai prashnach navta. Tyamule kon hi yaava, kon hi gaava.]

The board on the door of Trinity Club says "for members only." When asked how one became a member, Balasaheb explained:

If we had to run Trinity Club, what would be the entry fee? We decided that anyone who is regular is a member. The ones who come regularly and play the tabla, sing or play the harmonium, and mingle with the people. Therefore, there was no membership fee. Regular attendance was the membership. This is how it started, and soon it became popular among people that there there's a place like this in Girgaum, and we should go there and sing. [Aani ulat Trinity Club chalvaicha mag tyala he kai pravesh fee kai? Tar amhi tharavla ki pravesh fee kahi nahi. Zo regular yeil toh member. Zo regular tithe yeil, aapla tabla vajan kareil, aapla gayan kareil, peti vajan kareil, chaar lokan madhey mix hoel, raheel vaigere. Hyacha karta membership nahi. Hi membership aahe. Tar ashya tarahne te chalu zhala aani mag lokancha madhye naav hoila lagli ithe jaaga ashi aahe Girgaon madhaye hi ashi zaaga aahe tevhaan aapan tithe gayla basuya.]

Balasaheb's wife, Sumathi Tikekar, a singer of natya sangeet until she had an accident that affected her voice, added, "*Ani Club ha* commercial *navta tyamule kai*" (The club was not commercial, so). "*Paisha vishyacha prashna nahi*" (So there was no question of money), continued Balasaheb. Concluded Sumathi Tikekar, "*Ganya cha fakta pahije*" (We wanted only music people).[38]

Musicophiliac as Organizer and Collector: Kishor Merchant

Now in his sixties, Merchant comes from a family of Kutchi-Bhatia businesspeople who have lived in Walkeshwar in south Bombay since they moved to the city five generations ago. The family originally had a huge bungalow, which was later redeveloped into a high-rise building with apartments.

"We were one of the few famous merchants who used to keep the house concerts," said Merchant. "We were famous for the full-night concert. Concert would start after dinner. There would be two breaks in between, but it would go on until early morning. And there have been many such concerts, many great singers." When asked who some of the singers were, Merchant mentioned Begum Akhtar, who sang there in 1952, and Ahmadi Begum Chopra, a fine ghazal singer in the classical raga format, trained in the Bhendi Bazar Gharana—"she remained a name known only to musicians, because she did not want publicity." He continued, "Siddheshwari Devi a couple of concerts, again so, these types of names were there with my grandfather, father, all big, big time." Would the family approach the singer, or was it the other way around? "See, the name became so famous that the singers would approach my grandfather, and they would want to perform."

The house baithak was held in this way: "We had a very huge hall. It was wooden flooring and huge. We used to have special gaddis and bolsters for the concert which used to be stored in a big godown. They would be brought in during the day. We would put these white covers on them, and they would be ready for the evening." Although they had a harmonium and tanpura in the house, for the concert they would make sure to have the right accompanying instruments.[39]

Having grown up in this atmosphere, Merchant always liked Indian music, but drifted into "English music" when he was in college. At some point, though, he became close to Hindustani music again. The moment he talked about also marked the beginning of his passion for collecting music. "There was a gap of quite a few years and then all of a sudden I heard a very beautiful *abhang* [devotional song] of Bhimsen Joshi on the records. From that time onwards, I started collecting all Bhimsen Joshi's records, Kishori's records, Mallikarjun Mansur." Merchant was collecting only records at that point, but an incident made him start collecting live recordings: "Veena Sahasrabuddhe performed at NCPA. There was a hori she sang in Adana. It was a ten-minute hori. I approached the person who I had seen recording there. 'Can I have only the hori? I don't want anything else.'" His request was turned down. "I said, why, as a listener, and I as a good listener, should not be getting hold of that live recording? That is when I made up my mind that I will collect live recordings and I will disseminate them. He didn't give me that hori. That made me energised to start my own collection. I not only want [these recordings for] myself, but I want to give it to youngsters. Maybe, maybe I feel one of the reasons why Indian classical music has not survived on a high level is maybe because these collectors did not learn how to disseminate our music." Merchant makes his recordings freely available, especially to young musicians, because he feels that their musical growth can be enabled by wide listening. Parallel to this interest in encouraging musicians who are of the younger generation, Merchant managed to find private sponsorship for many months to organize a small concert series in a prime Walkeshwar venue to showcase young talent. This effort finally ran aground because it could not attract enough listeners to fill the 150-seat hall.

Musicophiliac as Collector, Teacher, Organizer: B. R. Deodhar

From being a student at Vishnu Digambar Paluskar's GMV at Sandhurst Road, Girgaum, in 1918, B. R. Deodhar, the Professor, went on at the urging of his guru to set up his own music school after Paluskar's had to close down. Deodhar's contributions to institutionalizing Hindustani music teaching reveal many facets of his musicophilia: his School of Indian Music, established in 1925, enabled thousands of children and young people to start learning music; he started an eventually successful campaign to get Bombay University to teach Hindustani music; his school's weekly concerts as well as the annual Paluskar death anniversary concerts were legendary for the musicians he invited, who were the objects of devotion of generations of musicophiliacs. Deodhar ran the music magazine *Sangeet Kala Vihar*, wrote copiously on musicians and music, took part in music experiments with the European scientist Scrinzi, obsessively learned new compositions and notated them in his own style, and developed bonds of great affection with a range of musicians, from the "mad fakir" Sinde Khan to the hugely popular performer Bade Ghulam Ali Khan to Kumar Gandharva, the prodigy who first studied at Deodhar's school. Deodhar's book *Thor Sangeetkar*, in Marathi, profiles leading musicians of his day, with insights based on his personal relationships with them.

Recalling his habitual evening strolls to the beach with Ghulam Ali Khan, Deodhar writes,

> Whenever we engaged in a chitchat on Chowpatty sands, a small crowd of music lovers would invariably gather around us. On one such occasion Khansaheb started singing. Within a short time he had an audience of thirty or forty people round him. They were all greatly delighted with his music. Khansaheb's glance happened to fall on a *paanwaala* who had also left his stall to listen to him.

Khansaheb said, "Did you see how music makes you forget everything? This paanwaala has been standing here for along time oblivious of the fact that he must sell paan to make a living. The crowd will melt away when the show is over but the poor chap would have lost the evening's business. I must do something for him."

He then called the paanwaala to his side and asked him to serve paans to every one of the thirty or forty people present, at his expense.[40]

Organizer and Collector: Nitin Shirodkar

Nitin, now in his late fifties, is a Girgaum resident from a kalavant family that moved to Mumbai in the early twentieth century, in his grandmother's time. He still lives in the house they occupied in the 1930s. If there is one word that might capture Nitin's demeanor, it is *utsaahi* or enthusiast. For decades, he has listened to Hindustani music in a variety of venues, organized small music events, collected records and cassettes, and been an amateur historian of his musical neighbourhood. At one point, he even tried to learn music from the eminent Kirana gharana singer Firoz Dastur, who was teaching a couple of his friends. As Nitin put it reverentially, "My fascination for Panditji for his purity in singing was there, so I used to go and wait for him while he was training [his disciples] inside for hours." Dastur told Nitin that he was starting too late, and besides his voice was more suited to light music, but he did teach him for a while. Nitin has a photo of Dastur on his mantelpiece, just like musicians keep pictures of their gurus. One of the events he is very proud of having organized is a celebration for Dastur's seventieth birthday where he had invited the other disciples of Sawai Gandharva, Bhimsen Joshi and Gangubai Hangal, to speak. He says no one sang on that day, but everyone spoke about music. A widespread form of musicophiliac activity of which Nitin too is an accomplished practitioner is the retelling of stories about the guru and the guru's guru. Nitin is also an officeholder of the Gomantak Maratha Samaj, which is how the kalavant community renamed itself. He has helped raise funds for the Samaj through organizing concerts by community members like Kesarbai Kerkar and Kishori Amonkar.

From the time he was quite young, Nitin has been collecting gramophone records of Hindustani musicians.

NS: Well, in my house, other than me, my *mama* [maternal uncle] also used to buy records. And he had that gramophone with that handle, one 78 rpm, and you know the box of pins used to be there, metallic box—you have to go and put that pin, and they used to take utmost care of these records. And once the LP and all started, I had the Phillips turntable and the Garrard changer. My father was that way very obliging. He gave me all those gifts, and he gave me the pocket money to buy these records, and we used to always wait for the sale . . . clearance sale at Rhythm House.

When normally one record would cost about 50 rupees—when they had a clearance sale you got three LPs for 100 rupees—that's the time I used to go and buy all my classical records of Bhimsenji and all. So I broke the ice with Bhimsen Joshi. There's a photograph of mine wherein I went with all the records to tell Bhimsen that I'm your great fan and I want to learn from you, and he obliged me by signing each and every record that I had carried that day.

This photograph of mine with Bhimsenji is on seventeenth April [19]82 at the Indian Merchants' Chambers of Commerce where he had gone to perform. So I had carried all his records, this abhang vani, *Purvi* and all that, and he did sign and give them to me. With me was my friend Sudhir Joshi—and absolutely an unassuming person Bhimsenji was—and because of Bhimsenji then I came in touch with Firoz Dastur and all the [other musicians].

Bhimsen Joshi never actually taught Nitin, but visited his house frequently to taste his wife's South Indian cooking and speak to them in Kannada, his mother tongue.

Learning to Sing: The Amateur and the Professional

This chapter has explored musicophiliac subject formation by discussing how the madness of loving music manifested in Mumbai over the twentieth century. From the person who was all ears and got pleasure out of listening to music, we move to the person who used to "sing with his ears." The musicophiliac spectrum includes at the far end the music lover who actually decides to learn how to sing. The genealogy of this practice can be traced back to those new urbanites who from the 1870s on tried to learn music, including lawyers, accountants, doctors, and even the occasional judge. Here are the profiles of three Mumbai men and women for whom just listening was not enough.

Murli Manohar Shukla, now in his eighties, came into music as a very

Figure 3.2. Record from Nitin Shirodkar's collection: D. V. Paluskar. Photo: Aashay Gune.

Figure 3.3. Photograph from the Shirodkar collection. Center: Nitin Shirodkar; seated, right: Bhimsen Joshi. Photo: Aashay Gune.

young child, and went on to make his living from teaching music, performing, and being a music administrator. He still teaches regularly in his home in Tardeo near Mumbai Central Railway Station, a stop away from Grant Road, where he grew up. He spoke in Hindi throughout the interview.

As far as music is concerned, from when I was four years old, my father used to make me listen to the radio. Then he told me . . . that I started sleeping less and started listening [to music] more. [Rahi baat sangeet ki, toh chauthe baras se mujhe radio sunaate thae woh aur main sunta tha. Aur baad mein pitaji ne mujhe kaha ki baad mein mera sona kam ho gaya aur sunna zyaada ho gaya. Neend kam ho gayi.]

I'll tell you how my sleep decreased. Since I was a boy, I used to go wherever there was a harmonium. If someone had a sitar, I would do the same. A bansuri, a violin, any instrument, it didn't matter which one. [Woh neend kaise kam hui main bataata hoon. Jab main bachha tha tab kisi ke yahaan harmonium hota tha, toh main jaake baithta tha. Kisi ke yahaan sitar ho, toh main jaake baithta tha, kisi ke yahaan bansuri hai, violin, kuch bhi ho.]

Some people asked me, "Do you want to learn [music]?" I was still very young, and those people were about thirty or forty years old. I must have been about eight, nine, or ten. I said yes, I'll learn. Someone taught me the scale: *sa re ga ma pa dha ni*. And they said to me, "*Arrey* you started playing this?!" In reality, I had no instrument of my own—no harmonium, nothing at all. It was only later that my father got all of that for me. So, I started playing. My grandmother, by the time I was eight or nine, started taking me to Talmakiwadi, here, near Bhatia Hospital. There all our people live. They are there to this day. There's a Dutt mandir (temple) there. In the holy period of Chaturmas [four months from July to October], kirtans are sung. I used to be the harmonium player! [Kuch logon ne mujhe kaha ki, "seekhoge?" Abhi chhota tha main . . . aur woh log bade thhe umar mein 30–40; ab main 8–9–10 ka tha. Bole haan main seekhoonga. Kisi ne mujhe "sa re ga ma pa dha ni sa" sikhaaya. Toh ve bole, "arrey tu toh bajaane lagaa?!" Asal mein mere paas harmonium, koi instrument, kuch bhi nahi tha. Baad mein pitaji ne sab laa ke diya. Toh bajaane laga mein. Meri grandmother mujhe jab main jab 8–9 saal ka hua, toh Talmakiwadi mein le jaane lagi . . . yahaan Bhatia Hospital ke paas, wahaan humaare hi log sab rehte hain. Abhi bhi hain. Wa-

Figure 3.4. The author with Murli Manohar Shukla at his home. Photo: Sohnee Harshey.

haan mandir hai, Dutt mandir. Wahaan Chaturmas mein 4 mahine keertan hota hai. Harmonium waala main.]

I don't know how I acquired *swar gyan* [knowledge of the notes], but whichever instrument was given to me, I could play it. That's where I had reached. Singing was still far away. Someone put a violin in front of me; someone brought a sarod. . . . I started playing it on my own . . . because I had marked how they played it and I had listened to a lot of music. [Uss samay tak pataa nahi mujhe swar ka gyan kaise hua, magar koi bhi instrument detey aap mujhe, toh main mila sakta tha. Yahaan tak pahunch gaya tha main. Abhi gaana door tha. Toh woh violin laake kisi ne rakha, sarod laake rakha, maine bajaana shuru kiya apne aap. Kyunki unlogon ko main mark kiya aur suna bahut tha.]

In those days at least twice a week there were classical music baithaks in Mumbai at one place or another. My father used to take me to them. There's a small hall called Laxmi Baug in the Opera House area—several famous musicians used to perform there. I've heard all the Agra gharana people there. I've heard all the Kirana gharana people too. I've heard Amir Khansaab. I've sat next to him. I've spoken to him. [Hafte mein us samay do din toh kam se kam Shashtriya Sangeet ki baithak Mumbai mein kaheen na kaheen hoti hi thi. Pitaji mujhe le gaye. Opera House mein Laxmi Baug ek chhota sa hall hai. Wahaan bade bade kalaakar gaate thae. Agra gharana ke sab logon ko wahaan maine suna hai. Kirana gharana ke sab ko suna hai. Amir Khan saab ko maine suna hai. Unke saath baitha hoon, unse baat bhi hui hai.]

And the whole world's musicians used to come to B. R. Deodhar's place. I've also studied there. Given all of these things, I had already cultivated my musical sensibility even before I went to a guru. [B. R. Deodhar ke yahaan toh poori duniya ke kalaakar aate the. . . . Main bhi waheen se seekha bhi hoon. . . . Toh aisi baatein hui toh kaafi sanskaar aise pehle hi ho gaye, guru ke paas jaane ke pehle.]

Unlike Shukla in his postretirement years, Ramdas Bhatkal, now in his late seventies, never had to make a living from music. From a Konkani-speaking background (Chitrapur Saraswat, like Shukla), he grew up in Mumbai in the 1930s and '40s in a musically inclined family with at least one famous musician, his uncle Chidanand Nagarkar, who went on to become the principal of the music school of Bharatiya Vidya Bhavan. Bhatkal spoke in English and Marathi, with occasional Hindi phrases.

The Bhatkal family owned a publishing house and bookshop, and Ramdas's father sent one of his employees to the house to teach the eight-year-old boy a bit of tabla. "[Music] was . . . somewhere in my system, so that even when I was not trained or training I would keep on singing within myself, and, if I may use the term, *mi kaanani gaato* [I sing with my ears]." For example, if he listened to a great musician like Faiyaz Khan, he could then "play [that music]" in his ears. When he was about nine, his sister

> started going to Deodhar School of Music and, while she was eleven by that time . . . she was very shy, *aani jataana ti mhanali, arrey chul tu ye re jara majhya barobar* [and while leaving she said, you come with me], so I went with her. And there was Harshe Master teaching there, and I don't know why he felt—I was hardly nine—maybe my fingers were, you know, giving him that signal. He said, "*Tabla yeto ka?*" [Do you play the tabla?] Now maybe I was so immature and foolish I said *yeto* [I know], so he asked me to give the *theka*. It was a

first-year class, so it was basically *dha dhin dhin dha*, which I knew, so for one year I played tabla with that class without singing at all, but I was listening.

Through the 1940s, Bhatkal listened to many famous and not-so-famous musicians performing at the Deodhar School. He thought, however, that some of the performers were "second-rate." "Maybe indirectly that gave me an encouragement that maybe I can also sing someday." Before his voice changed, Bhatkal studied at the Bharatiya Vidya Bhavan. At the time, he aspired to be like his hero Faiyaz Khan: "*Mala Faiyaz Khan vhaiychay* and I'm still dreaming about it." After this period, Bhatkal had a very long break from training, all of thirty-five years. He returned to music only in his mid-forties. He remained connected to music through regular listening on the radio, and always singing "with his ears."

Though I was not having formal training I was with [music]—and there are two interesting things about it. One is, since my business was publishing, I would visit the printers, and the printing press in those days or probably even now, the rhythm *toh aata hi hai* [it comes] while it is printing *thak, thak, thak*. The other is it gives a sound, so it gives you *shadja*. So unconsciously sitting there I would start humming and singing to that tune. So that way, and of course these festivals and listening to music otherwise, live, was also very much there, and in those days that area—Grant Road where I lived—was really very vibrant.

In the 1970s, Bhatkal, at his son's urging, went to his earliest teacher, S. C. R. Bhat, who laughed at him but agreed to do a test of his musical knowledge. The swar gyan (knowledge of notes) given to him by S. C. R. Bhat was so firm that after more than three decades Ramdas Bhatkal was able to pass the test with ease. Bhat began to teach him two or three days a week, and this arrangement continued for twenty-seven years, during which time Ramdas also began to sing in concerts. He never felt that he should be a professional performer. He had his writing obligations and his publishing business, which restricted the time he could spend on music.

However, although he doesn't earn a living from it, Bhatkal is still keen to perform on stage, even in his late seventies.

There are two things which have helped me sing a little better than I would have otherwise. One is that I don't have to sing. So I sing because I want to sing, and I take pleasure in it. *Tyamule te dalan dalna mhantat ki jasa lecturer kinva* [it's not a compulsion like a lecturer] who has to give eighteen lectures every week, that kind of a thing. I don't have to do that. So that is one great advantage. The second is that I'm not trying to achieve *ki mala kahi tari radio var jaoon mala B grade cha A grade karoon ghyaycha aahe, kinva vagere asa hi kahi nahi* [not trying to get graded as an artiste by All India Radio], so this my pleasure, and the listener's pleasure is what is important for me. That helps me do a little better.

Referring to music, he says,

I don't think it is complete unless it is communicated to somebody or the other, whether it's one person, one hundred persons, or the whole world, but unless that communication is completed, the art itself is not complete, because you really don't know what its impact is. So from the beginning that was my feeling. My wife keeps on telling me that "you are not a professional. You should be happy just singing [by yourself, at home]." I said no, no, I want [to] make others happy, whether they are five, five hundred, or five thousand; whether it's once a month, or once a year, that's not material, but it has to complete the circle and only then will I also feel what I'm doing.

Bhatkal's love of singing is matched by Farida Sabnavis, now in her early fifties, a Parsi woman who grew up listening to Hindi film music. After her marriage to a Marathi-speaking musicophiliac, she too got involved in Hindustani music. Her first exposure was through the CDs her husband played at home.

And then we started attending concerts, and slowly I got hooked onto it. So then I even wanted to listen to classical music at home. Then, I was busy in my corporate life. At thirty-five, I decided to take a break from the rut, which is . . . you know . . . corporate life, and I said I want to do part-time. And then I said what else do I want to do, and I always wanted to learn singing. So I said if I have to learn singing, I was very clear that I have to start and . . . it's like, your foundation should be strong. So I was very clear that I wanted to learn classical music. Start with classical music, and then, you know, if you know classical, light forms become easy.

After the 1940s or so, Parsis in Mumbai—with rare exceptions like Aban Mistry, a woman who played the tabla, or Jal Balaporia, guru of Farida's gurus—seem to have turned almost entirely to Western music, although they were among the earliest inhabitants of the city to become fascinated by Hindustani art music. Farida's entry into learning classical music was thus different from those of the other two people profiled in this section because of her complete lack of connection to it when she was growing up. When she first approached her teacher Sharmila Shah at the age of thirty-five, the teacher was shocked to find out that her newest pupil had never learned Indian music before, either in her school or through private music classes. Farida's Parsi background had denied her the exposure that could have been taken for granted with Hindu women of her age. She recalls the moment when she first met her guru:

> So she told me that she'd make me sing *sa-re-ga-ma*, and then she'll take a call on whether she can or cannot teach me. So the first two turns were really on an experimental basis. So I said fine, I was willing to give it a try. And then she told me later on that when she made me sing she found that my taal was perfect. Not that I knew at that time what was *sur* and what was taal. But she felt that I could pick up taal fast. She felt that I was dedicated, which I was, because if at thirty-five you decide to learn something, either you do it well or you might as well not do it. So that is how she actually started with me, and I can tell you that the first time we did taan, or the first time we did *taraana*, I was wondering why I ever wanted to learn classical music.

Unlike the other musicophiliacs in this chapter who began to learn music, she began relatively late. This is perhaps why the steps of the journey of acquiring music are quite vivid for her, unlike someone who has studied music since childhood.

> That's really been my journey and I've been doing this now for fourteen years. Anybody who wants to start music—and everyone thinks, oh it's so easy, but it's like—for the first ten years you don't know what you're doing. You think you're practicing and practicing and practicing, but nothing—because your mind knows. Because I was interested, I know what you should say. But the throat is not moving! Because it requires that practice, it requires that thing. And then suddenly one day, after ten years, I don't even know in which year, your throat is responding to your mind.
>
> And when that happens, it's bliss. That's the beauty of classical mu-

sic. When you touch a note, you know whether you've touched it or not. When you touch a note, you can feel the vibrations. I mean, I can feel the vibrations when we end a raga or when we end a composition—when I'm practicing with my guru—and I do it in this room. I can feel that around me. And that really gives me a high. When you're doing badly—it's not that everyday... you also go through ups and downs. When you're doing badly you know it's not coming out right. So classical music has really helped me. So now if you give me any light composition, it's really very easy for me to pick it up. Because I know the basis of the raga, re-ga-re-sa and all moves very fast because your throat is... used to that. And you know you can sing well. It gives you confidence to sing. I think that's really been the thing.[41]

What is most obvious about Farida Sabnavis's involvement in music is her ability to focus on her learning in spite of her high-stress corporate life. While she is not the first musicophiliac in this chapter who had a working life separate from music, her articulation of her involvement in music is imbued with the vocabulary of New Age styles of leadership training.

> FS: If I do not practice for one week, for whatever reason, I'll feel something is missing from my life. At the same time you can be under any amount of stress, you know, whether it is traffic stress or some personal stress, but the minute you say *sa* and you are in sur, you forget everything. You have to. Because I'm still at a stage where if I do not concentrate hard, the sur slips. So all your concentration is on that and you forget the world and you're so happy. Actually it's almost like a meditation session for me and then I come out of it and I feel I'm ready to take on the world.
>
> And I'm very clear that when I'm practicing, no phone. I mean, it's just switched off. The cell is put in one corner. When there was a world without cellular, you existed. You cannot be checking messages and singing. It just doesn't make any sense to me. Nowadays in concerts you see people on stage, on stage—forget in the audience—with cell phones. And I find that the purity is missing. And I think that's what's important. For me, it's more [about] concentration. Because you have to focus.
>
> TN: I think what comes across when you speak about music is what a singular and individual connection it is.

FS: It is. Let me tell you, I have been absolutely focused about learning. If it means that ... I have given a time [for the class] to my guru, both our track records ... she is as dedicated as I am and Rameshbhai [Farida's earlier guru, who passed away] was as dedicated. We have a 90 percent track record of ensuring that we meet and we do it. And this has been across fourteen years. Only 10 percent of the time ... specially if there's been a medical emergency that I've canceled the class. If both of us are in town, we definitely meet. And it can be so easy for me to say I cannot meet. Because you know how the demands on your time are. Oh you can do this, and you can do that, and whatever. And I've had client meetings where I've gotten up and people have said, "So what are you going to do?" and [I said,] "Oh, music, *arre* ..." You know how it is. "Oh you're going to learn music? You can always cancel it. Shift it to another day." As far as I am concerned—I say, I'm sorry, if your meeting is important, my music is equally important. I have been extremely strict about that. ... There have been times when there were meetings fixed with CEOs and I say I'm busy, I'm not coming.

If you decide that this music is not important, you can again slip into a day-to-day life and forget about why you started to learn music. And my thing is very clear. If at the age of thirty-five, I decided I was learning music, I didn't do it just for laughs ... to say arrey, I'm also learning music. It can be ... it's almost like a tick mark sometimes for people. "I'm also learning music." No, I *really* want to learn music. So if you want to learn, and you're starting from a blank background ... please understand I had no one in my family who was there. ... My mom also loves music. ... She had a harmonium. She learnt a few bhajans and all. But I don't come from a musical background or from a musical family. If I had decided that I want to learn music, I had to give it the same concentration I gave my career.

TN: When people say they love music, how is that manifested? Usually it's manifested by [going] to every single concert; they dedicatedly follow certain singers. They will collect stuff about the music, and they will collect music itself; they will listen to music; they will go out to listen to music. In your instance, I don't hear a lot of that. In your story about your relationship to music, it's much more about cultivating yourself and your practice as a singer. I find that very remarkable.

FS: Because most people don't bother to get to that point where they have to then learn music. They always put that off, saying maybe one day or maybe it doesn't matter. Because I'm manifesting my love for music in different ways. So I said let me try to learn, and I can tell you that if my gurus had not supported me, if my husband had not supported me, through the early years, maybe it would just have remained, like for most people, oh I love music. Even now when I talk to people who like music and who attend concerts, they say, but, oh how did you decide to sing? I said, I decided to sing, because I decided to take the plunge. And I tell everybody, try it out. Maybe if not voice, maybe it's an instrument. But if you like music, then you should learn to either sing or play or whatever, because it gives you so much of joy. And I believe I have grown as a human being because of music. I believe I have become patient. I also believe that because I do the practice and because, you know, I focus on that, I get away, I have "me" time. If suddenly after that, there's a pressure, there's a crisis, I'm able to handle that better because I've had that "me" time. I've had that time to concentrate. I've had the time to get away from it [all], so I can then tackle a crisis far better than if I was not learning music.

So actually . . . music has brought a lot of positivity in my life. So when you [ask] what music means to me, that's really what it means . . . and the fact that at thirty-five I said I want to sing, and then now at fifty I know I can sing. I mean it's been a journey. To me one of the greatest thrills in my life [has] been when people turn and say you have a good voice. And only I know what I have done to slog on that voice . . . when I started at thirty-five I was laughing and telling my friends that not only do I have to exercise my body, I'm exercising my voice also. I have to do both things simultaneously.

She now performs regularly on light classical music platforms, sometimes with her teacher, singing bhajans and devotional songs.

THIS CHAPTER HAS looked at the musicophiliac in Mumbai over the long twentieth century and has presented some of the manifestations of the intense passion for music that gripped a large number of Mumbai's inhabitants. I ended with showcasing three people who did not come from hereditary music backgrounds but made a musicophiliac decision to actually learn Hindustani music through discipleship to an established vocalist. Their love of singing is a mark of the performative modernity through which the social subjecthood of Mumbai's musicophiliacs is manifested. The implication of taking the deewaana (the person mad about music) seriously as a performer of modernity is this: we see that the experience of loving music in a non-Western colonial metropolis like Mumbai is not predicated on the individualized normative subject of Western modernity but on the subject forged in sociality, through the coming together of those similarly enchanted by music. This might well have implications for how we think about subject formation in such contexts, and indeed about sociality itself, compelling us to see them as co-constituted rather than separately analyzable. Part of the modernity of learning music in the twentieth century was the development of a number of pedagogic processes by which music training was imparted to nonhereditary musicians. The following two chapters focus on the training process—taleem—to see how the continuance of musicophlia was secured.

4

TALEEM

PEDAGOGY AND THE
PERFORMING SUBJECT

Alladiya Khan stayed at Kesarbai Kerkar's place and taught her for ten years. He would teach her all day long, different ragas according to the time of day. The teaching would go on until midnight, with two breaks for lunch and dinner, and then she had to wake up again at 5 a.m.
—**Dhondutai Kulkarni** (February 15, 2014)

Suppose I've uploaded a file ... I have to factor in all the possible faults [the student] will meet with when playing that, because he's not meeting me on a daily basis ... So I'd articulate in an email each and every thing.
—**Aneesh Pradhan** (February 13, 2014)

The metropolitan unconscious that took shape in Mumbai during the long twentieth century includes, at the one end, the pedagogic practices of the Muslim ustads who migrated to the city and, at the other end, the contemporary forms of cyber teaching. The musicophiliac who was drawn to Hindustani music then and now may be engaged in somewhat different forms of sociality and different kinds of listening environments. But a musicophiliac who decides to learn to sing or play an instrument in the present is compelled to engage with the sedimented cultures of learning that music pedagogy in the metropolis draws upon, even as it reconfigures the past through repeated retelling.

A fascinating description of the taleem of a major twentieth-century musician, Khadim Husain Khan, who lived in Mumbai for most of his adult life, comes from music-lover Jayavanth Rao, who based his account on intimate conversations with the Khansaheb over a number of years. Kallan Khan, Khadim Husain's guru and great-grand-uncle, was in his late seventies when he began teaching Khadim Husain, who was about ten.

> The ustad would get up at six o'clock in the morning even though his shagirds and he usually went to bed only at three or four o'clock in the morning. He would, however, see that the shagirds were left undisturbed till about 9:00 a.m. The ustad would go for his constitutional till the shagirds were ready after breakfast by about 10:00 a.m. Then there would be three or four hours of intense teaching till lunch time between 1:00 and 2:00 p.m. After lunch the ustad would rest while the shagirds would run errands and do their own riyaaz, recapitulating what their ustad had taught them during the previous night and that morning and making notes where necessary.
>
> Early dinner by about 7:00 p.m. would be followed by almost eight to nine hours of talim right up to the small hours of the morning. That was when the new ragas were taken up, special *cheezas* were taught and the subtle differences between close ragas were explained in great detail. The ustad would let them go to bed only after 3:00 a.m. and often 4:00 a.m.[1]

We hear similar accounts about the training of several other early and mid-twentieth-century vocalists and instrumentalists, whether it is Kesarbai Kerkar's taleem with Alladiya Khan, Bhaskarbuwa Bakhle's with Natthan Khan, or, in a later period, Dhondutai Kulkarni's with Kesarbai. As Daniel Neuman observes, there is a good deal of wistful imagining in any musician's remembered past, but it nonetheless remains true as an "affective reality."[2]

This chapter explores the process of imparting and acquiring taleem, the name for the pedagogic process that has to be strengthened through sustained individual practice or riyaaz. The idea is to investigate how the taleem process plays a crucial part in shaping the performing subject. This subject, as earlier chapters have argued, is a social subject, and here I lay out the connections between the acquisition of performative techniques, the guru-*shishya* (disciple) social relationship, and the musicophiliac audience that has to be won. Through in-depth interviews with musicians whose lives and those of their teachers stretch from the nineteenth century to the twenty-first, I draw out their understanding of the nature of taleem imparted to them. Although the interviews include occasional references to music school modes of teaching, such as those pioneered by Vishnu Digambar Paluskar in his Gandharva Mahavidyalay from the early twentieth century on, the teachers and students discussed in this chapter are engaged in forms of teaching as well as learning that exceed the fixed syllabus or the examination-oriented curriculum.[3] While it is probable that music classes, as they were called, used to be and still constitute the main source of exposure to Hindustani music in Mumbai, students who aspired to a performing career—even if they had attended a music school when young—usually shifted after a few years to a one-on-one form of training, also known as *sina-basina* or heart-to-heart.

Compared to the development of modern modes of pedagogy in Carnatic music, the process of pedagogic change in Hindustani music does not appear as clear-cut. Lakshmi Subramanian suggests that as Carnatic music moved to Madras city (now renamed Chennai), *sabhas* or gatherings formed by middle-class patrons became hugely influential in regulating and transforming not only performance but also pedagogic modes. According to Subramanian, the motifs that recurred in music appreciation and music criticism—to do with tempering noise and excess in executing the melody—marked the dramatic shift in pedagogic setting from the *gurukul* (literally, home or family of the teacher) to the school or university in the twentieth century.[4] The elaborate nature of curriculum development and pedagogic reform chronicled by Subramanian for Carnatic music seems not to be paralleled in Hindustani music, in spite of the efforts of codifiers like V. N. Bhatkhande, who did produce new resources for students. Instead, parallel streams of training in schools and one-on-one instruction coexisted, and continue to do so today.[5]

In the previous chapters, I have argued that the act of listening together to Hindustani music marks the moment in which sociality and subjectivity take shape in a co-constitutive mode. I have suggested that the metropolitan unconscious that emerged in Mumbai from the late nineteenth century on provides the psychosocial context for the formation of the musical subject. Some elements of the co-constitutive process are also to be found in the music school mode of pedagogy, where students often learn together by singing together.

But in the ustad-shagird (Urdu) or guru-shishya (Hindi) form of pedagogy, where only one student is taught at a time, the act of learning seems almost to break free of the sociality of the listening experience, even when that learning is predicated on a heightened form of listening, where the student has to hear every microtone in order to be able to reproduce it. In one-on-one training, the pedagogic process works toward cultivating the interiority demanded by the khayal form that established itself firmly in the twentieth century as the dominant form of Hindustani music. However, the production of interiority is strengthened not by making the student unique so that he or she then expresses that uniqueness, but by making the would-be performer as similar to the teacher as possible. Paying attention to the taleem process gives us an insight into how the repetitive scene of instruction is transformed into the performative moment when, as I mentioned in the introduction to this book, remembering gives way to knowing.

Sonic Materiality

The pedagogy that helps create the performing subject is laid out in minute detail here. To present center stage what usually remains in the quotidian exchanges between teacher and student is to lay bare the sonic materiality of the metropolitan unconscious even as we begin to understand how one end of the musicophiliac spectrum was able to reproduce itself.

Finding a suitable form for this chapter has not been easy. I have tried to step away from the objective, social-historical mode of description/analysis and instead pulled the many voices in my head into these pages. It felt important to hold on to the hesitations, the pauses, the repetitions, the ritual invocations of the guru's greatness, as the musicians I spoke with tried to find ways of making their experience of taleem intelligible. It was important also to bring in the many tongues in which the musicians talked about Hindustani music—Kannada, Marathi, Urdu-Hindi, English. The effort throughout is not just to showcase the factual details of taleem but, crucially, to point to how people remember, reflect on, and represent their experience of it.

In all three of these modes, remembering, reflecting, and representing, what is evident is the elaborate cultivation of a certain kind of vidya (learning) and the striving to become a performer of that knowledge/practice. The moment of articulation and of performance is the moment when the musical subject is formed, in the engagement with the musical archive that is part of the metropolitan unconscious. And it is precisely through this well-schooled engagement that the musicophiliac singer achieves the rupture of improvisation, to be applauded by the fellow musicophiliacs who are part of the *wah-wah mandali*. "If one tries to calculate how much time it would take an average music student of today learning for three hours a week to pick up all the musical *vidya* that an ustad like Khadim Husain Khan absorbed from his guru for about 12 years at the rate of 12 hours a day, it would work out to an incredible 300 years or more!"[6]

None of the people interviewed, even those who had received taleem from khandani or hereditary musicians, had had direct experience of this kind of training, although the effect of reality produced by multiple retellings cannot be discounted. However, they had obviously imbibed elements of what was accomplished differently in the past—say, in the mid- to late nineteenth century—but were taught perhaps with a new reflexivity and focus that the hereditary musicians brought to their craft as they devised new methods of imparting musical performative knowledge in the twentieth century. As chapter 3 tried to show, the desire for this knowledge animated the musicophiliacs of Mumbai, who not only attended Hindustani music performances but tried to learn music themselves.

For convenience, the material in the following section is divided by gharana, although anyone who engages seriously with Hindustani raga music is aware of the fluidity of the distinctions between the modes of singing and of the give-and-take of compositions and presentational styles across gharana divisions, and in some instances even the merging of two gharanas, as it happened in the case of the Agra and Atrauli gharanas when people intermarried, exchanged compositions between families, and studied with different teachers. The name of each gharana was derived either from a founder's birthplace (such as Abdul Karim Khan's Kirana) or the location where leading musicians of the lineage had been based (such as the princely states of Gwalior or Jaipur).

The standard writing of gharana history is an exercise that identifies the specific features (taan patterns, mode of elaboration, voice modulation, overall mode of presenting the raga) obtaining in the present-day practice of those claiming to be from a particular gharana, and then examines the performative style of the teacher and the teacher's teacher—either through available recordings or through hearsay evidence and anecdotes—to determine whether the features existed in the older musicians also. Although gharana histories are often presented as beginning with a legendary musician recognized as the founder of that gharana and then discussing his musical descendants, it is only in the present that the gharana becomes recognizable in the practice of twentieth-century singers. Thus the impulse to consolidate the idea of the gharana is related to the conditions of musical modernity in which, as I mentioned in chapter 1, music comes to be taught outside the extended family of the performer.[7] In his acclaimed book on musical life in North India, Daniel Neuman observes that the gharana concept provided a "social identity, an identity which distinguished not only musical styles, but groups of musicians and their disciples."[8] While an earlier version of gharana was established on the basis of hereditary lineages of musicians and the criss-crossing marriage lines of an endogamous group, in the twentieth century a gharana was more ethnically plural, as is evidenced also by the careers of the vocalists with whom I spoke.

The fact that so many gharanas were visible in the musicophiliac spaces of Mumbai is indicative of the migrant histories that feed into the metropolitan unconscious. The emergence of gharanas indicates the pressure to create and maintain distinctiveness in the performative and pedagogic spaces afforded by the new forms of patronage in the city. But they are also evidence of how the performing subject creates a genealogy of musical training that includes herself, thus transforming both the present and the past, a constitutive gesture I discuss in the introduction.

The Taleem Process

Kirana Gharana

The oldest Hindustani musician I spoke to was the legendary Gangubai Hangal (1913–2009), age ninety-three when I interviewed her in Hubli in 2006. We spoke in Kannada, although she broke into Hindi while relating conversations from incidents that took place outside Kannada-speaking regions. She was also conversant with Marathi, as are many people in the northern Karnataka region, which was part of the Bombay Presidency before India became independent. Due to her great age when I spoke with her, she was not able to recollect many details about her taleem, and only spoke about those things and events she had already found a language for, and had spoken about to journalists and writers who had interviewed her before.

One of the reasons to start with Gangubai is also to reference my own personal route into researching Hindustani music in Mumbai. In the mid-2000s I was working on the Hubli-Dharwad region, trying to understand the possible role of Hindustani music in forging a link between an emergent nationalism in the early twentieth century and the love of the Kannada language that first began to be formally articulated in this region.[9] Talking to Gangubai made me realize how significant Mumbai was to any discussion of Hindustani music in modern times. She and fellow Dharwad musicians took the meter-gauge train to Pune and changed to the broad gauge there to complete the journey to Mumbai. They visited the city twice a month or more frequently, and were able to sustain their households only with the higher concert fees that Mumbai offered (Rs. 125 as opposed to Rs. 25 in Hubli).[10] Gangubai told me there were at least twelve "arts circles" in Bombay in the 1930s, and they often came up with joint programs so as to share the cost of the artiste's travel.

Gangubai studied with Ramachandra or Rambhau Kundgolkar, otherwise known as Sawai Gandharva (1886–1952), student of Abdul Karim Khan (1872–1937), from about 1930–31 onward, when she was about eighteen or nineteen years old. The taleem took place approximately eight days in the month, at least two hours each day; she took the train to Kundgol from Hubli at 5 p.m. and traveled back on the 9 p.m. train. Since Sawai Gandharva was mostly in Mumbai in those days, staying at a friend's house and running his company, she learned from him only when he was in his hometown. "When my guru's theater company came to Hubli, my mother got our family friend Dattopant Desai to ensure that the rehearsals of the play were held at our house. Whenever my guru sang during the rehearsals, my clever mother used to identify the ragas, write down the notation, and teach me the compositions which were all based on Hindi cheezes."[11] Presumably the guru was singing in Marathi in the play, but because the sangeet natak songs were all based on Hindi compositions, through learning the songs Gangubai was also familiarizing herself with the Hindustani ragas on which they were based.

Her guru never told her the meaning of the words in the bandishes he taught her; she had to figure out what they meant by herself. The Kannada-speaking singers who became major names in twentieth-century Hindustani music, like Mallikarjun Mansur, Bhimsen Joshi, Kumar Gandharva, and Gangubai herself, are likely to have had their struggles with the linguistic aspects of the compositions. Most overcame it by gaining familiarity over time not just with spoken Hindustani but also with Braj, Awadhi, and the dialects of music, as well as Marathi, which was either the mother tongue or the shared tongue of the growing audiences for Hindustani music. I have argued in chapter 1 that a lingua musica, a common language drawing on Hindustani music, took shape in Mumbai from the late nineteenth century, and we could extend this to parts of the Bombay Presidency too. Gangubai had enough Hindustani to be able to sing, but there is some doubt as to how proficient her spoken Hindi was.[12]

Because of her Carnatic music training, her mother was very good at notation, and used to notate everything she heard. This was later of help to Gangubai, who also depended on the Bhatkhande volumes of *Hindustani Sangit Paddhati* for new bandishes and even ragas. From 1936 on, she started singing regularly on the radio and went frequently to Bombay for live broadcasts. Artistes had to present three times per day—morning, afternoon, and night—with the ragas appropriate for the time of day. They were supposed to give All India Radio a list of twenty-five ragas from which a selection would be made, taking care to avoid repetition with what other musicians were singing. The taleem with Sawai Gandharva being slow-paced and intermittent, Gangubai sometimes had to acquire what she called "bookish" knowledge. Once she had to present Raag Bibhas on the radio at short notice, and prepared it by refering to the Bhatkhande book. While returning from Mumbai to Hubli by train, she met her guru traveling in the same compartment. He had been in Mumbai for a concert and had heard his disciple's broadcast. He asked her to sit down next to him and proceeded to admonish her:

> Do you call that Bibhas? In our gharana, we employ *Teevra Dhaivat* [the sixth pure note in the octave], but you sang with *Komal Dhaivat* [the flat version of the sixth note]. Your *Megh Malhar* was also faulty. *Radio daaga haadokkintha munche nanna kade bandu kalthukondu hogabaaradenu?* [Why didn't you learn the raag from me before singing it over the radio?] Gangu, *jana nanaga hesaridthaara, heenga kalisyaanenu eekeya guru antha* [you sing something as you please and people ask—is this how he taught her]?[13]

He then started giving her taleem in the train, with him singing and her following him, in front of their curious fellow passengers.

From 1937–38, Gangubai's lessons became more regular when her guru returned to Kundgol for good, having left the theater company in Bombay. Gangubai took the train from Hubli to Kundgol everyday for her taleem sessions, which she said were "almost like a *tapasya* [meditation, spiritual discipline]."[14]

Pedagogy and the Performing Subject · 135

> Guruji would ask me to sing a few notes of Puriya Dhanashree and practice them arduously for hours together. "Ga Ga Ri Sa Ni Pa, Ni Ni Dha Pa Ma Ma, Ga Ga Ri Sa, Ni Dha Pa, Ma Ga Ri Sa." I had to sing the same notes again and again till I got tired of repetition. But Guruji, even if he was otherwise engaged in some other part of the house, would be listening attentively. It was like incessantly rubbing sandalwood on a smooth stone—no discordant notes, the purity and elegance of notes [*surel-pan*] to be maintained—an essential feature [*jeeva lakshana*: life feature or characteristic, the life of our style] of our gharana. The correct movement of notes in the alaap of the raga and the systematic slow elaboration of the raga to be ensured. All the notes not to be elaborated [she used the word *kharcha* or spent] in haste. Guruji's advice, "Be economical with the notes, like a miser. Keep the audience anticipating the next note and let them experience the thrill when the change-over is made in the notes." I slowly understood the mystery. *Raagada jeevala swaravannu hachhuva tanaka shrotrugalannu kutoohaladinda kaayisa beku* [Until you reach the most important notes of the raga, you should keep the listeners waiting in anticipation].[15]

Thus her guru taught her the mode of presentation of the raga. "Onde raagavannu varsha gattale riyaaj maadidaaga ondu bhadra bunaadi haakidantaagi, mundina raagagala abhyasakke daari sugamavaaguthithhu" (When one practiced the same raga for years on end it provided a firm foundation for the acquisition of other ragas after that).[16]

"Guru was god for us. When he used to teach a new raga, explaining the different notes and their elaboration, I was so timid that I dared not ask the name of the raga."[17] Gangubai was terrified of singing in front of her guru, but the radio was a different kind of platform. Here the guru often heard her sing, but she did not have to see him in person. Sawai Gandharva had a strange way of expressing his appreciation:

> Whenever I was broadcasting over the radio in Bombay, my guru happened to be in town either for his own concerts, or for giving taleem to Firoz Dastur, or for his own radio programs. But he would never tell me how my program went.... If he told the victoria driver to turn toward Kalbadevi [an area in Girgaum, the native town of Mumbai], saying, "Gangu, let's go and have a glass of masala milk," it meant that he was happy with me. The masala milk shop was his

"patent shop," where the man made the milk with almond and pure saffron.... If he didn't like my program, he would only tell me by and by what the problems were.[18]

Perhaps it was Sawai Gandharva's involvement in Mumbai's metropolitan music platforms, where he interacted with well-known singers with a devadasi or naikin ancestry, like Mogubai Kurdikar and Kesarbai Kerkar, that made him accept a female disciple from a similar social background. Gangubai was one of very few women from her region in her generation who became classical singers, and perhaps the only one to achieve the kind of national prominence she did. Although Gangubai's mother was a Carnatic vocalist, the interest in Hindustani music came from Gangubai's own musicophilia, developed from listening to gramophone records in her childhood. And the discipleship to Sawai Gandharva, perhaps because Gangubai was a woman singer—a rarity in the region at the time—learning art music, was one of musical apprenticeship only. It did not involve other kinds of service to the teacher that a male disciple like Bhimsen Joshi was expected to do—such as carrying water over long distances or cleaning the house—but which also gradually disappeared. We see in Arvind Parikh's account of his relationship with Vilayat Khan, discussed later in this chapter, how an earlier form of discipleship was replaced by the kinds of assistance that a wealthy musicophiliac student could offer, such as helping out with acquiring a new home, driving the teacher everywhere, going with him to the cinema, and paying his various expenses. Parekh's story is perhaps unusual in that it sounds more like a patron's than an aspiring performer's, but it is driven by musicophilia nevertheless.

In Gangubai's story, the train is both central to her taleem and an important mark of mobility: it takes her from Hubli to Kundgol for her music lessons; it takes her to Pune, where Sawai Gandharva stayed for some time, and to Mumbai, where she recorded and broadcast her singing and gave concerts; it also becomes her classroom on occasion when she runs into her teacher, who is upset with her performance of Raag Bibhas on the radio (a raga she learned from the Bhatkhande books) and sits her down in the compartment in front of the other passengers to correct her mode of enunciation. Supplementing her lessons by dipping into Bhatkhande's volumes, shifting constantly between a notation-less mode of instruction to an autodidactism where she reads the notated bandishes and teaches herself the raga, being constantly vigilant about the treatment she receives and what that might indicate about her place in society as a woman from a devadasi family, using her professional stature to command public respect for herself and other musicians—these challenges reveal her taleem as embedded in the social circumstances and ancestry that made a musical career thinkable while at the same time constraining her choices in a number of ways. The choices had to do mostly with the need to appear respectable, in spite of accepting her ambiguous position as the non-Brahmin wife of a Brahmin man who later married someone from his own community. He had many failed ambitions that led to financial problems, and with his demise, Gangubai became the person to support both her own children and the family of the other wife.

Niyaz Ahmed Khan (1924–2003), best known for his *jugalbandi* or duet singing with his brother Faiyaz Ahmed Khan, was a prolific Kirana teacher in Bombay, a hereditary musician who adapted his pedagogic techniques and pace for teaching amateurs. Theater director Anmol Vellani, whose mother used to learn music from Niyaz Ahmed Khan, told me that his method was to teach the same bandish or composition for four to five years, with extensive elaboration of the notes, never shifting to another raag until the student had mastered that one.[19]

On this account, Niyaz Ahmed Khan's style of teaching does not appear very different from Sawai Gandharva's—working extensively with just one raag, elaborating the raag with the same bandish for four to five years, teaching simple taan patterns to help the student grasp the melodic features of the raag. As a performer, Gangubai in desperation had to learn other raags from the books, because she was called upon to sing something different for each radio performance. For wealthy female students who did not perform in public, there was no such compulsion, and they could afford to stay with the single raag the ustad decided to teach. But this teaching mode is likely to have induced boredom in the not-so-serious student, leading her to abandon her classes eventually. While Gangubai learned raags from notated compositions, even though she never mentions doing notation while learning from her guru, the amateur singer depended on this form of recall. As Vellani told me, the Khansahebs who taught in his house had no objection to notation, although they would not write it themselves, instead allowing the student to note down things, which Vellani's mother did in Devanagari script.

Writer Sheila Dhar, who studied music with Faiyaz Ahmed Khan and Niyaz Ahmed Khan, points to the pedagogic inventiveness of these Mumbai-based ustads:

My teachers prided themselves on the teaching skills they had learnt in addition to and as distinct from their musical training. Their sincerity and inventiveness in this area was remarkable.... They once cured a disciple who was chronically *kamsura* [singing below the actual note] by holding up three parallel fingers every time she touched the *taar sa* and telling her that her voice had reached only as high as the first finger whereas she actually needed to pitch her voice to the third one. They gradually adjusted her ear and her psychology until she got her bearings and readjusted her ear to the right pitch.

... Once, they succeeded in correcting the inflection and intonation of a typical phrase in the raga Mian-ki-Malhar by telling a student to actually sing the *mandra saptak pa* [fifth note in the lowest octave] while keeping her mind firmly on the sa [first note]! This took several hours of trial and error since it was not an old and tried remedy but one invented on the spot to solve an unexpected problem that had arisen.[20]

Gwalior Gharana

The Gwalior khayal gharana's founders are usually named as the Muslim musicians Haddu Khan and Hassu Khan, the grandsons of Natthan Pir Baksh, who settled in the princely state of Gwalior, which was ruled by the Mahratta Scindias.[21] Haddu and Hassu Khan taught a number of singers, including the Maharashtrian Brahmin student Shankarrao Pandit in the 1860s.[22] Pandit's son Krishnarao Shankar Pandit became a court singer at the Gwalior darbar and opened a music school, Shankar Gandharva Vidyalaya, in Gwalior in 1914. He and his uncle Eknath Pandit both taught Sharadchandra Arolkar, who in turn taught, among others, Sharad Sathe and Neela Bhagwat, whom I interviewed. The three last named are also Maharashtrian Brahmins, besides being inhabitants of Mumbai.

Sharad Sathe (b. 1932) combines in his training the two strands of the Gwalior gharana in Maharashtra: the Krishnarao Shankar Pandit strand via Sharadchandra Arolkar, and the Vishnu Digambar Paluskar strand through D. V. Paluskar. His early training was with the latter.

At no time did he sit down and learn the basics of music, says Sathe. During our discussion, he focused not so much on the actual techniques through which he must have learned but on the general approach to music that his teacher had imparted. He spoke in English mostly, with occasional Hindi phrases.

Sathe was a musicophiliac from a young age, although it took him some time to enter a formal learning situation. He approached D. V. Paluskar, already well known as a vocalist, and began to spend time with him, picking up his attitudes and approach to music:

> He [D. V. Paluskar] loved me a lot and he used to take me on his tours. So, I have visited quite a number of places and I used to watch him, how he used to sing, and how he caters to the audience . . . how he is respected and the general setup of the mehfil and all these things, how decorum has got to be maintained and how discipline is very important, and how he maintained it throughout the concert and even after the concert, before the concert, during the concert. All these things made quite an impact on me.[23]

I asked him what it meant to maintain discipline in the concert performance. His answer did not touch on the musician's behavior, as I thought it might, but on the mode of presenting a raga:

> The raga, every musician has his own way of rendering it, so I used to pay attention for [to] the correct diction of the bandish and all these things and the connection with the rhythm and all these things were very important.

These things were not taught to Sathe but were picked up from observing the teacher:

> Nobody in Hindustani music comes and says, "Look, [this is how you do it]." He can only take you once and say, "This is the way how you should cross the road." He brings him back and says, "Now it is up to you. I have shown the way." It depends on you, how to do it, but this is the way it has to be done. So . . . he didn't actually tell me, now sit here, this is "sa," this is "re," and all these things.

Here we have a singer who obtained taleem from a leading figure in the Gandharva Mahavidyalaya, established by Vishnu Digambar Paluskar (D. V.'s father), and one of the earliest and most influential music schools. From his account, Sathe appears never to have gone through the initial training like other beginners did. He did not try to learn from a book, he says, a method that was inculcated in the schools. He never did the graded music exams, although he straightaway passed the highest examination—Visharad—when studying with Prof. B. R. Deodhar in Bombay. Even as he attended the Gandharva Mahavidyalala or the School of Indian Music, he sought out and was trained individually by eminent teachers like D. V. Paluskar and B. R. Deodhar. With his second guru, Sharadchandra Arolkar, with whom he studied from 1966 to 1994, Sathe says, "One day was like a year for me, it was so vast." It is examples such as Sathe's that confound any easy opposition between guru-shishya taleem and music school training in musicophiliac Mumbai.

His *guru-behen* (fellow student/sister-in-learning) is Neela Bhagwat (b. 1942), who spoke to me at great length about her taleem with Sharadchandra Arolkar. She occupies an unusual position as a woman who has made her living entirely from teaching and performing music, without a backup profession like some male musicians in Mumbai, and without assigning the sole responsibility for the household economy to her husband (himself a vocalist and music critic), like many other female musicians. I have studied informally with Neela Bhagwat since 2003 and thus am privy to her teaching methods. She spoke in English, with interjections in Marathi and Hindi.

She studied with Arolkar every day for the first eight years, starting in 1969, and more intermittently thereafter until his death in 1994. He taught her tabla, which she practiced at home.

TN: What did he teach you first? What raag did you start with?

NB: Yaman Kalyan. *"Avagunana kijiye gunisana."* Oh . . . that's a tough bandish. In teentaal. And my taal was totally bad, and I made several mistakes, and then I said, *Bua mala kharach nahi yeth* [Bua, I really don't know how to do this]. Honestly, I was telling him, *acchi baat nahi hain* [this is not good]—*mala kalatach nahi kay karaawa* [I don't understand what to do]. He said with your left, you have to count. I said, *Ho ka? Bar.* [Is that so? Okay.] So I started counting with my left hand, and in between I used to make mistakes, but I think it was his playing the tabla along with the singing that gave me gradually a sense of taal, a sense of rhythm.

Bhagwat's guru's guru, Krishnarao Shankar Pandit, although a court singer, was interested in an institutional mode of teaching. He set up a syllabus and modes of assessment for students and actually wrote down bandishes with notation.[24] At the same time, he wanted to retain the intensity of one-to-one training and the closeness of the student-teacher bond, both associated with a gurukul mode rather than with a modern music school. Here we see a pattern of instruction that attempts to combine depth with range, different from how the Kirana singers recall their taleem.[25]

NB: In Gwalior gharana, whether it was in the Vidyalay or with the other pupils of Krishnarao Pandit, nobody has stuck to one raag for several years. The only thing was that the bandish is very important. [The] first few years you have to teach the major thirty ragas, and the sargam and the bandish and the tarana. All these forms, in each of the thirty ragas you have to teach.

TN: When you started teaching beginners, did you follow the same methods?

NB: I followed [my colleague] Kaka Patwardhan's methods. The *alankars* (note patterns specific to a raag)—I wrote down about fifty-three alankars. Then I told the students to make their own alankars. It's fun to do that. If I hadn't created any interest, any fun, for students, they would have run away. As I always say, these are basic alphabets. And from the word formation, you travel to the abstract form.

TN: And the sequence—you would teach them alankars first, the consonants and vowels, and then *sargams*, is it?

NB: The consonants and vowels... very few students I taught that—I gauge in my own way and then go ahead—for those who are seriously interested in the sound form, I teach them sargam, then the bandish, simple bandish, and then I write down the notation. Arolkar never did that. He wrote down the bandishes and notation only for Jagdish Prasad Goenka. He used to teach him, that owner of Swan and Jubilee textile mills. To us, for none of us he wrote down the notation—he wrote the text of the bandish and we did whatever we wanted. I did the notations on my own.

In this story, Goenka is the rich factory owner who dabbles in music and perhaps could not pick up the music without the aid of notation. For his serious students, however, Arolkar made no such concession. Although there is evidence of different music teachers creating their own notation systems to help students even in the late nineteenth century, notation of Indian music has been a contentious topic—with many gurus against the practice or wanting to keep it to a bare minimum. Neela has firm views on the significance of notation, although her teacher did not encourage it. She sees notation as an aid to remembering and for achieving clarity of enunciation. This is very different from a Western score, where the notation represents the actual model for performance.[26] In Hindustani music, a raga cannot be performed by reading the notation, since the latter is simply an aid to memory of the repertoire, which has to be elaborated afresh and improvised in each presentation. So in the face of such clear differences between the purpose of Western notation and that of the systems devised by Indian musicians, why did tensions around the practice of notation surface so frequently? Amanda Weidman argues that in the case of Carnatic music the contrast between orality and writing came to be seen as the fundamental difference between Indian and Western music.[27] I am inclined to think that the need to uphold this difference is what caused the tensions in Hindustani music also. In actual practice, however, even hereditary musicians who resisted the institutionalization of music pedagogy were known to have either permitted students to notate what was taught to them or do so themselves. Arolkar's own teacher, Krishnarao Shankar Pandit, a Hindu Brahmin second-generation singer rather than a hereditary Muslim performer, was one of the pioneers of pedagogic techniques—including notation—that could be used for nonhereditary musicians in music schools, but Arolkar himself was not known to have favored the practice.

TN: So he didn't mind your doing the notations?

NB: I never showed him, I never told him (laughs). There was no way I could think of telling him. It was very difficult.

TN: In your own teaching practice, why do you feel that notation is crucial to the understanding of the student?

NB: Because the students go wrong. In the bandish, if there is "re" and the student is singing "ga," or there is "sa" and the student is singing "ni"—how can that be? You have to give the precise note, and which meend it falls. All that structural precision is very essential for a bandish. So that—I have to teach that.

TN: But you didn't learn in that way, right?

NB: No, I didn't, but I thought *I* must do it. I know how to do it. And Bua never wanted to know whether I knew how to do it.

I asked Neela about the breathing exercises, and those for clearing the nostrils, which she teaches in her music workshops, wanting to find out whether she used these to train beginning students of hers. She responded,

Yes, but in the old traditional way they don't teach it. You take care of your own breathing and your own cold and cough. Bua was not worried about that. See, the whole process of teaching was more guru oriented. I am more student oriented. I would see to it that the student gets something. One hour of teaching [the normal duration of her class].

Neela is fully aware of the contractual agreement that undergirds modern music training, where students pay fees and the time spent with them is strictly regulated. But at the same time, she is concerned about passing on everything she has learned.

You see, time is so short and the vidya is so great—how can you pass it on to the students and how can they become singers, how will this Gwalior gharana survive, if I don't teach, and I don't make things clear? *Mera kuch* perspective *hi alag tha. Unka aisa tha hi nahi.* [My perspective is quite different from his.] He was not worried about whether the gharana survives or not. He was worried about the pure, authentic art form of khayal—thumris, tappas, taranas, all that he was so involved in. Not that we are not, but I also see it in a larger perspective, in a different context. This enriches our culture, and I'm a vehicle to carry forward the music. If I don't do it, *kya hoga uska? Kahi mar jaayega, kahi chalaa—chala toh gaya hi hain, aur aur bhi jaayega.* [What will happen to it? It will die somewhere. It's already going, gone, and will disappear further.]

Neela often speaks bitterly about the secretiveness of the older generation of musicians, which meant that they did not teach their students everything they themselves had learned. This practice of withholding ragas and compositions was evidently prevalent in northern India, as documented by Daniel Neuman in relation to hereditary musicians. This is strangely mirrored in the many archival efforts taken up, often by musicians themselves, who are unwilling to share freely what they have collected, or reveal it only on rare occasions, a little bit at a time. Aligning herself with modern pedagogic initiatives like Bhatkhande's, even as she never misses an opportunity to criticize his classificatory modes, Neela Bhagwat has now shared her notated bandish collection on the internet and is urging fellow musicians to do the same.

Jaipur Gharana

After studying with Bhurji Khan, Alladiya Khan's son, as a young girl in the princely state of Kolhapur, Dhondutai Kulkarni (1927–2014) went on to learn from Laxmibai Jadhav, and eventually with the help of the Khansahebs' family, she was introduced to Kesarbai Kerkar (1892–1977), a Goan from a kalavant or performing background who had by the 1950s become one of the leading Hindustani singers. Dhondutai was Kesarbai's only disciple, and Kesarbai was already seventy-two years old when she began teaching her. Since Kesarbai was a wealthy woman, she refused to take any money from Dhondutai.

Dhondutai's narration of her taleem with Kesarbai Kerkar wove in and out of the story of Kesarbai's taleem with Alladiya Khan. Talking about Kesarbai's taleem, Dhondutai said how Alladiya Khan was of the opinion that music should not depend on the voice; *damsaas* (breath control) is important. You need a technique by which to sing so as to prolong the note.

Interestingly, breath control is the only clear pedagogic objective Dhondutai mentions in her entire story of how Kesarbai obtained her taleem. As I discuss later in the chapter, Dhondutai was unwilling to talk about how the teaching proceeded, except to describe it in terms of duration.

DK: For ten years Kesarbai got nonstop training from him, every minute of the day—I don't think anyone else has learnt like this. Khansaab said, "I have to teach you alone, but you have to pay as much as I need to take care of my family because I'm just teaching one person. How will I take care of my family?" And Kesarbai paid for all his expenses, and she learnt with him, and she would wake up again at five in the morning and start again. [Toh Kesarbai ne aise dus saal unke paas ek minute ka bhi kuch bandh nahi aisa sikha, aise kisi ne sikha hi nahi, kisi ne. Ek toh kya hai ke jab Khan Saab ne kaha ke "tumko akeli ko hi sikhana hai toh mujhe jitna meri grahasti chalane ke liye jitna paisa lagta hai utna aapko dena padega, ek hi admi ko main sikha raha hoon nahi toh meri grahasti main kaise chalau," toh utna sab kharch karke sab deti thi, woh aaram se sikhte thae aur subah paanch baje phir uth ke karte thi.]

She would tell me, "I don't know how I would take a bath at noon, and when I would eat lunch and fall asleep. I would have a bath half asleep, have my lunch like that, and fall asleep after that." Again she would wake up at four o'clock and Khansaab would train her again till eight o'clock. At eight he would stop the training and have dinner, and again at night from nine to ten o'clock he would start teaching again. [Woh mujhe kehti thi ki "dophar 12 baje main kaise nah ti thi aur kab khana khaake sona chahiye toh mujhe maloom hi nahi padta tha, main aise aankh band karke hi nah ti thi. Waisa hi khana khaake soti thi." Phir 4 baje uthte thae Khansaab phir taalim dete thae 8 baje tak. 8 baje band karte thae thoda khana wana hone ke baad raat ko 9–10 baje gaana sikhana shuru karte thae.]

Until the song "sat in her throat" Khansaab would not let her sleep and the next morning she had to wake up at five. So it was after ten years of this kind of training that Kesarbai was ready. No one else would have learnt like this or got this kind of training. And Alladiya Khansaab said music should not depend on the voice, so he developed certain techniques. Kesarbai got all those techniques. The foundation of this gharana, for every raga the variations in the notes, and damsaas. [Toh jab unke gale mein jo baithana chahte thae woh pura nahi hota, tab tak Khansaab usko sone ke liye nahi chodte thae. Aur woh subah phir 5 baje uthna hi hai. Toh aise 10 saal seekhne ke baad woh Kesarbai tayyar ho gayi. Aise kisi ne seekha hi nahi, aise kisi ko aisi taalim hi nahi mili. Aur Alladiya Khansaab ne awaaz ke upar apna gaana depend nahi hona chahiye isiliye ek tarika kuch banaya tha. Woh sab tarika Kesarbai ko mila tha—yeh iska gharane ka foundation, har ek raga ke shruti ke sur aur damsaas.]

Dhondutai says only that Kesarbai was taught all the *tarika* or techniques developed by Alladiya Khan, without ever saying what those techniques were. Here, even though she is a modern student of music, she echoes the concerns of hereditary musicians regarding the sharing of proprietary knowledge. The need to achieve distinctiveness in urban space created new boundary lines: what was earlier shared only within the family was now shared within the gharana, which included nonfamily members, but could not be revealed to outsiders, whether they were musicians or just musicophiliacs.

Azizuddin Khan (Baba), Burji Khan's son and Alladiya Khan's grandson, who taught Dhondutai for some time and felt responsible for her future, felt that Kesarbai would be a good teacher for her. When he spoke to Kesarbai, she said, "If someone is ready to learn like I did, practice hard like I did, bring that person to me right away and I will teach her." ("Jaise mein seekhi, jaise maine mehnat ki, waise koi tayyar ho to mere paas laake abhi de do, mein sikhaoongi.") But in the beginning, Kesarbai seemed reluctant to teach her much.

> DK: After two years she felt that I really wanted to learn, so she took me to her bungalow in Lonavala. So we went there to stay with one servant. So during that time the way Alladiya Khansaab trained her, she trained me. [Do saal ke baad jab unko laga ki, sach maaniye, mein inko Sikhana mujhe . . . Lonavala mein bangla tha unka. Toh wahan jaake hum log rahe ek naukar leke. Toh uss waqt jaise Alladiya Khansaab ne unko taalim di thi, waise taalim mujhe de diye.]
>
> How should you present a raag? First, when you sing the shadja [the first base note], you should be able to captivate all the listeners [*haat mein aana chahiye*—they should come into your hand]. Second, how should you increase breath control? Both these things she taught me at Lonavala. But she didn't teach me anything for two years before that. It was a test. [Ek raag kaisa present karna chahiye? Ki shadja lagane ke shuru karne se baad se shrota sab apne haat mein aane chahiye ek. Dumsaas kaise badhana chahiye? Yeh dusri baat thi aur yeh dono cheeze mujhe unhone Lonavala jaake wahan sikhayi. Magar do saal pehele kuch nahi sikhaya, do saal. Pariksha.]

Dhondutai also talked about aspects of the taleem that are manifested not in technique but in the overall approach to musical training, such as Kesarbai's emphasis on punctuality:

> So from the first day itself, she was so particular about time—I would go to her place at five. I should ring the doorbell at five sharp. One day I was late. It was 5:05, and she showed me the clock, asking, "See, what is the time?" I said only five minutes late, not more. But, she said, "When we sing, can we mark the *samm* [first beat] after five minutes?" So from that day I made sure to reach at five sharp. So . . . discipline. The one who has no discipline in her music cannot sing. [Tar pehle din itni time ke baare mein woh itni perfect thi main paanch baje unke ghar jaati thi na paanch baje maine barabar ghanti bajana chahiye. Ek din 5 baje se 5 minute mujhe der ho gayi unhone mujhe ghadyal dikhaya, "Dekho time kitne baje", 5 hi minute ho gaye jyada nahi. "Magar jab gaate hai toh sam dete hai toh 5 minute ke baad sam dene ko chalega kya?" aise. Us din se maine dekha

Figure 4.1. Kesarbai's image in Dhondutai's house. Photo: Tejaswini Niranjana.

ke 5 baje jana chahiye. Toh phir . . . discipline. Woh kehti thi ke jiske gaane mein discipline nahi hai woh gaa nahi sakta.]

Kesarbai's own training with Alladiya Khan, who stayed at her house and taught her throughout the day, seems to have been different in time perception from the way she taught Dhondutai. The Khansaheb was, in Dhondutai's narrative, precise about starting times, but then the lessons stretched across the entire day, for ten years, until he felt that Kesarbai was *tayyar* or ready. In contrast, Dhondutai had to arrive on the guru's doorstep at the appointed time and leave when her lesson was done. It was only when Dhondutai went to the hill resort of Lonavala, after two years of studying with Kesarbai, that she was given access to the special voice production techniques of the gharana, in an instructional mode that was presumably not regulated by the clock in the way her earlier lessons were. The point of Kesarbai's insistence on punctuality was not just to make sure Dhondutai came on time, but her way of enforcing musical discipline, as is evident from her analogy of reaching the samm or first beat five minutes late.

Rutuja Lad (b. 1992) obtained her taleem from Dhondutai Kulkarni and has recently started learning from Ashwini Bhide Deshpande, also of the Jaipur gharana. When I interviewed Dhondutai, Rutuja was also present, making tea for us and passing snacks around. We filmed part of her taleem, although it ended up being a scene crafted for the film rather than a documentation of a routine lesson that was taking place. Dhondutai was a reluctant presence throughout. Rutuja sang in front of her guru, who only very occasionally corrected her. Whenever Dhondutai was asked about some pedagogic detail, she ignored the question or side-stepped it. Rutuja, a good sixty-five years younger, understands what her teacher did that day, and now that the guru is no longer alive, she discusses what and how she learned in a mode that acknowledges her teacher's reticence with some embarrassment.

Rutuja's taleem with Dhondutai gives us a glimpse of how pedagogic techniques must have developed through the twentieth century as they passed through three or four generations of modern musicians. As Rutuja talks about her training, the discussion is populated by other scenes of instruction that bleed into the twenty-first-century one: Kesarbai teaching Dhondutai, and Alladiya Khan teaching Kesarbai.

I asked if Dhondutai made her do alankars (note patterns), and Rutuja replied that the focus of her riyaaz or practice was not to memorize patterns, but to be able to produce each sur or note in a strong way, an open-throated way. "And did you do sargam?" (a singing exercise with a string of notes), I asked. Rutuja said her gharana did not use sargam, although if she was not able to get a palta (a string of note permutations for a particular raga; used in riyaaz), Dhondutai would ask her to notate it, or write it down for her. For more than seven years Dhondutai did not allow her to write down anything, but after that time she asked Rutuja to write the words of the compositions, as well as the notations, so that she would always remember how they had been taught to her.

TN: Did she ever write down the bandishes that she knew?

RL: Yeah, she did, she did. She had a book. She never opened that book in front of us. Looking at the book and then teaching, that was not the case.

TN: She never showed any of you the book?

RL: She showed me the book, but then the thing is she never used the book for our taleem. That means she had everything in her head. Of course at times what used to happen, she used to forget a word—you know, *ek shabd* missing *hain* [one word was missing]—then she would refer to her diary. That's what she did.

Here again, in a pedagogic practice devised for nonhereditary musicians, starting with Kesarbai, born in 1892, a hundred years before Rutuja, we see no avoidance of notation, although there is no evident dependence on it. Musical knowledge was acquired not from the book but from the teacher, even as the book remained a reassuring presence in the musician's life. The status of the book is somewhat different in the Carnatic pedagogic mode that was emerging in the twentieth century, where, as Amanda Weidman has it, notation was seen as a mark of literacy, "and therefore of classical status, and as a transparent and legible representation of orality, and therefore of Indianness."[28]

I wanted to know if Dhondutai recommended any exercises to improve the quality of the voice. Rutuja misunderstood the question to refer to clarity. Perhaps for her this idea of exercising for better voice quality was intelligible only through what was implied and experienced versus what needed to be explained.

RL: That's a difficult question to answer. We did not have that systematic way of telling a student. So I can't [for example] just tell ki "*asa asa he kar*," then this will happen, do like this then this will happen—this sort of explanation was never given to me. It was all implied, and it was all experienced. But she always used to make it a point to tell me that when you are practicing taans, practice at a very slow speed. Make it correct. Just listen to your own taans first. Make sure that each and every sur is pronounced correctly—speed is not important; clarity is important. That's what she always told us. We are like, at a younger age we are just behind speed, that's the tendency, na? That was not practiced in our taleem. Speed *apne aap ho sakta hain.* [Speed comes by itself.]

TN: So clarity is about distinguishing one swar from the other, right?

RL: Yeah, so for example I am singing a simple taan—*pa dha pa pa ga re sa sa* [sings it]. This is the taan. So when you're practicing, it should not be [sings it very fast]—*ek gaya. Ek ek sur suna hi dena chahiye, matlab* [sings it again, twice]. Each and every sur should have that clarity. This is a palta, from Raag Bhoop. This pattern you can

Figure 4.2. Rutuja Lad with Dhondutai Kulkarni. Photo: Tejaswini Niranjana.

see across all the ragas which have similar surs [notes]. You can sing this in Yaman also. In any raag that has *pa* and *dha*. That is a kind of a link—*pa dha pa pa*. So these kinds of important phrases she made us practice.

Rutuja demonstrated for me the *gamak* taan (where a certain force is added to notes), and the *sapaat* taan (where the notes are placed in the order in which they appear in the octave).

RL: *Tabla ke saath hum log gaate thae* [we used to sing with tabla accompaniment] *matlab, ek ek ek taan* was composed in that *avartan* [rhythmic cycle], you know. And that kind of building the continuity of taans, that practice, we got it from that time only.

TN: Did she ask you to compose the taans yourself?

RL: Yeah, yeah—later that spontaneity—*apne aap ko ban jaata hain na?* [You get it by yourself, no?] You internalize the process, you in-

Pedagogy and the Performing Subject · 151

ternalize the approach, of the presentation. So then the spontaneity is established after that.

Here Rutuja acknowledges that spontaneity is the product of a long and intensive training process that brings the aspiring vocalist to the point where she knows how to sing rather than worrying about what to sing.

Agra Gharana

At the age of seven or eight, Lalith Rao (b. 1942) started learning from Ramrao Naik in Bangalore. Naik was the disciple of Ata Hussain Khan, son of Mehboob Khan "Daraspiya" and brother-in-law of major twentieth-century musician Faiyaz Khan, to whom he provided vocal accompaniment in concert, and from whom he also learned music. Naik never taught Lalith Rao in a grammatical way and was quite casual in his approach, perhaps, as she says, because she was a little girl at the time. He did not prescribe *paltas*, but taught her a few songs in each raga. He came to her house three times a week for an hour. Although she sang publicly in her teens, music was just one more hobby, along with sports, acting, and debating. She went into engineering and moved to Canada in 1965 to earn a master's degree. After marriage in 1967, her husband, Jayavanth Rao, persuaded her to give up her engineering job and devote herself full-time to music. In 1967–68, she studied with Dinkar Kaikini in Delhi, and then they moved to Bombay.

Lalith Rao had already decided to become Khadim Husain Khan's disciple. She had encountered him once before when she was fourteen, and he had blessed her after a private concert, even as he drew attention to an incorrect enunciation that he thought could be improved upon. She calls him a "wonderful teacher." He did not "make her practice"—*riyaaz karna tumhara hai*. "If you didn't practice, that was your problem," she says. Since she was an advanced student, Khadim Husain taught her one raga a week, whereas a beginner would have spent a year or two on a single raga.

I asked Lalith Rao what the differences could be in the way taleem takes place in different generations of musicians. What was the difference between how Khadim Husain Khansaheb was trained and how he trained her? And what was the difference between that and how she trains her students? What did the similarities and differences mean?

> For Khansaab it was maybe listening and imbibing and repeating, when they were young; not even imbibing, just repeating until you

got it right. Because they were taught six or eight or nine to ten hours, that's what they say. Khansaab said his taleem started at ten at night and went on until three and four in the morning. So it must have been a very intensive training.... Many of them were uneducated. Maybe they couldn't even read and write, I don't know. Some of them couldn't, some could. How much they wrote down, how much they didn't, I don't know. If at all, like me, just the words of the bandish.

Although her comment was about the family in general, in many ways echoing a modern attitude toward hereditary—in particular Muslim—musicians, I pointed out that somewhere in *Sajan Piya* (Jayavanth Rao's book on Khadim Husain Khan) it says that the Khansaheb did actually write down all the compositions.

He has written them down, but whether it was then or later I don't know. They [the musicians in her teacher's family] had very little formal schooling. With so many continuous hours of teaching, I think you know it became part of the system. It was something they would never forget. I didn't ask him in my case, whether he wrote it down then. I did write down the words [of the composition], and he did not give me what you'd call the *aaroh* and *avaroh*, the scale going up and down. He said that had no contextual reference to the raag. Because the same notes can be sung in different ways. It is mainly the swar patterns, which combinations you take in which raag, and [that] you can write down.

Here Lalith Rao talks about what can and cannot be written down. A music school teacher would begin by dictating the aaroh and avaroh, which define the nature of a raga. But in Khadim Husain's understanding, this does not really help, because the exact same notes "can be sung in different ways." The note patterns and the combinations that could be made with them, rather than the scale, defined for him the unique features of a raga.

LR: So he gave me what was roughly called a *chalan*. Chalan means—roughly—going up and down, but not just the sargam. And then, most important was, how much time you spend on each note, how much emphasis you give on each note, how you connect notes, and which patterns are to be used more, which patterns are to be used less. Where you take a breath, and where you stop. These make up, these give you, the three-dimensional quality of a raag.

TN: Do you know if he had to create these ways of teaching, or this is how he was himself taught?

LR: He also might have been taught like that, I don't know... because the earlier way of remembering the raags was through the bandish. You sang the raag as to how the bandish was phrased. You looked at the raag through the bandish. So if you knew the bandish exceptionally well, then you would explore the raag through these avenues.

Although Hindustani musicians usually say that what they are presenting is the raga and not the bandish or the composition, which is more or less incidental, Lalith Rao suggests that "the earlier way"—presumably before the phenomenon of musicophilia changed the audiences and practitioners of Hindustani music—was to remember the raga through the bandish.

TN: So if there were many bandishes, would you use all of them to explore the raag?

LR: Not necessarily. They'd say—if you were singing a particular bandish, you explore the raag as it is in that bandish. If you are singing another bandish, with a slightly different perspective, you can do that also. But in the final analysis you combine all of them together.

TN: So your taan patterns or your phrases that get repeated would be across the bandishes, right?

LR: There would be slight variations on how you take combinations of notes. I was thinking Khansaab must have learnt the same way. Because you know that incident involving Ghagge Khudabuksh?

Ghagge Khudabuksh was a senior musician of the Gwalior/Agra styles of vocalization, his nickname "Ghagge" deriving from his voice, which used to be strikingly hoarse before it was transformed by vocal training. The story goes thus: someone came to visit Ghagge and said he would like to learn Raag Jait from him. Ghagge is supposed to have said that he didn't know Jait. The other musician got quite angry, and said, "Achha, you don't even know Jait, then you have no right to keep the tanpura with you." So he walked away with Ghagge Khudabuksh's tanpura. Later, the singer's sons came back and asked what had happened. Ghagge said, "Somebody came here and asked me to teach him Jait, and I said I didn't know what Jait was, and so he took away my tanpura." The sons said to the father, "But you know five of the bandishes in that raag," and they named the bandishes, and Ghagge said, "Oh, is that called Jait? How am I to know?"[29]

> LR: This is a pointer to the fact that they didn't give importance to the raag. Through the bandish, the raag remains safe. You don't need to know the aaroh and avaroh—just see Deshkar and Bhoop, for example. They have the same notes. But when you sing them they sound totally different. Aaroh-avaroh therefore wasn't important. So Khansaab taught me the same way.
>
> TN: But when Khansaab taught you, he did place a lot of emphasis on the bandish itself, right?
>
> LR: Yes. He said, you learn the bandish, and that will open up the whole raag for you. He did teach me a bit of the raag also. In the sense, the *aakaar*, and the *nom tom*, and the sargam—that would be done. But the alaap, etc., went *through* the bandish.

Lalith Rao's explanation for why this teaching method came into being had to do with the insecurity of life in northern India, "due to the many invasions, and the continuous wars between various kings and the British and the Moghuls." Through this description, she echoes the modern Indian's perspective on "those days."

> You must have read how Khansaab's family had to flee Gondpur, throwing their books and everything into the well. Then you try to preserve whatever treasure you have. You think of the best way of preserving it. So what happens? You remove things you think are unnecessary. And they [might] have said then that aaroh-avaroh can be gathered later. You can always pick it up from a book or from someone else, but the bandishes, and the way the raag is presented through the bandish [are] the most important. That is the nucleus of the vidya [knowledge].

She too teaches her students by giving them the chalan, and by giving them elaborations of the raag.

She commented on how there is now a shift to the student's own initiative and ability to practice independently, with the reduction in the number of hours the student spends with the teacher. But listening to her recorded lessons and repeating was not enough for an aspiring musician, who had to be guided by the guru in voice production.

Figure 4.3. Khadim Husain Khan teaching Lalith Rao. Photo: Mansaram.

LR: Even if you listen and sing, there are certain things you don't get absolutely right. For example, breath control or *dumsaas*. Dumsaas is very very important. But you know Khansaab had a very informal way of teaching. He only said: "Lambi saas lo, aur jitna tum usko rakh sakthe ho usko kaayam karo" [Take a deep breath, and hold on to it for as long as you can]. So *lambi dumsaas* is necessary for all music. No matter to which gharana you belong. Voice culture he did emphasize a little bit, but more importantly he emphasized how to pronounce the word, how to bring emotion into your gayaki, the inflections, how to bring modulations and where not to use them.

TN: Did you ever write down the notation for any composition?

LR: Khansaab said, *mere paas na kitab na pustak* [I don't have any books of any kind]. He trusted me not to write them down, so I didn't. I've now forgotten some compositions [as a result].

Did the Khansaheb not have any books because his family had thrown them into the well as they fled from the attacking armies? Were those

Figure 4.4. Lalith Rao performing in 1989 in Darbar Hall, Baroda. Collection of Jayavanth Rao.

books filled with the text of bandishes, or did they have notation also? From what I have seen in Lalith Rao's master classes where she instructs several students simultaneously, she does write down for them not only the words of the composition but also the notation. However, as the master class gathers pace, no one there is reading off the notation from a photocopied sheet. Instead, they are listening and responding to the teacher's verbal cues.

Etawah Gharana

Born to a wealthy industrialist family in Ahmedabad, Arvind Parikh (b. 1927) came to Bombay for his higher education and became the lifelong disciple and friend of Vilayat Khan (1928–2004), with whom a chance meeting had prompted his decision to move to Bombay. Vilayat Khan was a sitarist of the Imdadkhani or Etawah gharana, and Parikh studied with him from 1944 to 2004. Inayat Khan (1894–1938), Vilayat Khan's father and his first teacher, is known for having reshaped sitar playing to gayaki *ang*, approximating the vocal khayal bandish format, following the practice of his own father, Imdad Khan (1848–1920).

Pedagogy and the Performing Subject · 157

AP: I used to listen to a bit of *been* also, sitar, and then I was listening to all kinds of sitar players all over India through the radio, so I heard Shiraz Ahmed Qureshi, Mohammed Sharif Poonchwale; All India Radio, Lahore, started at that time. Then Haider Hussein Chugtai from Delhi, Iliyas Khan from Lucknow, Waliullah Khan from Dhaka.

I started listening to these sitar players—and then I heard Ravi Shankar-ji. And I knew this was something very different. The language is different, and so on, and then of course I heard Vilayat Khan. I went to Vilayat Khan-saab by chance.

TN: Where did you meet him?

AP: I met him in Bombay. Actually, I had come to Bombay to give an audition on the radio. And one of my relations met me at the railway station, and saw the sitar in my hand, and said, "What are you doing here with this sitar?" I said, "I have come to give audition in All India Radio." He said, "Do you want to meet Vilayat Khan?" I said, "Of course I want to meet him. Is he in Bombay?" He said, "He is very much in Bombay, and he is coming to teach me at eleven." So I went to his house at eleven. It was just a chance meeting, and . . . I could never believe this is Vilayat Khan.

Because a young man comes with a blue kurta, and a Craven-A *dabba* [packet], and cigarette—smoking away—and shaded glasses, and I said, how can this be Vilayat Khan? Because I imagined Vilayat Khan with sherwani, and beard, and I just couldn't believe it. And he was seventeen at that time, and so was I. I told myself, this is not Vilayat Khan. Then of course, we started chit-chatting. He said, "Do you play?" I said, "Yes I do," and so I played a little bit for him. When he heard me he knew I am definitely going to fail in the audition, because I was just no good.

But I thought I am very good, so that was a problem. But anyway, he taught me a little bit, which I picked up very fast, and he was very impressed, and he said, "Why don't you come to Bombay . . ." I was very, very good at academics. I used to always stand first-class, first all throughout. So I got admission in Elphinstone College and I had my maternal uncle's flat—as I said they were very rich people—so I stayed there.

Parikh is a widely read man and an astute businessman, in addition to being a reputed sitar player. He uses a distinction between conscious and subconscious that is not often used by Hindustani musicians to describe their craft:

> My teacher tells me that, Arvind, when you play sitar, your fingers should have vision. That is a beautiful sentence. It means, when your fingers should have vision, your subconscious mind is guiding you.
>
> So what really has to be done for a musician [is] that the conscious mind creates music, and the subconscious mind executes it. When you reach that stage you have made it. And when your conscious mind is creating a [subconscious], there is a dichotomy, and there is no tension. When your conscious and subconscious both are focused, there is tremendous tension. When you bifurcate your conscious mind, and your subconscious is executing, there is no tension. There is no stress. And therefore all musicians are doing paltas.
>
> Why are they doing paltas? Not for getting proficiency only. Proficiency is one thing, but after you play your paltas fifteen times, twenty times, thirty times, fifty times, then your mind starts wandering, and you do this automatically. It's not automatic—it's your subconscious mind doing that. So the role of palta, if you understand it really, what is that role, you have to gradually withdraw your conscious mind, and your subconscious executes it.

Parikh's founding distinction appears quite different from that suggested by Dard Neuman, who also talks about sitar playing. Neuman's teacher, Ustad Shujaat Khan, who happens to be Vilayat Khan's son, insisted "that the capabilities of the fingers should always be ahead of the mind." Neuman coined the phrase "body-instrument" to refer to how the improvisation process is built up, through conversations between repetitive phrases, the mind, and the player's active fingers. In contrast, Parikh does not address the issue of embodiment, but instead applies distinctions such as intellectual versus emotional or conscious versus subconscious. These are neither musicological distinctions nor those used by hereditary musicians, but those of the modern musicophiliac who speaks about music through the terms more commonly used by the educated person in everyday life.[30] Following an idea elaborated by Weidman, we can see that these distinctions that turn away from embodiment actually create the idea of an interior self which then strives to find expression in performing.[31]

> TN: Did Vilayat Khansaab teach you complete ragas for years on end, or did he teach you different kinds of techniques—what was the

process by which you learnt? And a related question is, what kind of taleem do you give your students? Is it very similar to how you learnt?

AP: Muslim Ustads, the way they teach is there are two sitars, one they have in hand and one the student has. They play and you have to follow. Very few Ustads, barring my own Ustad, like to have questions. Why is it so? Arre, *hamare abba karte thae is liye*, why is it so *ka kya baat hai*, what are you talking [about]? My father used to do it. I am doing it. Where is the question [of why]? In olden times, I am told, not in my time, students were banned from asking questions.

Vilayat Khansaab, although we were close, when he used to teach, I was afraid of him. Believe me, I was afraid of him. But if I asked a question, he would not say, why are you asking this question? He would give me an answer. He taught me all the right things, and I was a good student. But it was not easy to learn from him, honestly.

The number of ragas [he taught me] were not hundred[s], just a few ragas, and taals also were few; but he gave me such intense insight into my vision of music, it was completely molded by him. One day he tells me, take a piece of paper and pencil, draw a line. [Then he asks,] "What is this, Arvind?" I said, "It's a line." He'd say, "It's not a line. It's a string of a sitar. How are you looking at this string? What is the affection? How are you touching it? How are you plucking it? From what angle you are plucking it?" *Kaunsi jagah se* . . . you know, the complete vision that the man had was divine grace, even completely unique at that young age.

Even as Parikh claims that his guru had a "complete vision" of music, it was not based on "reasons." He suggests that it is only through the student's analysis of the taleem that the scientific principles underlying Vilayat Khan's teaching method could be brought out:

So he gave me a vision. He exposed me to a great many other musicians, and he taught me in the manner that I described. He taught me without giving the reasons, which I found when I analyzed his [taleem]. Why should we wear the [sitar plucking ring] in this way? What is the scientific reason? You hold sitar at 45-degree angle. *Koi neeche nahin hona chahiye koi upar nahin hona chahiye* [it should not be higher or lower]. Why 45 degrees? Because scientifically it is proved that gravitational force is least at a 45-degree angle. If you hold it [vertically] like some do, then gravitational force going up becomes difficult.

In the right hand [which plucks the strings], which are the sources of strength? This is not a source of strength—this is a hinge. There is one source of strength here, one here, and another here. [I figured these out.] So when I am teaching I use this method.

Parikh also prides himself on the mode of analyzing students that he has developed:

> Once in a year at Gurupurnima we organize a two-day festival. All my students play—about thirty of them play, and I sit from 9:30 in the morning up to 7 p.m. making notes [about] each student. Usually no guru listens to the complete recital of a student. But during the Gurupurnima festival, I make notes [about the weaknesses of each], and I type them out, give a copy to the student and keep one copy for myself. I've got a file for each student.

Parikh's guru, Vilayat Khan, is known to have been utterly dismissive of music school teaching, even commenting once in disgust that "these schools are mushrooming like urinals."[32] So even while Parikh's pedagogic practice is based on the assigning of rational explanations that hereditary musicians did not offer, his effort is to reimagine sina-basina training rather than adopting a classroom approach. We have seen other attempts in this chapter to produce explanations for how musical training works, especially in the interview with Neela Bhagwat. I suggest this is a feature of musicophilia-driven teaching and learning in metropolitan space, where Hindustani art music is pedagogically encountered in both music schools and guru-shishya training, and where the latter sometimes uses concepts from modern education to render musical pedagogy intelligible to a student who is immersed in that education system for acquiring most kinds of knowledge except that of music.

This chapter has looked closely at the minutiae of Hindustani music training, embedding them in the larger social context in which tensions over older and newer forms of education were manifesting themselves. Chapter 5 presents a few more sites where the tensions are exacerbated or resolved.

5

NEARNESS AS DISTANCE, OR DISTANCE AS NEARNESS

As the space of teaching and learning music expanded to different sites through the long twentieth century, and as performance opportunities and venues also changed, face-to-face training acquired new complexities. In the case of Neela Bhagwat, it had to do partly with ideological orientation and partly with the student's ambition, although it manifested in the actual give and take of music compositions. In the section "Taleem by Other Means," musicians speak about how they expand their performative repertoire (through gramophone records, the radio, and now digital archives and YouTube) and how they do their riyaaz or practice in performance, so to speak. The concluding section of the chapter discusses the recent proliferation of cyber teaching, asking whether geographical distance comes to be digitally resituated as a new form of intimacy.

A Complicated Relationship

The tensions in twentieth-century guru-shishya relationships were many, as we can sense from the accounts of Neela Bhagwat talking about Sharadchandra Arolkar, or Dhondutai Kulkarni talking about Kesarbai Kerkar. Others did not talk about the tensions, either because the sense of devotion and awe dominated, or because in their understanding of the guru-shishya

Figure 5.1.
Sharadchandra
Arolkar. Photo:
Sateesh Paknikar.

relationship it was not something that could be spoken about. In stories about hereditary musicians, we do hear about arguments and enmities between musicians, but not between teacher and student.[1]

Among the musicians I met, the ones who were willing to speak about the complexity of the guru-shishya relationship are also, interestingly, those figures who represent a transitional moment—from the mid-twentieth century to a later period in which what was allowed and what was not got reconfigured. So although the conflict is embodied in persons and personalities, and is often understood as manifestations of different psychological makeups, it is indicative on the one hand of the changing social and political economy of music in our times, and on the other of the changing formation of the social subject of musicophilia.

Neela Bhagwat spoke about her strong ideological inclinations toward feminism and socialism and how her guru disapproved of them. She also spoke about Arolkar's reluctance to teach her compositions, which was one of the reasons she started going to Jal Balaporia of the same gharana.

TN: So does this mean that as a singer passes away, the bandishes [compositions] also disappear?

NB: Yeah, yeah it does.

TN: Do you have any idea how many he would have known and how many you did not learn?

NB: Bua had learnt 1,064 compositions of the tradition. Now I know only 337 of them. Of the 337, a few I have learned from Jal-saab [Jal Balaporia], since Bua was not willing to teach me everything. He had a different idea. He said, *Tula ya pithawar basaiche* [You have to sit on this stage]. He said, you have to become like a guru, you have to preserve the knowledge, you have to analyze, you have to become the resource person for Gwalior and the khayal and the aesthetics and all of it. I used to say to him, But I also want to sing. I feel like singing and I enjoy singing. He used to say, *Theek hai, gayacha tar gaa pan he tujha kaam hai* [Sing if you must, but this is your real work]. He allotted this role to me, whereas I also wanted to sing. I was performing and I was enjoying [it]. I also started composing my own stuff. In about five years' time I was composing. I never showed it to him. I never told him.

She spoke about the fear that imbued the student-teacher relationship:

There was a little fear [one felt around] him. Because suddenly if he is annoyed with you, then he will certainly not teach. Otherwise there's a chance that you get to learn something, so you had to please him. Now in a way that guru-shishya relation was creative for me, because I composed a lot and whatever little I learned, my other . . . the other poor students did not get to learn even that much. And some of them said, *Arre, tum ne jhagad jhagad ke itna toh leliya, accha kiya. Humko woh bhi nahi miltha hai.* [You fought with him and got this much. You did well—we don't even get this much.]

I asked her whether Arolkar wrote down all 1,064 bandishes he had learned, and she said he had. But when asked whether she had access to them now, she talked instead about the day Arolkar died:

NB: He had told his nephew and his wife to burn that book along with him. So when he passed away, he died in the morning, and then the nephew called me up: "Neelatai, *chala* [come]," so I went and I saw that the book was there near his feet. Then I said, *Ithe kaa thevlele* [Why is this book there]? He said, *Annani sangitlay, majhya barobar he jaloon gelela pahije* [Anna has told us, this should be burned with him]. *Ti vidya aahe, jaloon deta kama nahin* [This is vidya (knowledge); we can never allow it to be burnt]. *Pan Anna mhanale tasa* [But that is what Anna said]. *He bagh, Anna mhanaale, the thyancha-purta theek aahe* [Look, this is for him to think]. It's for him to think like that. Not for us. We have to think differently. I'm going to keep it aside. So I lifted that book, and I kept it away. And that's how we saved it. And now I'm not getting that book again [laughs ruefully] because it's with my elder *guru bandhu* and he is just not giving. This is the property relation.... I have no property. I'm giving it to everyone, but that's me. People are different.

TN: And with Jal-saab, how was the interaction? Where had you heard him sing?

NB: I used to hear him everywhere, because he came for Arolkar's concerts. He came for Krishnarao Pandit's concerts, Gwalior *ke log hain toh aapas mein itna toh milna-julna hota tha* [this much meeting up the Gwalior people used to do], and Jal-saab used to sing behind Krishnarao Pandit, so I had heard him. I had heard his concerts also. I organized his concerts, and I used to get lots of people for his concerts. So all the other guru bandhus used to say, Baalu Patwardhan for example, he said, *Ata Jal kade zaayla paije—thyachya kade khub bandishi aahet* [Now you go to Jal: he has many bandishes]. *Ani tya aapan shikhun ghetlya pahijet* [And these I have to take from him through learning them].

So I thought, let me now ask Jal-saab if he will teach me. He said, yes, he will teach. These two had a lot of bickerings about each other. Arolkar Bua hated him, and Jal-saab always said that he [Arolkar] learnt from Dr. Moghe and he doesn't acknowledge him as his guru, so that's very bad. It's a sin for a musician to do it. I used to hear it and keep quiet. I did that for nearly three to four years.

TN: Where did you go? You went to Andheri, to Jal-saab's house?

Figure 5.2. Jal Balaporia at his guru poornima celebration, 2011. Photo: Tejaswini Niranjana.

NB: I went to Andheri. He used to teach one bandish in one day. I used to go on Saturdays. He taught a bandish, and on the way back in the train I used to immediately make the notation so that I don't forget. I used to keep humming. Sit in the Andheri train, which leaves from Andheri, so there is nobody in the ladies' compartment, except some women who had finished their work and were going back; it was nice to meet them at that time. And I used to hum and I used to write down the notation, that was really wonderful. Like that I learnt fifty-six compositions from him.

TN: What kind of raags?

NB: The same raags, but different compositions which Arolkar Bua had not taught. I knew them. I had heard them from all these Gwalior people, but Bua never taught me. So I learned them from Jal-saab.

Neela related the acrimonious exchanges she had with both her teachers about acknowledging publicly who her guru was:

Jal-saab was angry with me: he said, you don't give my name as your guru. I said, but I do that. Then I had to show him the writing, the press clipping—*bagha mi ithe dilela aahe aapla naav* [Look, I have put your name here]. And then Arolkar Bua used to say, *Tu tyacha kade zaates?* [You go to him, do you?] I said, no, I don't go. Then he said, *Tyaani tyaacha nao guru mhanoon lihile aahe* [But his name has been written as your guru]. [I said,] *Mala mahit nahi kasa lihile te lihinya-varcha kaam aahe* [I don't know how it has been written. That is the business of whoever wrote it]. *Mi kahi jaat nahi* [I don't go to him]. [He said,] *Tyacha kade gelis tar khabardar* [I forbid you to go to him]. *Majhya kade mag paool takaycha nahi* [Then don't set foot in my house again]. *Yeoo nako* [Don't bother to come to me]. *Ti ghaan aahe Gwalior chi* [That is the filth of Gwalior]. [I said,] *Pan Bua tumhi asa kaa mhanta?* [But why do you say that?] *Changla gaatat te* [He sings well]. *Chaan watta* [I feel good]. *Tumhala kalat nah mhanoon tumhi asa mhantaat* [You won't understand, so you say this]. I realized that it's some conflict between the two which I'm sandwiched between, and I have to bear with it and keep quiet.

Even Neela's early sessions with Arolkar were fraught with the tensions she felt more intensely later on in their relationship. She spoke about how Arolkar taught her, how he first started her on Raag Yaman Kalyan—a *bada khyal* (a slow or vilambit composition that is more complex than the *chhota khyal*).

> He [first] taught me, *Avaguna na keejiye*, then I started counting the beats with my left hand, and I could manage that. Then he said, now you should learn *Bana re banaiyya*, so I learnt it—all these in Yaman Kalyan. Such a great bandish, and Arolkar taught it to me within the first month of learning from him. Then he taught me so many great bada khyals, and I was so happy and impressed by all that. And like a stupid fool, I used to say, oh this bada khyal is like that, and there are such differences, there is sa-re-sa-sa there and sa-re-sa-sa here, and then what allusions it makes. I used to make my analysis and give out my aesthetic understanding, and he didn't stop me. Then later on he said, "Because you understand music and the aesthetics of music, I was teaching you. But now we have to stop." After three-four years he stopped. That was the time he realized [that] this girl is picking up very fast. She is performing, she is singing, and if she learns everything she will go away. So then he slowed down the

Figure 5.3. Neela Bhagwat. Photo: Elton Pinto.

process, and so many things he didn't teach me at all. Because I was singing well!

Neela then relates an incident that still causes her much pain, in which Arolkar accused her of reducing him to an accompanist:

> And what he used to do, he used to play the tabla—*Ab toh badi ber, Saade naala ve* [compositions in Raag Bhimpalas], all these I performed in his presence, and he played tabla with me. Once he got very angry with me. I thought I was singing very well, and singing so much like him. I understood the way to go ahead in the khayal, and I paid so much attention to the bandish. He said, "Why are you singing so much? Do you think I'm a tabla player?" It was quite a jolt to me. I respected him so much. It didn't even occur to me that I was doing this. Then I realized that, oh, he gets hurt. Let him decide what he wants to do. Then I never asked for anything after that. Some rare

times, if I really felt like learning something, I said it to him. After two months he used to teach me that [raga or bandish].²

In spite of the interpersonal tensions that Neela remembers so clearly even twenty-five years after Arolkar's passing, she sees herself as a true inheritor of the Gwalior musical legacy and assiduously performs the acts of memorialization—commemorating Arolkar's death anniversary, publishing cassettes and CDs of his music, writing about his life and work—that are expected of a good disciple in musicophiliac Mumbai.

Taleem by Other Means

There exist a variety of learning situations in which musical training is imparted, but these are not strictly part of the actual taleem setting. These learning situations were not specially devised for nonhereditary musicians, but they developed in the musical milieu of metropolitan Mumbai and elsewhere in India.

Learning by Accompanying

Several of the musicians I spoke to emphasized the importance of learning the nuances of the gayaki through accompanying (giving *saath*) their guru in concert performances. There is also the phenomenon of what Jayavanth Rao calls "Faiyaz Khan disciples." Faiyaz Khan (1886–1950) had a busy performing schedule and did not give taleem like other ustads in his gharana.

> Many are the musicians who derived considerable benefit by associating themselves with Faiyaz Khan. Almost all the younger ustads and musicians of his family and several others used to provide him vocal assistance and thus acquired many aspects of his gayaki, both its mechanics and its aesthetics. Others merely listened to him long enough to absorb a part of his singing style. Some have even imbibed a bit of his style by just listening to his records and recordings over and over again. Those who have been impacted call themselves his disciples.³

Ramdas Bhatkal, the musicophiliac turned musician discussed in chapter 3, says he dreamed of becoming Faiyaz Khan.

Arvind Parikh about Vilayat Khan. "He allowed me to play with him, at the back, in concerts. I must have played at least twenty to twenty-five concerts sitting behind him. It's a great, very great taleem, because after five minutes or ten minutes, he'd say, 'You come along, play a little. You have not played at all, and your hands are steady.' So suddenly you start [providing saath], and that was a great taleem for me."[4]

Aneesh Pradhan. Pradhan spoke about providing tabla accompaniment to vocalists: "I think more of my information about that material came when I really went outside and sat in on taleems of other musicians. For instance, my guruji's daughter Tulika Ghosh, she used to learn from Khadim Husain Khan Saab of the Agra gharana, so I would accompany her in those taleem sessions at his home. So I got to hear a lot of that material. And similarly, while accompanying so many musicians across gharanas and across forms of music, you get to hear [a great deal]. Of course you have to be open and receptive; otherwise you can just be a timekeeper. So I decided to be open and absorb as much as possible."[5]

Learning by Listening: Shravan Shiksha

Learning how music works through the act of attentive listening is an important part of the taleem process. Musiophiliacs shared this in common with those who went on to become performers, even if the experiences below come from those who belong to that more restricted category. Listening happened in concerts, by going to the sangeet natak, through the radio, and through records; in the twenty-first century, it happens increasingly with the help of YouTube.

Gangubai Hangal. "On my way back from school, I used to listen to the gramophone records played in the *kiraane* [grocery] shop. I remember liking Zohrabai Agrewali in particular. I used to imitate the singers and sing their songs. Because of this, my mother realized that I liked Hindustani music and had an aptitude for it."[6]

"Shri Shripadrao Tamhankar, a harmonium player, was quite closely known to us. Apart from repairing harmoniums, he used to sell gramophone records in his shop. I used to listen to the gramophone records in his shop for hours together, forgetting everything else. I liked a particular song, 'Anban Jiya Mein Mila' [should be 'Lago' instead of 'Mila'] so much, and listened to it so many times, that I learnt it by heart."[7]

Sharad Sathe. "Ustad Faiyaz Khan was my inspiration. I must say he inspired me a lot. I used to listen to him, without knowing anything of music, but somehow.... This is records, in those days, gramophone records. Also,

Vadodara radio, every Thursday, they used to have his broadcast then. I hardly missed any broadcast."

Neela Bhagwat. "Radio, yes, radio also was another thing, and in fact in my childhood I was very sick, and lying down for four months. I had pleurisy. I was not to move, and I was bedridden. But I used to listen to radio and make notes on whatever I heard: *amkyani kasa gayla* [how someone sang], *hyachat bhav hota, hyachat taana hota* [there was *bhaav* here, there were taans here], all that, writing criticism—it began since that. I was in the eighth standard. That means, I must have been twelve years old."

Arvind Parikh. "I was about eight or ten years old. Ahmedabad being a textile center at that time—and we belonged to a business family—there was hardly any worthwhile music atmosphere there, environment there, or even good gurus there. So really speaking, my real guru was the radio. I used to listen to the radio, unbelievably, two to three hours a day. At that time, the radio used to publish what they called "Indian Listener," and I used to mark out all.... Curiously, I was attracted to instrumental music, rather than vocal music."

> TN: What year would this have been? When did you start listening to All India Radio?
>
> AP: This was in 1936. I was born in 1927, so at the age of ten years, twelve years—1936–38 up to almost 1943–44. I shifted to Bombay in 1943–44. But in that period I listened to a lot of radio, and my good teacher was really All India Radio. Originally, I started playing several instruments: I started with *dilruba*, then I started playing the flute, then the violin. I played mandolin, I played *jaltarang*, all kinds of instruments I tried to handle—and at the age of twelve, I think, I started sitar.

Amarendra Dhaneshwar. "I belong to a family where music was liked by everybody, and my parents—my father was not a musician—he was a government servant but he was a music lover. He grew up during times when the gramophone record had just started coming, so he used to always sing songs like, "*Tum bin meri kaun khabar le govardhan giridhari...*" or "*Radhe Krishnabol mukh se. Radhe Krishna bol na na na.*" That was Narayan Rao Vyas's. So I have grown up listening to his humming these songs, and these songs were sung by classical singers.

"In Bombay we had no radio set at home, but we used to go to Poona for holidays, and Poona electricity... I think that house got electricity in 1957... '56–'57. So Radio Ceylon every day. *Purane Filmon Ke Geet* they would switch on, and without fail I would listen to the K. L. Saigal song, and all those songs, I still know them by heart. Later on, natya sangeet [theater music] is a major influence for Maharashtrians because... I mean [it was an] introduction to classical music, so Natya Sangeet I was listening to.... There were singers like Sripadrao Nevdekar. He was a male actor who used to act opposite Bal Gandharva in male roles. He was my favorite singer. I had seen Bal Gandharva, but I had never seen him act. He had already retired by then.

"During the Emergency [1975–77], I was in jail for about fifteen months in Bombay jail—Arthur Road [He was a political prisoner]. We were provided with a radio set, because that was allowed. I used to listen to music over there, and there used to be National Programme and everything. I used to listen to it because that was a nice way of spending time apart from reading."[8]

Aneesh Pradhan. "When I was a kid, the radio was one major source of entertainment and engagement and so, it was always on—whether you had programs for workers or folk music programs or even Western classical music lunchtime concerts, so the radio was constantly on, and I grew up listening to diverse kinds of music."

Girish Sanzgiri. "Kirana gharana singer-vocalist Girish Sanzgiri had considerable exposure to records of good musicians. When Sanzgiri's guru Firoz Dastur happened to be free on a Sunday (when he had no travel, and no programs), he would call interested students home and play them gramophone records, of Abdul Karim Khan, Sawai Gandharva—all the Kirana singers, and also Amir Khan, and Balkrishnabuwa Kapileshwari."[9]

Neela Bhagwat. Bhagwat spoke about becoming acquainted with Hindustani music through the Marathi sangeet natak.

> NB: Plays like *Saubhadra* and *Samshay Kallol* and *Sharada*. We were living in [the suburb of] Thana at that time, and my father was treasurer in some school's committee which used to organize plays to raise funds. So [all of us in the family] got a chance to see the plays.
>
> TN: And which were these natak companies? Were they from Bombay? Were they from somewhere else?

NB: They were from Bombay itself. Lalitkaladarsha, and some other groups. I don't even remember their names. But *Saubhadra* was enacted, and Ram Marathe and Suresh Haldankar, they were acting and singing in those plays. And Prabhakar Karekar, who is now over sixty, he used to sing, very well at that time. He was a pupil of Suresh Haldankar, and what a fantastic voice he had at that age.

TN: So that was your first exposure to the theater?

NB: Yeah, yeah, and I used to dream of singing and . . . sometimes my parents would say *aaj natkala nahi jaycha udya tujhi pariksha aahe* [No theater today—tomorrow is your examination]. *Pan mazha abhyas zhaala, mee yete* [But I have finished my studies. I will come]. They would say, "Nothing doing. You have to sit at home."

TN: Did you learn those songs, from sangeet natak?

NB: I used to sing them. I used to perform them.

TN: Did your family have a gramophone player?

NB: No, but we had a tanpura, we had a harmonium, we had a tabla. My father used to sing, all my aunts used to sing. They used to sing in the music squads for the pre-Independence movement. They all used to sing in that. So we grew up hearing, "*Vijayi vishwa tiranga pyaara*" [Victory to the tricolor flag we love], something like that. And "*Yaare saare ithe gama hya jhendya khaali*" [Come all, under this flag]. And we made fun of those songs as children, because we tried to put it on the floor *Thoooraaa asa*. Funny! We used to say that. We were naughty kids, and we were making fun of those songs. But that was bringing us up.

Aneesh Pradhan. "When I was growing up as a musician, I made a conscious decision that in my free time I would go and listen to as many concerts as possible, and so if I was not performing I was listening and I was listening and I was listening; I would go to the NCPA [National Centre for Performing Arts, Mumbai] library to either listen to their archival stuff or I would listen to the LPs there. I became a member there, and I was also referring to their books. All these were conscious decisions, you know. It was not like one fine day I just decided, let's just go out there. And that's the way I tell my students also to engage themselves with music.

"I tell them to keep a notebook and make notes. What concert have you heard? What raag? What taal? I make a conscious effort of asking them because that's what my guru did with me too. So he would say, what concert did you go to? Then I would say so-and-so. Who was the artist? Okay, so-and-so. What time did it start? And who was there in the audience, and what did they perform? I had to be really observant, you know. So I think my students also try to do that, and some of them do take notes even when they go to the NCPA library."

Rutuja Lad. Lad and I shared this exchange on WhatsApp:

TN: Did you listen to music on TV, YouTube, or other media to get a sense of how others are singing?

RL: Yes, today there's a lot of influence of YouTube on my listening, while growing up it was relatively less. YouTube listening gives us a wider scope to be able to listen to a wide range of artists and different stylistic techniques.

TN: Thanks, that's good to know.

RL: [☺] [thumbs up emoji].

Cyber Teaching and Learning

In the early 2000s, voice-over internet protocols were being developed worldwide, and within a few years of the introduction of the Skype platform in 2003, Hindustani musicians were teaching online. The singers I spoke with did not teach anyone they had only met online but simply continued to teach their students who were no longer in geographical proximity, although they maintained occasional face-to-face contact too. As Amanda Weidman points out in the case of Carnatic or South Indian music, "practices of listening and performing, and ideas about listening and performing subjects, change in conjunction with technologies of sound reproduction."[10] While her comment in this instance is about recording for the radio and the gramophone, it could be equally applicable to internet platforms, where musical sound not only is reproduced within the virtual pedagogic setting but is also recorded by the student with all its jaggedness and cyber interruptions.

On Skype, the singular pedagogic moment and the singular space of face-to-face or sina-basina teaching multiply into three: the teacher's location, the student's, and the internet platform in which their voices and images come together. Weidman suggests that the use of radio lessons helped the classical music student to avoid the "socially complicated process" of finding someone to teach her, and "removed the student from the scene of teaching."[11] Internet lessons, on the other hand, are cast in a more conventional guru-shishya mode. The voice may simultaneously be disembodied through the technology as Weidman suggests, even as it is digitally re-embodied in the cyber images of teacher and student.[12] In an essay, "The Internet Guru," ethnomusicologist Jeff Roy speculates on how to embody musical knowledge "when the *body* is gone."[13] However, in my interviews with Hindustani musicians who cyber taught from their homes in India, there was never any sense of bodies being absent, since the virtual images produced by Skype and FaceTime are acknowledged as signifying those bodies, and the closeness to the screen of both teacher and student even produces a feeling of physical proximity that was not to be experienced in the offline pedagogic setting.

Lalith Rao, whom I interviewed on Skype about this topic, teaches online one student in Singapore, one in Dubai, and yet another in London, apart from her regular students in Bangalore. I asked her what the challenges are when she teaches online.

> LR: Of course internet problems are there, but the main problem I find is—but you can easily get over it—is the time lag. Otherwise I'm quite happy, because we never sing together. I teach and then they sing, or they sing and then I correct.
>
> TN: And do you play the electronic tabla and tanpura on both sides?
>
> LR: The student plays when she's singing, and I try to hear—I try to adjust mine when the samm is coming. Make it softer so I don't disturb her, but I know what she is singing.
>
> TN: So you have the electronic instruments switched on, on both sides.
>
> LR: But I keep it soft when she is singing so it doesn't disturb her, and when I sing she keeps it soft so it doesn't disturb me. But she gets an idea which beat we are on.
>
> TN: Do you also have face-to-face contact with these people?
>
> LR: Whenever they come to Bangalore, they come and learn from me.

TN: And that's important, you feel, right? To have both.

LR: Yes. That's important. Because then you know you work on whatever doubts they have, whatever they have missed out on. Their parents live in Bangalore, so there's no problem.

TN: Do they ever record anything and send it to you for your checking?

LR: No, they don't. But sometimes when I teach, they do record it. Even here [face-to-face] some of my students record [the session] when I teach. Though Khansaab would never have allowed it.

Another musician who has been teaching on Skype for some time is tabla player Aneesh Pradhan. As a musician who is also a highly qualified historian, Pradhan brings an unusual angle to thinking about pedagogy, since his own practice is strongly informed by his understanding of the strategies of hereditary musicians as they entered the spaces of musical modernity:

> How were practitioners—hereditary performers—looking at their own practice of teaching when they needed to teach a larger number of students than before? I think (learning about what they did) helped me renegotiate my own space [as a musician]. So, for instance, when I was teaching on Skype, it was very different to teaching in a live situation. First of all, there's at least a three-second delay, so we can't play together.

When Pradhan was learning from his guru Nikhil Ghosh, the sessions typically involved the student following the teacher, without much spoken communication. This changes in the internet lesson:

APN: So I had to really, you know, capture as much as possible in that moment, but we could play together. I could play along with him. In a Skype situation you can't do that. You have to wait for the person to finish and only then [can you play], so it changes the very sound of music that you are hearing. You are not hearing your teacher's instrument or medium along with yours.

TN: So a certain temporality comes into that sound.

APN: Yeah . . . yeah, so that is one aspect—the technology. The second thing is, supposing I have uploaded a file. Let's say it's a composition. Now I have to factor in what are the possible faults that he will meet with when playing that, okay, because he's not meeting me on an everyday basis. Maybe once a week or something we'll exchange notes, so I would articulate in an email each and every thing, and I made a conscious effort of doing that because I felt that, let me see, challenge myself and see how much I can articulate the faults that somebody may encounter, and even if you encounter the fault, how are you going to, you know, correct yourself? So we've exchanged many emails like this. Sometimes [the student] would say, "No, Aneeshji, I cannot understand this," or he would say, "Okay, I've got it."

After many decades of teaching students face-to-face, Neela Bhagwat began in 2013–14 to take on Skype students. However, these were all people who had learned from her for a while in Mumbai and then gone away to different countries, or—like me—traveled extensively for work. In 2014 she made a large content donation to the Wikisource platform, which now hosts all of the Gwalior gharana's traditional compositions, written in Devanagari and Roman script in Neela's handwriting, and with complete notation of each composition.[14]

After seeing the books on Wikisource, more people approached Neela for Skype lessons. Having direct access to the compositions and notation meant for the student that one of the important activities of the conventional music taleem session, where some teachers, including Neela, write out these things, can be bypassed, and the training intensifies in a different direction.

> TN: Now you teach so much on Skype and you have these different time zones [UK, US, Hong Kong] you work in—I want to know how it has changed your teaching. Or, when you teach on Skype, how is it different from teaching offline?
>
> NB: I don't think there is much change.
>
> TN: Really? But all the difficulties, the time lag, the internet connectivity problem . . .
>
> NB: That happens. But it's there for a minute, and then it gets back to normal. When you teach, you have to teach the taal structure, the melodic structure, the meaning of the poetry, the voice modulation, and all the other things about the raag also. And I also try to give a certain background of the bandish. All that I do whether we are in an actual class or a Skype class. It is the same.

TN: Any one difference that you see?

NB: The only difference is that on Skype when the taal [referring to the beat of the electronic tabla] is on, there is a time lag in the rhythm, and that makes it difficult. But if a student knows Tilwaada taal, for example, and I can explain the spacing of the bols [the actual words of the composition], the student can manage on her own. And she has the notation from my books. [Further progress] will depend on the student and her imagination.[15]

Neela's resolute refusal to acknowledge that Skype might transform her mode of taleem perhaps comes from decades of teaching in a style that she has taken a long time to perfect in all its nuances. Perhaps she also has a sense that some of her online students are extremely serious about becoming performers, so she would not want them to feel they are not getting the same kind of attention and instruction as the students who live in Mumbai. So she has to think of the intermittent breakdowns of the broadband connection as something to be tolerated and overcome, even if it means reconnecting multiple times in the course of one session, which routinely happened when she was teaching me on Skype. In offline teaching, Neela is often interrupted during taleem sessions by the cook, the cleaning woman, the doorbell, or the telephone. After each of these interruptions, which have a routinized quality to them, she reconnects effortlessly to the taleem, often in mid-composition. The Skype reconnections are perhaps for her not very different from those necessitated by the domestic chores. My plaintive cries punctuated our Skype sessions—"Are you there?" "Can you hear me now?" "Should I call back?" "I see only video—the audio's gone"—but the frustration seemed to be only on my side.

HOW DID THE relationship between teacher and disciple affect the nature and development of the taleem process in the twentieth century? What did musicians hold on to, and hold back, as the musicophiliac sought to learn from them? What might have been the economic and other compulsions for holding back?[16] After all, none of the performers with whom I spoke—from the oldest to the youngest—came from a hereditary musical background. How did the acts of giving and taking of musical knowledge play out in the formation of the musicophiliac subject? How did the social press in on the individuated transaction between teacher and student? What was the nature of the student's struggle as a modern subject to acquire a training that presented itself as something only available through a rigorous apprenticeship and forms of knowledge that did not seem amenable to modern pedagogic modes?

The community of practitioners to which the musicophiliac subject who was trying to become a musician sought entry continually invoked a world in which the number of ragas and the length of riyaaz kept diminishing. This idea of the shrinking of the musical repertoire surfaces repeatedly in the narratives of taleem in this chapter. While it is always invoked in an idiom of loss and lament, its ubiquity converts this affective reality into a signifier of the modern pedagogic process. It is almost as if the musicophiliac recognizes this as the only way by which she can render musical knowledge graspable and configure it as something within the reach of the nonhereditary musician. The music school and the sina-basina taleem rub up against each other in Mumbai, as they did elsewhere: the former paying its respects to the latter but creating pedagogic techniques not favored by it, and the latter holding the former in disdain even as notation, sometimes covert, became a feature of taleem and an aid to riyaaz, to one's practice.[17]

WHILE THE PROCESSES discussed in this chapter are not unique to Mumbai, the concentration of musicophiliac students in the city prompted the development of new pedagogic modes and made possible new kinds of relationships between guru and disciple. Here, the metropolitan unconscious brings together the histories of migrant musicians and newly urban musicophiliacs alike, and in the repeated telling of musical stories and anecdotes that form part of the taleem process, the present creates for itself a past that it reconfigures in the telling.

Appendix: Teacher-Student Lineage

I have listed the dates below to provide a glimpse of the long twentieth century, which goes back into the 1830s when Lalith Rao's teacher's teacher, Kallan Khan, was born, and stretches into 2016 when some of the conversations discussed in this chapter took place. An attempt has been made to list at least two generations of musicians related by lineage to those interviewed in my project, so as to lay out the web of connections that gains visibility in the music taught in Bombay in the twentieth century. The dates below are the year in which a musician started his or her apprenticeship.

1914	Khadim Husain Khan (1905–93) from Kallan Khan (1835–1925)
1922	Kesarbai Kerkar (1892–1977) from Alladiya Khan (1855–1946)
1930–31	Gangubai Hangal from Sawai Gandharva (1886–1952)
1939	Dhondutai Kulkarni (1927–2014) from Bhurji Khan Azizuddin Khan (1957–60 from Laxmibai Jadhav)
1944	Arvind Parikh (b. 1927) from Vilayat Khan (1927–2004)
1949	Lalith Rao (b. 1942) from Ramarao Naik (1909–1998)
1950	Babanrao Haldankar (b. 1927) from Mogubai Kurdikar (1904–2001)
1950	Sharad Sathe (b. 1932) from D. V. Paluskar (1921–55), then from B. R. Deodhar (1901–90) from 1956 to 1966, then Sharadchandra Arolkar (1912–94) from 1966 until 1994.
1959	Babanrao Haldankar from Khadim Husain Khan
1959	Nayan Ghosh (b. 1956) from Nikhil Ghosh (1919–95)
1962	Dhondutai Kulkarni from Kesarbai Kerkar
1969	Neela Bhagwat (b. 1942) from Sharadchandra Arolkar from 1969 to 1994, and from Jal Balaporia (1927–2013) from 1989 to 1992
1970	Lalith Rao from Khadim Husain Khan
1972	Aneesh Pradhan (b. 1966) from Nikhil Ghosh
1980	Ramdas Bhatkal (b. 1935) from S. C. R. Bhat (1918–2008)
2001	Rutuja Lad (b. 1992) from Dhondutai Kulkarni, from 2001 to 2014, and from Ashwini Bhide Deshpande (b. 1960) from 2015 onward

Jal Balaporia from Eknath Pandit and H. G. Moghe

Firoz Dastur (1919–2008) from Sawai Gandharva

Ashwini Bhide Deshpande from Manik Bhide (b. 1935), student of Mogubai Kurdikar

Afterword

In the Hindi film *Dastak,* or *The Knock* (written and directed by the noted novelist Rajinder Singh Bedi, and released in 1970), Salma and Hamid are a young, newly married Muslim couple, recent migrants to Mumbai of the 1960s. They are having a difficult time finding a place to stay in the big city. Hamid, played by Sanjeev Kumar, works as a clerk in the municipal corporation office while Salma, played by Rehana Sultana, keeps the house. Part of their difficulty in finding a dwelling has to do with their meager income combined with Hamid's insistence on their social standing as *shareef* or respectable people. They are tricked into renting a two-room apartment in an old building in a rundown neighborhood, and find out very soon that their place used to be occupied by a tawaif called Shamshad Bano. Salma stays at home while Hamid goes to work and soon becomes the object of the neighbors' prurient curiosity, with two young men trying to catch glimpses of her bathing and dressing, or apparently talking to a guest with whom she plays cards and drinks tea. Old customers of Shamshad Bano keep knocking on the door at odd hours of the night, and strains of thumri singing accompanied by dholak are heard close by.

Early in the narrative, on their first day in the new house, the couple hears clearly someone singing a thumri: "*Baiyyan na dharo o balamaa, na karo mose raar*" (Don't twist my arms, beloved, don't fight with me). After listening to this, sung in Mishr Khamaj in the traditional style of the genre, Salma says this thumri should be presented differently. She goes on to sing the entire composition in a modern mixed style that has come to be identified with Hindi film music's invocation of the classical.[1] When she finishes singing, Hamid tries to touch her feet reverentially. "What's this?" she asks, alarmed. "The *salaam* is not for you but for the music," says Hamid. "*Kuch der se mein jaanwar tha, tumne insaan bana diya*" (For some time I was an animal, but you've turned me into a human being). Touched, Salma says, "I will always sing for you."

When they go to Salma's hometown for a vacation, somewhere in northern India, we meet her old father in his decrepit but once-grand house.

He talks about the time that he was a well-known singer. "*Kabhi hamaare sangeet ki qadr hoti thi, badi badi majlison mein log bulaate thae—aur hum Tajdar Khan Ustad kahe jaathe thae*" (When our music was held in regard, people used to invite me to perform at major forums, and I used to be called Tajdar Khan Ustad), says the father. But now times have changed. "*Magar yeh tiya tabba sangeet shuru hua, hum Taja Miya hokar rahe*" (Now that this rubbishy music has taken over, I have become merely Taja Miyan).

Meanwhile, in Mumbai, Shamshad the tawaif pays the unsuspecting and bored Salma a visit, and invites her to visit her kotha, perhaps with the intention of getting the young woman to join the sisterhood. Salma is not sure what to make of two young girls she glimpses dancing suggestively; Shamshad closes the door on them, saying it's merely her daughters practicing. Shocked at seeing a sex worker and her customer, Salma runs back to her own house. Hamid is waiting, annoyed by her absence, and suspicious about where she has been. After a series of unpleasant incidents involving lustful neighbors, bad news from Salma's home, and Hamid's continually frustrated attempts to find another house, there is one more knock on the door at night. A well-dressed man eases himself into the house, asks for Shamshad, and is told by Hamid, who has just had another financial reversal, that she doesn't live there anymore. "I'm from Bhavnagar," he says, "*mujhe sirf gaana sunne ka shauk hain*" (I just like listening to music). Then we hear the sound of Salma's tanpura being strummed. The man from Bhavnagar slips into the next room and sits on a stool in front of Salma, who is seated on the floor, her head covered with the edge of her sari, her eyes averted. She begins singing a thumri: "*Hum hain mataa-e-koocha-o-baazaar ki tarah*" (I'm like a commodity for sale in the marketplace. Every look is that of a buyer). As she comes to the end of the song, the paan seller from their street, who earlier tried to court her and has now followed the music up the stairs, raises his arms in a gesture of appreciation, saying, "*Subhanallah*" (Praise be to God). Meanwhile, Hamid, who has picked up a knife, has been slowly moving toward Salma. Hearing the paan seller's appreciative exclamation, Salma throws the tanpura at him in rage, and it breaks. Seeing the knife in Hamid's hand, both the paan seller and the man from Bhavnagar rush out of the house in fright. The film ends with Salma indicating that she is pregnant, and Hamid declaring that they will not go anywhere, but live and die in this house.

In his book on the ideology of the Hindi cinema, M. Madhava Prasad reads *Dastak* as a story of the emergence of the bourgeois female subject in India, one who is a desiring subject but with her husband as the primary object of that desire. According to Prasad, the tawaif represents illegitimate sexuality, while Salma stands for the domesticated sexuality of the respectable middle class, with sexual desire contained within the marital framework. Reading this narrative through my formulations about the subject of musicophilia, I foreground the music sung by both tawaif and housewife, which appears to be the same music, albeit differently sung. It is the fact of Salma's singing that marks her out as sexually available for the gaze of the neighboring men, even with her outward trappings of respectability. The courtesan has been a central if shadowy presence in the story I tell about Hindustani music in Mumbai, whether it is in the discussion of the present-day mujra hall in chapter 1 or the exploration of the tawaif neighborhood in chapter 2, or the visit to the kothas in NB Compound and Foras Road by different people mad about music as described in chapter 3. We don't know if Salma has been trained by her musician father or whether she simply picked up music by listening to it as a young girl. If this were a realistic story rather than an allegorical melodrama, she could not—as a Muslim woman—have obtained taleem in her family, since that would have been reserved for sons, nephews, or younger brothers. For the film's narrative, the brief invocation of the old musician in the village and the fact that Salma is his daughter is enough to suggest that what she sings stands in for the repurposed classical.

Dastak, then, is in my eyes the story of Hindustani music's resituating, after the decline of princely patronage, in the bazaar of the city. But because it is a musician's daughter and not a son who brings the music to the city, the making-respectable of the music is represented through the conjugal fantasy of modern middle-class marriage in which the singer is supposed to sing only for her husband.[2]

The music schools that proliferated throughout Mumbai in the twentieth century and that continue to be popular today have allowed women from different classes to gain access to musical learning. The emergence of the schools, as I discussed in chapter 1, was fueled by the intense musicophilia that developed in Mumbai from the late nineteenth century onward. The location of the music shifted from the *diwaankhaana* of the kotha to the concert hall and the drawing room, where both singers and listeners include women as well as men. There has also been a transition from music as occupation to music as vocation, perhaps also a consequence of the widespread nature of musicophilia. We obtain glimpses of this transition in the discussion in chapter 3 of those musicophiliacs who have become amateur singers. The fact that many more middle-class women learn Hindustani music today than a hundred years ago could be seen as a mark of dissociation from the musical culture in which the tawaif played an important role. But, as I have argued in chapter 1 in relation to the content of musical presentations, the fact that these middle-class women learn thumri is part of their performance of modernity. Salma in *Dastak* can sing the same thumri as the tawaif and invoke the musicophiliac's passion, but she refrains from becoming sexually vulnerable by remaining within the domestic space. Also, her mode of presentation is distinguished from that of the tawaif, as evidenced by her insistence at the beginning of the film that the thumri heard from afar should be sung differently.[3]

Even when the signs of domesticity and middle-class respectability are firmly and recognizably in place, however, sedimented ideas about singing women lurk just below the surface. Some years ago in Mumbai, I was assisting a senior woman musician to carry her tanpura back home after a concert. We hailed a kaali-peeli taxi and bundled everything into it for the short ride to her flat. My male companion got out with her to help carry the instrument and her bags. While I waited in the taxi, since we were going elsewhere, the middle-aged driver turned to me and asked how old she was. I told him. "Ah, and she's still singing?" he said with a leer.

This book has explored the extraordinary phenomenon of musicophilia that swept through Mumbai in the long twentieth century, with its roots in the 1860s and reaching into the present. Complex intersections of migrant histories produced a metropolitan unconscious through which new social subjects were formed. These subjects engaged in what I have called the pradarshan (exhibition, display, performance) of modernity, a modernity uniquely marked by the musical repertoires and cultures of learning that were mobilized by Hindustani music.

An important task of the research was the assembling of the archive of materials through which my questions could be framed and my key concepts generated. I can only think of the word "rummaging" to describe the process of assembly: rummaging in people's memories, in the filing cabinets and cardboard boxes of personal archives, in bookstores to find dusty volumes that had long been out of print. Through the long conversations with musicophiliacs of different generations, I built a narrative of their engagement with Hindustani music and the many kinds of activities they undertook to show their love. The greatest challenge was not to reproduce the musicophiliac's often hagiographic account of musicians, whether the latter were encountered in the mehfil or in the taleem room. Instead, the critical task I assigned myself was to examine closely the pauses and hesitations in the story even as I tried to remain sympathetic to the force and feel of those utterances.

I was aided in my grasp of musicophilia's significance by a thorough exploration of Girgaum's spaces of music. I found references in somebody's memoirs to a particular building and went off to look for it. In an interview, a musicophiliac would talk about a concert hall in a tiny lane of the native town, and I would keep asking the shopkeepers in the neighborhood until I could locate it. To be standing inside Trinity Club with the huge black-and-white photographs of musicians looking down and gather in the music of over a century sent a strange shiver down the spine. Thus, understanding what musicophilia means requires that you be a musicophiliac yourself. Additionally, in this instance of Mumbai's musicophilia, there is also a love of music's spaces in the city that is intimately tied to the love of music itself. One sees this in most of the interviews I draw upon throughout the book.

My methodology was informed by a form of interdisciplinary collaboration that is not commonly found in standard critical practice. The initial collaboration was with the filmmaker Surabhi Sharma, with whom I had made *Jahaji Music: India in the Caribbean* between 2004 and 2007. Unlike that instance, where the film followed the book (although it ended up reorganizing it), in the case of the Mumbai research the film shooting was an integral part of the exploratory research and provided me with interviews as well as rich visual documentation of music spaces.[4] Even when the funding for the film was exhausted, I continued using the method in several other interviews, replacing the elaborate setup of the film crew with a hand- or tripod-held video camera.

As the film shooting and the research process fed off one another and continued side by side, our growing interest in built space made us seek the help of architect friends to better understand the physical places that music occupied. Brought on board in 2014, Kaiwan Mehta and Sonal Sundararajan, both of whom have taught at the Kamala Raheja Vidyanidhi School of Architecture in Mumbai besides being trained there, started joining us on walks through the native town of Girgaum, discussed as a musical precinct in chapters 2 and 3. The architects brought to the project a greater focus on the structuring of neighborhoods and the social-cultural moorings of how buildings were constructed, whether it was the chawl or the wadi or the concert hall. I learned from them how an architectural motif or ornament on a facade could be a reminder of where the homeowner had migrated from. This idea of a tangible past set afloat in the present gradually grew into my concept of the metropolitan unconscious, and became translated into how the subject of musicophilia gets formed.

The Exhibition: Making Music Making Space

In the early twenty-first century, the museum or even the art gallery has become a privileged space for public exposure that also positions filmmaking, architectural objects, or academic research in such a way as to draw the kind of attentive gaze normally reserved for the more conventional visual arts object. Inspired in part by international events such as the Documenta in Kassel, which has been bringing social science research into conversation with the visual arts, many practitioners across the world have been situating their work in the museum, the Biennale, or the gallery as an adjunct to other platforms they would normally use.

Adding a designer to our collaborative team, we began to wonder what the effort of working toward an exhibition would do to our different forms of practice. Unlike other exhibitions that showcased a selection of finished objects, for our exhibition, we decided to create new objects that would speak to our research concerns. The raw materials we collected for the exhibition also came from our diverse disciplines even as they fed into our collaborative sense-making of the project's larger arguments around music and sociality. The materials included live recordings of performances from the 1950s to the present in a variety of public and private venues; images of early twentieth-century postcards representing musicians and other performers; early twentieth-century photographs of Bombay city; early twentieth-century maps of Bombay; newspaper advertisements from 1860 to the present; photographs from musicians' personal albums; concert advertisements and reviews (archival); digitized images of writings about music, in different languages; and copies of nineteenth-century Gujarati and Urdu plays. Additionally, we had extensive film footage from Surabhi Sharma's work in progress, the drawings of native-town buildings prepared by the participants from a workshop for architecture students, and the research videos already put up under the project name Mumbai Music, available online at Pad.ma (https://pad.ma).

Each of us began working with the primary materials to conceptualize an exhibit that was also a research output. Studio X, our quasi-gallery space in an ancient South Mumbai building, had long and narrow windows looking out onto some of the spaces we had researched.[5] Capitol Cinema, about to be torn down, could be seen from the windows. So we picked

Figure 6.1. Inside-Outside. Photo: Tejaswini Niranjana.

out for this installation an announcement for Abdul Karim Khan's performance at the Gaiety Theatre—renamed Capitol Cinema in 1927. The screen-printed white chiffon curtain hangs between line drawings of the actual arch of the theater (figure 6.1).[6] Thus this one advertisement was showcased in such a way as to embody the connection between musicophilia and metropolitan built space that was central to the exhibition as a whole. We took a decision to keep the information outside the frame, so that the actual installation, gesturing toward the space occupied by musicophiliac audiences, could function as a trigger for personal memories and aesthetic responses that converged in the metropolitan unconscious. Apart from word of mouth, advertising was an important means by which musicophiliacs came to know about concerts they could attend. While the advertisements were carried not only in the English press but in Marathi-, Hindi-, and Gujarati-language papers also, my collection is primarily from the *Times of India*, established in 1838 and known as one of the oldest English-language newspapers in the country.

Another important preoccupation of the collaborators was the issue of layering, of image, text, and architectural motif. We worked with the layering of sound in two installations, *Soundspace* and *Of Silences in the Present*, seeing the act as performing a labor similar to the layering of texts in *Singing in Tongues*, described below, to show the auditory materiality of the space occupied by the social subject of musicophilia.

In figure 6.2, in the panel on the top left, Rutuja Lad is doing her riyaaz in front of her guru, Dhondutai Kulkarni; on the right, Nitin Shirodkar, Girgaum musicophiliac, is listening appreciatively to records of Kesarbai Kerkar that the singer had given to his mother; in the bottom panel on the left, Kalyani Puranik, whose father was Abdul Karim Khan's disciple, is teaching her students inside the Saraswati Sangeet Vidyalaya on Lamington Road; and on the right, Rutuja Lad is checking the quality of her recorded voice in Laxmi Baug auditorium.

In the black box shown in figure 6.3, the projection enveloped the spectators and drew them into the filmed spaces of buildings that have been central to the musical and social history of the city—Trinity Club, Laxmi Baug, Blavatsky Lodge, Congress House, Jinnah Hall, Brahman Sabha. Looped single shots created a soundscape where all you heard was ambient sound leaking in from the outside, because the interiors, as we filmed them in the present, have been long empty.[7] The silent interiors form an important part of the film, *Phir se Samm pe Aana* (Returning to the first beat), where long takes inside the Girgaum buildings are accompanied

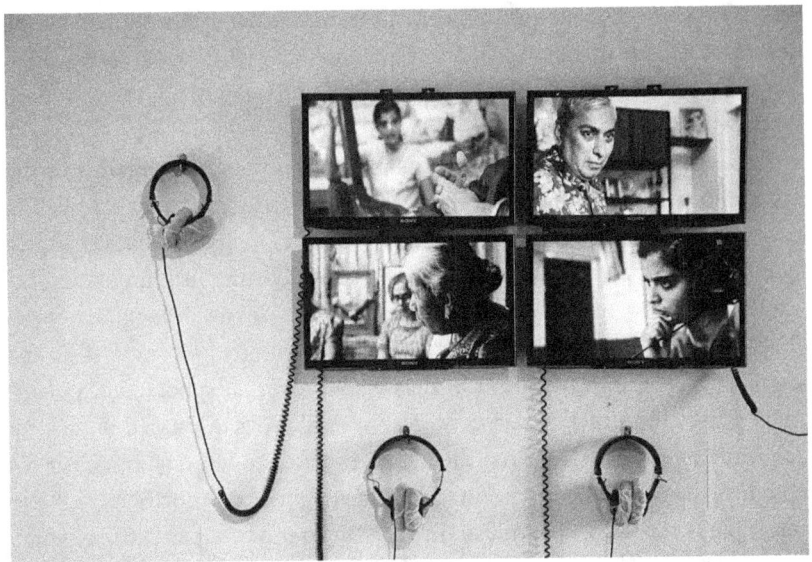

Figure 6.2. *Soundspace*. Photo: Tejaswini Niranjana.

Figure 6.3. *Of Silences in the Present*. Photo: Tejaswini Niranjana.

only by street noises: the sound of a car horn, the suburban train clacking across—in the frame but outside the building, the whine of an arc welder, the shout of a vegetable vendor, pigeons cooing. The music draws attention by its very absence from this installation.

Called *Singing in Tongues*, this installation in figure 6.4 references the fact that those who practiced Hindustani sangeet in its classical as well as lighter genres in Mumbai came from a variety of linguistic backgrounds. But although the classical genres were primarily sung in Hindustani, including its different dialects, the light genres were in other languages too.[8] From the time of the earliest proscenium plays in the 1860s, both the Parsi Gujarati theater and the Marathi theater put together spectacular performances in which music played a central role. But, as discussed in chapter 1, within a few years the Parsi theater had shifted to Hindustani/Urdu for reasons of wider appeal, and invited playwrights from northern India to write plays for them. The music in Parsi theater as well as sangeet natak drew on the melodic structures of Hindustani ragas. Again, as elaborated in chapter 1, the widespread attraction of Hindustani music in Maharashtra and the formation of a listening public that was musically literate can be traced back to the use of raga music in theatrical compositions. And in the early twentieth century, when a new generation of classical musicians emerged, it included a number of performers whose mother tongues were Marathi, Kannada, Konkani, or Gujarati, although they sang in Hindustani, the lingua musica I talk about in chapter 1.

The large translucent sheets that formed this display, hanging curtain-like in the main hall of the gallery, showed extracts from Parsi theater in Gujarati and Urdu: a Marathi-language excerpt from the memoirs of Govindrao Tembe, actor and composer for the sangeet natak and subsequently the cinema, and another from the Kannada autobiography of Gangubai Hangal, where she speaks about her involvement with the musical scene in Mumbai.[9] The visual motif of a hanging screen covered with text is echoed toward the back of the hall, where the advertisement for Abdul Karim Khan's performance hangs in front of the glass window through which the actual concert hall can be seen. These screens function not to obstruct the musicophiliac's vision but instead to add another layer of collective memory that becomes the doorway to engagement with music and space in the present.

An integral part of musicophiliac culture was the obsessive recording of one's favorite musicians using the technology of the day. Music lovers went from concert to concert documenting on a range of equipment the voices of their favorite musicians.[10] What they recorded decades ago is now part

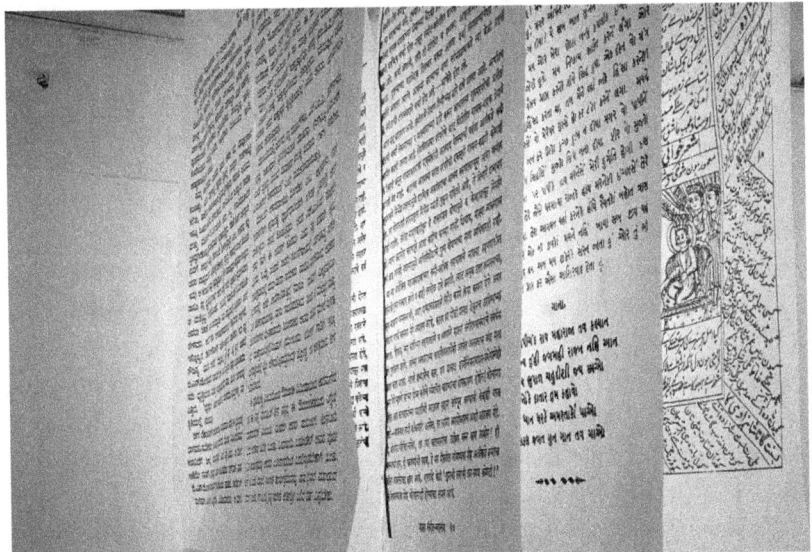

Figure 6.4 *Singing in Tongues*. Photo: Tejaswini Niranjana.

Figure 6.5. Listening to live recordings. Photo: Tejaswini Niranjana.

of the anonymous gift economy, the sharing made easier today by digitization and portable hard discs or flash drives.

Live recordings from the 1950s to the 1970s played on three suspended speakers: recordings of concerts from Girgaum, Santa Cruz, and Dadar-Matunga, the hubs of Hindustani music in the twentieth century; of guru poornima (tribute to the teacher) and barsi (death anniversary) sessions, often performed in more intimate spaces than the public concert; and of private baithaks in the homes of patrons and fellow musicians. This audio installation sought to draw attention to the fact that private recordings are a significant part of musicophiliac culture, often ranging far beyond the official commercial recordings even though they circulate only in informal networks. Like the young man in figure 6.5, many exhibition visitors stood listening until the entire loop in each speaker ran its course, absorbed in receiving the gift.

Through projection mapping, the musical walk through the native town linked past and present, viewer and performer, the history of metropolitan space and the history of music. These were the spaces where musicians lived, practiced, taught, and performed. Edited video footage of these spaces was projected onto the white-painted surface, a laser-cut plywood map shaped according to the contours of the native town (figure 6.6). As blue markers began to light up each space on the map, the moving images connected to that space began to draw in the viewer.[11] The aim was to connect the visualization of spaces with the particular geography of Girgaum, represented here by the bumps on the plywood sheet. Around the projection map we had suspended speakers, each playing a sound story, narratives in different voices culled from our research interviews, each referencing music spaces in the native town, each recollecting intense moments of musicophilia. The idea was to transform the present-day experience of music through this immersion in sonic and visual materiality, even as the visitor's understanding of the past was altered.

On this map (shown in figure 6.7), executed by Sonal Sundararajan, we presented Greater Girgaum, our name for an area overlapping partly with the old native town and broadly defined to include Kalbadevi, Thakurdwar, Prarthana Samaj, Jagannath Shankarseth Road, Lamington Road, Grant Road, Foras Road, Kennedy Bridge, Phanaswadi, Bhangwadi, and French Bridge, and stretching up to Forjett Street and Nana Chowk. Girgaum, as I discuss in chapter 1, was the earliest location in Mumbai to have music schools, music clubs, concert halls, and wadis where musicians were invited to perform. This is also where the first communities of music lovers began

Figure 6.6. Projection map of Girgaum, the "native town." Photo: Tejaswini Niranjana.

Figure 6.7. Map of Girgaum overlaid with exhibition visitors' comments. Photo: Tejaswini Niranjana.

Figure 6.8. Dancing girl postcard, from a private collection, London.

Figure 6.9. Birds over Girgaum. Photo: Anuj Rao.

to form, an important example being Trinity Club, established in the early twentieth century off Mughbat Galli, and featuring in chapters 2 and 3. From the mid-nineteenth century, theaters opened in Girgaum, the earliest being Grant Road Theatre in 1846. A host of music schools—the Gayan Uttejak Mandali, Balkrishnabuwa Ichalkaranjikar's classes, Vishnu Digambar Paluskar's Gandharva Mahavidyalay, Abdul Karim Khan's Saraswati Sangeet Vidyalay, B. R. Deodhar's School of Indian Music, and many others—were established between 1870 and the 1920s. The lanes and alleyways of the map were lined with picture cards with a few lines about the key institutions.

AFTERWORD · 195

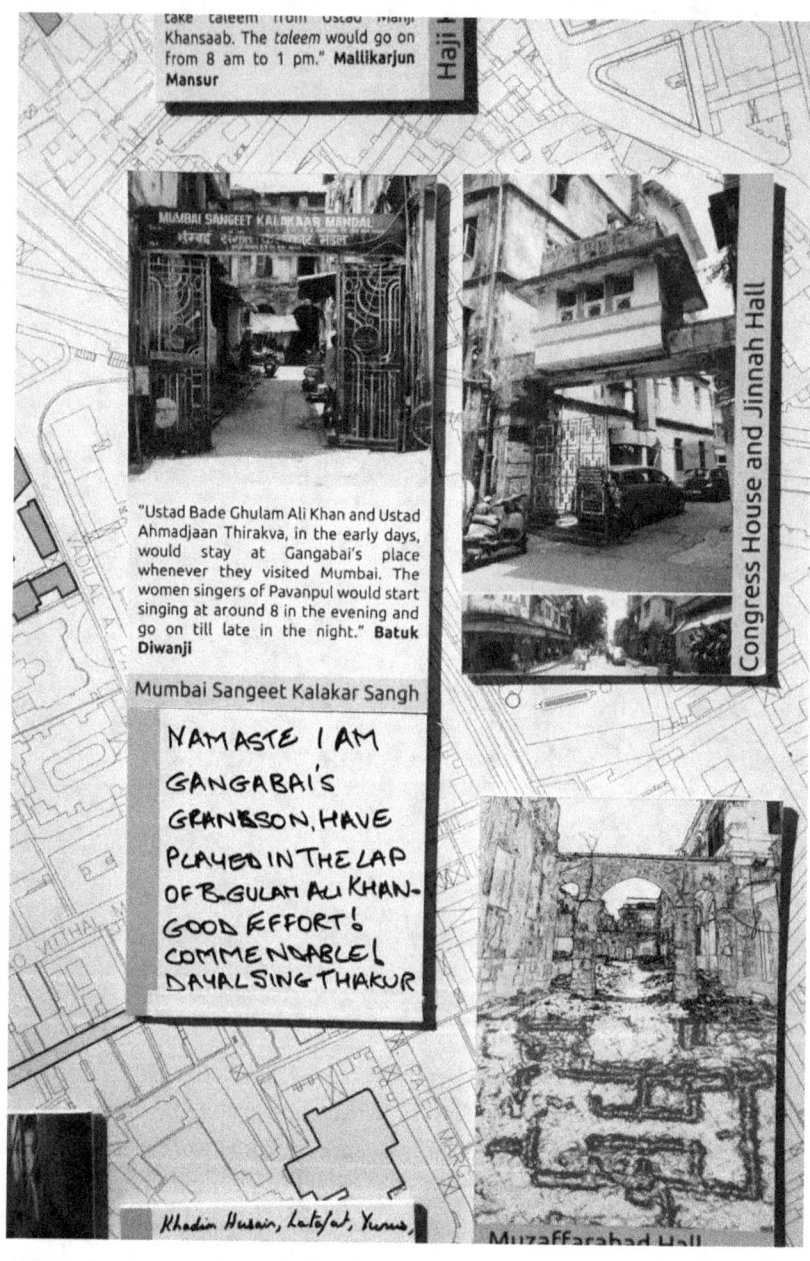

Figure 6.10. Picture of NB Compound from the Girgaum map, with a comment from the courtesan's grandson. Photo: Tejaswini Niranjana.

On the suspended speakers you could hear extracts from the project's research interviews, with references to places where music was performed and taught. On a side table we had placed blank cards and marker pens for visitors to add their own comments or memories to the wall map. By the third week of the exhibition, the map had become thickly populated with the contributions of members of the public. By placing the map at the beginning of the exhibition, we ensured that a visitor would see it again on the way out, in a sense revisiting all the spaces of music seen in the other parts of the exhibit. What then happened as a result of the map's positioning was a reinforcement of the idea of the social subject of musicophilia, who navigates the spaces of the native town where listeners gather.

The photographs that ran in a loop on the LED screens in the foyer or were blown up on the pulled-out panel are drawn from early twentieth-century postcards, research walks, and personal archives. The postcard images gave a sense of city space in the late nineteenth and early twentieth centuries, against which backdrop some of the performers who migrated into Bombay were also represented. The dancing girl in figure 6.8 was one such performer, as were her accompanists, who are shown here with sarangi and drums. Girgaum from the late nineteenth century on became home to many kinds of performers.

Although by the time the exhibition was mounted, most of the research for the book was complete, creating these installations in the gallery space opened up the work to new interlocutors, who were then brought into the research. The most exciting interlocutor of this kind was Dayalsingh Thakur, grandson of Gangabai, the courtesan of NB Compound who has appeared in several of my chapters. Thakur left a message and his mobile number on the wall map (figure 6.10).

Listening to Surabhi Sharma's interview with Dayalsingh Thakur, I was determined to find a way into the NB Compound and visit the mujra halls, which I eventually did in 2017. It was one of the very first places I had been intrigued by in Girgaum while location hunting for the film, the most difficult to research because of its seclusion from public space in Mumbai, and thus the last space of music I entered. Stray references in interviews were all that could be found for what was obviously a central location in the topography of the musicophiliac.[12] The figure of the tawaif with which chapter 1 opened returns here in this afterword in the discussion of *Dastak* and in the message of the tawaif's grandson. Appropriately enough for a book on the passion for Hindustani music, I return to the samm or the first beat of the rhythmic cycle.

AFTERWORD · 197

Glossary

The terms glossed here come from many different languages: Persian, Arabic, Urdu, Sanskrit, Hindi, and so on. No attempt has been made to specify the etymology, since this is well covered in the encyclopedic writing on Hindustani music. The main purpose of this glossary is to provide a ready reference to the reader of this book.

aakaar—Singing on the vowel "aa."
aaroh *and* avaroh—The ascending and descending scales that define the nature of a raga.
abhang—Devotional song in praise of the god Vitthala.
ada *or* adaakaari—Facial expressions and hand gestures used especially in courtesans' performance, conveying coquetry.
alaap/i—Vocalizing notes through the open vowel "a."
alankar—Pattern of notes used as ornamentation, and sometimes in learning exercises.
Anarkali kurta—Long frock-like dress with tight leggings. Takes its name from the fictional courtesan Anarkali from the eponymous 1953 Hindi film.
arre *or* arrey—Hindi interjection used as filler word, sometimes to express surprise.
asthan gayak—Court singer.
auliya—Saint, mystic.

bada khyal—A slow or vilambit composition that is more complex than the chhota khyal.
badath—Elaboration.
baithak—Performance while sitting down; earlier used for the performance of someone who sang rather than dancing while singing, but now customarily used for a concert with a small audience, often at a private home.
bandish—Composition.
bapu—Father.
barsi—Death anniversary.
been—A wind musical instrument, also known as pungi.
bhaav *or* bhava—Emotion or mood.
bhajan—A genre of devotional singing.
bhang—A drug prepared from the leaves and flowers of cannabis.
bhavai—Folk theater form of western India, specifically Gujarat.
bol—Mnemonic syllable (Wiki). Words of a composition.

bol taan—Melodic elaboration through the words of a composition.
brun-maska—Hard-crusted bread with fresh butter.

chajjiyas—Projecting eaves, often supported on brackets.
chalan—Movement of notes.
chaithi—Semi-classical songs sung in the season of Chait (March–April).
chaudhury—Chief; a female chief would be *chaudharayin*.
cheez *or* cheeza—Used to refer to a composition.
chhota khayal—A small khayal.
chowki—Station.
churidar—Tight leggings worn with a long kurta or top.

daad—Expression of appreciation or praise.
dabba—Box or tin.
dadra—A semiclassical form.
damsaas—Breath control.
dangal—Wrestling arena.
darbar—Court.
dargah—Shrine or tomb of a Sufi saint, visited by people of all religious backgrounds.
dayan tabla—The right-side tabla, smaller of the tabla pair.
deed taas—One and a half hours.
deewaanapan—Madness, insanity, state of being madly in love.
deewaana/dewaane—Crazy person/people.
deredar—Owner of the tent; chief performer.
devadasi—A woman dedicated to the gods, a practice from southern India. Not officially in use today.
devi—Goddess.
dhaivat—Sixth note.
dholak—A drum often used in folk music.
dhrupad—A musical form.
diwaankhaana—Drawing room.
doha—A verse form.
drut—Fast-paced composition.
dumsaas—Breath control.
dupatta—Long scarf draped over the shoulders.

farmaish—Request.

ga—Third note of the octave.
gaddi—Cushion.
gajra—String of jasmine flowers.
gala taapaila—To warm up the throat.
galli—Alley or narrow lane.
gamak—An ornamented or embellished note.

gamak taan—Where a certain force and repetition is added to notes.
gandabandh—Initiation ceremony.
Ganesh Utsav—Festival for the god Ganesh.
gayaki—Musical style; a style of singing usually associated with a gharana.
ghar—Home.
gharana—Like a school, with connotations of kinship.
gharanedaar—Belonging to a gharana; carrying features associated with this form of training.
ghazal—A semi-classical musical form.
ghungroo—String of bells forming an anklet; used in many south Asian dance forms.
grihast—Householder.
guru bandhu—Male fellow student of the same teacher; a female fellow student would be a *guru behen*.
gurukul—Home or family of the teacher.
guru poornima—Annual get-together of a musician's students to pay their respects through performing.
guru-shishya—Roughly, teacher-student.

hom—Ritual offerings placed in a sacred fire.
hori—Popular music genre sung during the Holi festival.

jalsa—A gathering.
jamaat—A gathering.
jugalbandi—Duet singing.
jumma—Friday; the sixth day in the Islamic week, a day on which Muslims pray together.
jumme ki baithak—Friday afternoon postprayer performance sessions.

kaali-peeli—Black-and-yellow taxi.
kalavant—Performer.
kamsura—Singing below the actual note or sur.
kaan-sen—Expert listener; pun on "tan-sen" (expert musician).
kajri—Semi-classical seasonal song associated with the rains.
khandani—a hereditary musician, one born into a khandaan, or someone who comes from a musical family that traditionally passed on the knowledge only to family members.
kharaj mehnat—Exercising the voice in the lowest octave.
khayal—Genre of what is considered to be classical Hindustani music.
kholi—Room.
kiraane—Grocery store.
kirtan—Devotional music genre.
kirtankar—Performer of devotional songs.
komal dhaivat—The flat version of the sixth note.
komal sur ka raag—A raga with flat notes.

komal swars *or* swaras—Soft or flat notes; both spellings acceptable.
kotha—Tawaif's establishment.
kuch thanda—Something cold, as in a cold soft drink.

lakh darwaza—A hundred thousand doors.
Lamington cha raja—King of Lamington Road.
latkaan—Metal globes.

ma—Fourth note of the octave.
maand—A style of folk singing, originating in Rajasthan in western India.
madhyam—Fourth note of the octave, same as "ma."
mahaul—Atmosphere or ambience.
mama—Maternal uncle.
mandra saptak pa—Fifth note in the lowest octave.
mangalsutra—A necklace (often made from gold and black beads) signifying that the wearer is a married woman.
matlab—Meaning.
meend—Musical glide from one note to another that is further away in the octave; the intervening notes are not separately articulated, but glided over.
mehfil—Concert.
mehfil maarna—To capture your audience.
mehnat—Effort or labor.
Mirasi—Traditional singing and dancing community, often Muslim by religion.
mujra—Song-and-dance performance by women from hereditary performing backgrounds.
munim—Clerk.
Musulman—Muslim.

naikin—A woman from a Goan family of performers.
natya sangeet—Music from a play; theater music.
nazakat—Conventions of hand movement that conveyed erotic longing.
nishad—Seventh or final note.
nom tom—Developing a raga through alaap using syllables of no specific meaning; common in the dhrupad genre of Hindustani music, but also used by some khayal singers.

paan—Betelnut, lime, and spices wrapped in betel leaf.
paanwaala—Paan seller.
padam—A form of musical composition in the Carnatic style, with the lyrics usually drawing on the Bhakti tradition.
pakad—Key phrases in Marwa.
palta—A string of note permutations for a particular raga; used in riyaaz.
phatka—A poetic form.

pradarshan—Exhibition, display, performance.
prahar—Unit of time, usually three hours.
punyatithi—Death anniversary.

qawwali—Genre of Sufi devotional music.

raag *or* raga—Melodic structure based on specific note patterns in a specified order.
rasa—What the musician intends to evoke or achieve as well as what the audience experiences while listening; juice, sap, essence.
rasika—One who appreciates.
riyaaz—Traditions of practice; individual practice.

saath—Accompaniment.
sabhas—Gathering.
samm—First beat of a rhythmic cycle.
sammelan—Gathering.
sampoorn swar ragas—Ragas with all the notes of the octave.
sangeet natak—Musical theater.
sanskaara—Cultivation
sapaat taan—Taan where the notes are placed in the order in which they appear in the octave.
saptak—Octave.
sarangi—Stringed instrument, used for accompanying vocal music.
sarega-regama—Basic notes.
sargam—A singing exercise with a string of notes specific to a particular raga.
sarvajanik—Public.
seva—Service.
shadja—First note of the octave.
shagird—Disciple.
shareef—Respectable people.
sheesham—Rosewood.
shishya—Disciple.
shravan shiksha—Training through listening.
shruti—Lyrics.
shuddha swaras—Pure notes.
sina-basina—Heart-to-heart or one-on-one form of training.
soota-bootaache gavai—The suit-boot singer. Referring to someone dressed in Western style, wearing a suit and shoes.
sthayi bhava—Stable emotion or mood.
sur—Note.
surbahar—Plucked string instrument used in Hindustani music.
surel-pan—Elegance of notes.
swararekha—Line of sound, of a note.
swar gyan—Knowledge of the notes.

taal *or* taala—Rhythmic unit.
taan—Sound pattern specific to a raga.
taar sa—Highest note in the upper octave.
Tabalji—Tabla player.
taleem—Training; the pedagogic process which has to be strengthened through sustained individual practice or riyaaz.
tanpura—Drone; a long-necked plucked stringed instrument.
tan-sen—Expert musician. Pun on "Tansen," the legendary Hindustani singer.
tapasya—Meditation, spiritual discipline.
tappa—North Indian folk song, incorporated into Hindustani music performance by some gharanas like Gwalior.
taraana *or* tarana—Medium- or fast-paced composition rendered through phonemes of Persian and Arabic origin.
tarika—Techniques.
tar saptak—Higher octave.
tawaif—Courtesan; a performer in the courtly tradition, from North India.
tayyar—Ready.
teentaal—Rhythmic structure with sixteen beats divided into four units of four beats each.
teevra dhaivat—The sixth note in the octave.
theka—Basic rhythmic phrase of a specific taal or taala.
thoda—Somewhat, a little.
thumri—Romantic and/or devotional song.

ustad—Teacher, guru.
utsaahi—Enthusiast.

vada—Large private home.
vidya—Learning, knowledge.
vilambit—Slow tempo; the performer begins exploring a raga by first singing it in this tempo.

wadi—A cluster of homes with a central courtyard.
wah-wah mandali—Idiomatic expression referring to the group of people who sit right in front at a concert and express their appreciation by saying "wah-wah."

Notes

Introduction

1. The rendering respectable of music and dance in southern India has been discussed extensively in Matthew Harp Allen and T. Viswanathan, *Music in South India: The Karnatak Concert Tradition and Beyond* (New York: Oxford University Press, 2004); Davesh Soneji, *Unfinished Gestures: Devadāsīs, Memory, and Modernity in South India* (Chicago: University of Chicago Press, 2012); and Srividya Natarajan, "Another Stage in the Life of the Nation: Sadir, Bharatanatyam, Feminist Theory" (PhD diss., University of Hyderabad, 1997). Similar processes around Carnatic music in particular are described by Lakshmi Subramanian, *From the Tanjore Court to the Madras Music Academy: A Social History of Music in South India* (New Delhi: Oxford University Press, 2011); and Lakshmi Subramanian, *New Mansions for Music: Performance, Pedagogy, and Criticism* (Abingdon: Routledge and Social Science Press, 2018).
2. Daniel Neuman wrote in 1980 about how women were the majority among music students in both North and South India, something that is still a social fact nearly forty years later. Middle-class nationalists, Neuman says, who shared with their colonial mentors an antipathy toward the performing arts and their practitioners, began to take an interest in learning music by the 1920s. He rightly suggests that this development is linked to the "public celebration of Indian civilization" inspired by nationalism. For more details, see Daniel Neuman, *The Life of Music in North India: The Organization of an Artistic Tradition* (Detroit: Wayne State University Press, 1980).
3. Tejaswini Niranjana, *Mobilizing India: Women, Music and Migration between India and Trinidad* (Durham, NC: Duke University Press, 2006).
4. Before 1947, we see more commonly the term "Indian music" counterposed to "Western music." This usage is to be found, for example, in English-language advertisements for concerts in Mumbai in the first half of the twentieth century.
5. Ernest Clements, *Introduction to the Study of Indian Music* (London: Longmans, Green, 1913); Ernest Clements, *A Note on the Use of European Musical Instruments in India* (Pune: 1916); Ernest Clements, *The Ragas of Hindustan*, 2 vols. (Sangli: 1918, 1919).
6. I borrow the term "musicophilia" from Oliver Sacks's eponymous work, *Musicophilia: Tales of Music and the Brain* (New York: Knopf, 2007), although his focus on human neural systems is not one that you will find in my book.

7   Lawrence Grossberg, *Cultural Studies in the Future Tense* (Durham, NC: Duke University Press, 2010).
8   Grossberg, *Cultural Studies in the Future Tense*, 264.
9   M. Madhava Prasad, "Public Modernity: Some Issues," review of *Consuming Modernity: Public Culture in a South Asian World*, edited by Carol Breckenridge, *Economic and Political Weekly* 33, no. 18 (May 2, 1998): 1020–23.
10 Partha Chatterjee, "Our Modernity" (Rotterdam/Dakar: SEPHIS CODESRIA, 1997), 20.
11 Kwame Anthony Appiah, *In My Father's House: Africa in the Philosophy of Culture* (Oxford: Oxford University Press, 1992), 157.
12 M. Madhava Prasad, email message to author, August 29, 2017.
13 From his 1980s work in *Subaltern Studies* to his more recent writings, Partha Chatterjee has explored what he has called a split in the domain of politics that creates different spheres of engagement for elite and subaltern groups. "Our Modernity" may well be an argument about elite Indians, and therefore seems to go against the spirit of Chatterjee's later concern with the politics of subaltern social groups, as in his *The Politics of the Governed: Reflections on Popular Politics in Most of the World* (New York: Columbia University Press, 2004). I suggest that when we foreground cultural practices like music, it becomes analytically difficult, if not impossible, to separate questions of affect for different groups that occupy the same metropolitan space. This is especially true of Hindustani music's melodies, which have appeared before the aural public in Bombay across different genres, from theater music to concert performances to film music.
14 "Mumbai" and "Bombay" are often used interchangeably in the book, since my references use both, and since it also reflects current usage.
15 I have benefited from reading, among others, the short fiction of the Gujarati writer Saroj Pathak, the novels of the Marathi writer Shanta Gokhale, the English novels of Kiran Nagarkar, and the short stories of the Kannada writer Jayant Kaikini.
16 According to music and theater historian Urmila Bhirdikar, "Classical music criticism appears more regularly in magazines from [the] 1920s. Magazines like *Sahyadri, Pratibha, Manohar, Vasundhara* and especially *Ratnakar* and later *Mauj* encouraged new avenues for music criticism, ranging from appreciative criticism to formalist analysis . . . several newspapers and periodicals carried news-reports and sporadic debates." Email message to author, March 30, 2018.
17 I borrow this notion of the "social subject" from Molly Anne Rothenberg's theorizing of the "excessive subject." See in particular Molly Anne Rothenberg, "Extimate Causality and the Social Subject of Excess," in *The Excessive Subject: A New Theory of Social Change* (Cambridge: Polity, 2010), 30–56.
18 Anjali Arondekar, "Subject to Sex: A Small History of the Gomantak Maratha Samaj," in *South Asian Feminisms*, ed. Ania Loomba and Ritty A. Lukose (Durham, NC: Duke University Press, 2012), 244–63.

19 Pierre Bourdieu, *The Logic of Practice*, trans. Richard Nice (Stanford, CA: Stanford University Press, 1990), 53.
20 Bourdieu, *The Logic of Practice*, 55.
21 Bourdieu, *The Logic of Practice*, 56.
22 Bourdieu, *The Logic of Practice*, 57.
23 Bourdieu, *The Logic of Practice*, 56.
24 Rothenberg, *The Excessive Subject*, 84.
25 Rothenberg, *The Excessive Subject*, 83.
26 Rothenberg, *The Excessive Subject*, 84.
27 See Nazir Ali Jairazbhoy, "What Happened to Indian Music Theory? Indo-Occidentalism?," *Ethnomusicology* 52, no. 3 (fall 2008): 349–77; also see his important early work, *The Rags of North Indian Music: Their Structure and Evolution* (Bombay: Popular Prakashan, 1971). Two other significant contributions to this field are Bonnie C. Wade, *Khyal: Creativity within North India's Classical Music Tradition* (Cambridge: Cambridge University Press, 1984); and Peter Manuel, *Thumri in Historical and Stylistic Perspectives* (New Delhi: Motilal Banarssidas, 1989).
28 I am indebted to Ashok Ranade's wide-ranging musicological writings and his conversations with me, which were always inspiring. Another important grammarian of Hindustani music is Deepak Raja, referred to in chapter 3.
29 See Aneesh Pradhan, *Hindustani Music in Colonial Bombay* (Gurgaon: Three Essays Collective, 2014). Subramanian's remarkable book *From the Tanjore Court to the Madras Music Academy*, cited in note 1, tracks the transformation of the Carnatic music canon as it moves from the court to the modern colonial city, arguing that the shifts in patronage and the ambitions of the new middle-class patrons helped performative arts become central to the cultural project of nation building. The author claims that her historical scholarship is different from that of earlier writers on music or performance in that it does not provide a historical account of Carnatic music's development, but instead is strongly informed by discussions on the social organization of music and its reception.
30 Amanda Weidman, *Singing the Classical, Voicing the Modern: The Postcolonial Politics of Music in South India* (Durham, NC: Duke University Press, 2006); Janaki Bakhle, *Two Men and Music: Nationalism in the Making of an Indian Classical Tradition* (New York: Oxford University Press, 2005).
31 Not to put too fine a point on disciplinary orientations, but to me what distinguishes Weidman's and Bakhle's works from several other ethnographic and historical writings is their demonstrated ability to critically engage with their disciplines or to ask questions in an antidisciplinary way when necessary. I see my own writing as inspired by such efforts.
32 Our film, *Phir se Samm pe Aana* (Returning to the first beat) premiered at the Mumbai International Film Festival (MAMI) in October 2017.

Chapter I

1. A comprehensive account is to be found in Madhu Trivedi, *The Emergence of the Hindustani Tradition: Music, Dance, and Drama in North India, 13th to 19th Centuries* (Gurgaon: Three Essays Collective, 2012). Even into the twentieth century, the music was simply referred to in English as "Indian music," the usage "Hindustani music" being more recent. Although today it is commonly referred to as North Indian classical music, I hesitate to use the term "classical" because in India it cannot be easily counterposed with something called popular, there being a spectrum of raga-based music ranging from what scholars have termed "art music" to that which is seen as "light music." For convenience, in this essay I use "Hindustani music" or "Hindustani art music" to refer to the music that first gripped Bombay's inhabitants in around the 1860s.
2. Aneesh Pradhan, *Hindustani Music in Colonial Bombay* (Gurgaon: Three Essays Collective, 2014); Jayavanth Rao, *Sajan Piya: A Biography of Ustad Khadim Husain Khan* (Mumbai: Sajan Milap, 1981).
3. Raymond Williams, *The Long Revolution* (London: Chatto and Windus, 1961).
4. For pioneering scholarship on the formation of an organization that tried to bring together descendants of kalavant families, see Anjali Arondekar, "Subject to Sex: A Small History of the Gomantak Maratha Samaj," in *South Asian Feminisms*, ed. Ania Loomba and Ritty A. Lukose (Durham, NC: Duke University Press, 2012), 244–63.
5. *Making Music Making Space*, which I curated, showcased video and audio installations and cartographic representations of Mumbai. It was held from June 15 to July 7, 2015, at Studio X, Kitabmahal, D. N. Road, Mumbai.
6. An early discussion on singing and dancing entertainers is to be found in K. Raghunathji, "Bombay's Dancing Girls," *Indian Antiquary* 13 (June 1884): 165–78. Aneesh Pradhan, in *Hindustani Music in Colonial Bombay*, summarizes some of the earlier literature and adds more material from his own interviews to explain the organization of sororities of tawaifs. Urmila Bhirdikar, in "The Spread of North Indian Music in Maharashtra in the Late Nineteenth and Early Twentieth Centuries: Socio-cultural Conditions of Production and Consumption," in *Music and Modernity*, ed. Amlan Das Gupta (Kolkata: Thema, 2007), discusses the discursive process by which the voices of naikins were rendered respectable, and women singers such as Kesarbai Kerkar and Hirabai Barodekar, from the 1930s on, were incorporated into the gharana system as classical singers. Anna Morcom, in *Courtesans, Bar Girls and Dancing Boys* (Gurgaon: Hachette India, 2014), points to the disappearance of courtesan performers by the mid-twentieth century.
7. For a discussion of the economic modernity of Bombay, indigenous capital, and the creativity of industry and trade, see Lakshmi Subramanian, *Three Merchants of Bombay: Doing Business in Times of Change* (New Delhi: Allen Lane, 2012). Earlier scholars who have addressed the issue of economic leadership include Christine Dobbin, *Urban Leadership in Western India: Politics and Com-*

munities in Bombay City 1840–1885 (London: Oxford University Press, 1972); and A. D. D. Gordon, *Businessmen and Politics: Rising Nationalism and a Modernising Economy, 1918–1933* (New Delhi: Manohar, 1978).

8 Amar Farooqui, *Opium City: The Making of Early Victorian Bombay* (Gurgaon: Three Essays Collective, 2006).

9 A very early understanding of the significance of migration for Mumbai's growth is to be found in the 1863 Marathi-language "urban biography" by Govind Narayan, *Mumbaiche Varnan*, available in English as *Govind Narayan's Mumbai*, ed. and trans. Murali Ranganathan (London: Anthem, 2012). Amar Farooqui's *Opium City* makes a strong case for understanding the rise of the metropolis through the history of the opium and raw cotton trade with China. Holden Furber's classic writings on trade in the "Orient" from 1600 onward provide a meticulously detailed analysis of the economic changes that led to the nineteenth-century prominence in colonial trade of a city like Bombay. See in particular Furber's *Rival Empires of Trade in the Orient 1600–1800* (Minneapolis: University of Minnesota Press, 1976), and *Private Fortunes and Company Profits in the India Trade in the 18th Century* (Brookfield, VT: Variorum, 1997).

10 *Census of India, 1891* (New Delhi: Ministry of Home Affairs Office of the Registrar General and Census Commissioner), accessed April 2014, https://archive.org/stream/cu31924023177268/ cu31924023177268_djvu.txt.

11 Rajnarayan Chandavarkar, "Peasants and Proletarians in Bombay City in the Late Nineteenth and Early Twentieth Centuries," in *History, Culture and the Indian City* (Cambridge: Cambridge University Press, 2009), 59.

12 Jim Masselos has written about the relevance of geography in the way Bombay developed, basically as a "native town" surrounded by "Raj areas": "By the mid nineteenth century Bombay, with its extended past and growing size, had become a complex entity: its sprawling geography of streets and buildings housed a wide diversity of social groups involved in an equally diverse range of activities. The mix was perhaps more various than elsewhere in India at the time, and continued to be so during the following century with Bombay's industrial base making it a target for migration from around the country." Jim Masselos, "Appropriating Urban Space: Social Constructs of Bombay in the Time of the Raj," *South Asia: Journal of South Asian Studies* 14, no. 1 (1991): 33.

13 Madhu Trivedi, "Music Patronage in the Indo-Persian Context: A Historical Overview," in *Hindustani Music: Thirteenth to Twentieth Centuries*, ed. Joep Bor et al. (New Delhi: Manohar, 2010), 65–93.

14 Ian Copland, *The British Raj and the Indian Princes: Paramountcy in Western India, 1857–1930* (Bombay: Orient Longman, 1982); Pushpa Sundar, *Patrons and Philistines: Arts and the State in British India, 1773–1947*. New York: Oxford University Press, 1995.

15 For more details, see N. K. Kelkar, *Bhaskarbuwa Bakhle* [in Marathi] (Mumbai: Karnatak Prakashan Samstha, 1967); Alladiya Khan, *My Life: As Told to His Grandson Azizuddin Khan*, trans. Amlan Das Gupta and Urmila Bhirdikar

(Calcutta: Thema, 2000); Govindrao Tembe, *My Pursuit of Music*, trans. C. R. Kuddyady (Mumbai: Bhavan's Book University, 2014); Mallikarjun Mansur, *Rasa Yatra: My Journey in Music*, trans. Rajshekhar Mansur (New Delhi: Roli, 2005); Gangubai Hangal, *The Song of My Life*, as narrated to N. K. Kulkarni, trans.

G. N. Hangal (Hubli: Sahitya Prakashana, 2003); Balkrishnabuwa Kapileshwari, *Abdul Karim Khan: The Man of the Times* (self-published, 1973).

16 Musician Dipali Nag, in her introduction to her biography *Ustad Faiyaaz Khan* (New Delhi: Sangeet Natak Akademi, 1985), suggests that the gharana concept is part of "the guild-craft ethos" in Indian music, and refers to musical continuity over three generations or more (ix).

17 The centrality of Bombay to the story of Hindustani music is quite evident in the concise account by Joep Bor and Allyn Miner, "Hindustani Music: A Historical Overview of the Modern Period," in *Hindustani Music: Thirteenth to Twentieth Centuries*, ed. Joep Bor et al. (New Delhi: Manohar, 2010): 197–220. An important work discussing the popularity of the singers of devotional songs or *kirtans*, the kirtankars, is Anna Schultz's book on the Marathi-language kirtan, where she showcases this composite performative genre and its role in presenting nationalism as devotion. See Anna Schultz, *Singing a Hindu Nation: Marathi Devotional Performance and Nationalism* (Oxford: Oxford University Press, 2012).

18 This phrase was used by eminent sitarist Arvind Parikh in describing the space in front of the musician that was reserved for aficionados who responded enthusiastically and with discernment to the performance. Interview with the author in Mumbai, February 16, 2014.

19 As Ashok Ranade points out in his interview with Deepak Raja, V. N. Bhatkhande's pioneering collection of khayals included 1,800 compositions, spanning Marwadi, Brijbhasha, Sindhi, Punjabi, Persian, Maithili, Bhojpuri, and several other languages and dialects. Ashok Ranade, "Dhrupad Represents the Precomposed Tendency in Hindustani Music," transcript of an interview with Deepak Raja on August 19, 1998, available at *Deepak Raja's World of Hindustani Music*, http://swaratala.blogspot.hk/2007/04/ashok-ranade-dhrupad-represents.html.

20 Janaki Bakhle, *Two Men and Music: Nationalism in the Making of an Indian Classical Tradition* (New York: Oxford University Press, 2005).

21 Also pronounced as *Khan Sahib* or *Khansaab*. When people are speaking, they slur the pronounciation so that it sounds like *Khansaab*; thus, in instances of quoted speech, the word is written as *Khansaab*.

22 Girish Sanzgiri, interview by Tejaswini Niranjana and Surabhi Sharma in Mumbai, July 3, 2013.

23 Stephen Slawek, review of *Two Men and Music: Nationalism in the Making of an Indian Classical Tradition*, by Janaki Bakhle, *Ethnomusicology* 51, no. 3 (fall 2007): 511.

24 Slawek, review of *Two Men and Music*, 509.

25 Amlan Das Gupta, "Rhythm and Rivalry," review of *Two Men and Music*, by Janaki Bakhle, *Economic and Political Weekly* 41, no. 36 (September 9, 2006): 3861–63.

26 I am indebted to Amlan Das Gupta for reminding me of this fact. Examples of Muslim musicians singing in temples abound in the biographical and autobiographical writings on Hindustani music. See, among others, Alladiya Khan, *Sangeet Samrat Khansahab Alladiya Khan* (Calcutta: Thema, 2000); and Kapileshwari, *Abdul Karim Khan*. Muslim ustads still perform at the Ganesh Utsav celebrations in Mumbai today.

27 Deodhar on Bade Ghulam Ali Khan's death in 1968: "With his death, I have lost a dear friend and a brother (I feel grief as though I have lost a brother)." B. R. Deodhar, *Thor Sangeetkaar* [in Marathi] (Bombay: Popular Prakashan, 1993). I thank Rutuja Lad for assistance with Marathi translations.

28 Deodhar, *Thor Sangeetkar*. It is unclear from Deodhar's account whether Rahimat Khan actually performed during the circus acts, but it is not unlikely, given the popularity of lineups that included music, dance, and acrobatics along with performing animals.

29 Nayan Ghosh, interview with the author in Mumbai, February 17, 2014.

30 It is not my contention that interreligious intimacy was not fraught with social tensions. N. M. Kelkar relates in his Marathi biography *Bhaskarbuwa Bakhle* how the Brahmin Buwa had to move from Girgaum Naka, where he lived in a Hindu-dominated chawl, to Papermill Lane, where his neighbors were Christians and kalavant women, because of objections to his house being visited by Muslim singers (147).

31 The first proscenium-style permanent theater in Mumbai was the Grant Road Theatre (also known as the Theatre Royal or simply the *pila* house, or playhouse), which opened in 1846. Its backers included major merchants like Jagannath Shankarseth, Jamsetjee Jeejeebhoy, and Framji Cawasji, who were able to obtain support from the colonial government for this public facility. Although the first plays performed there were in English, the playhouse soon became an important venue for Parsi theater and Marathi musical plays. More details in Kathryn Hansen, "Parsi Theatre and the City: Locations, Patrons, Audiences," in *Sarai Reader 02: The Cities of Everyday Life*, ed. Ravi Sundaram et al., accessed December 4, 2016, http://sarai.net/sarai-reader-02-cities-of-everyday-life.

32 The growth of Parsi theater has been extensively discussed by Somnath Gupt, *The Parsi Theatre: Its Origins and Development*, trans. and ed. Kathryn Hansen (Calcutta: Seagull Books, 2005), and Kathryn Hansen, "Languages on Stage: Linguistic Pluralism and Community Formation in the Nineteenth-Century Parsi Theatre," *Modern Asian Studies* 37, no. 2 (2003): 381–405. Most of the light classical genres on the stage drew on the courtesan repertoire of the Mughal empire and its successor regimes, including the "native state" of Awadh. The *qawwali*, however, is from Sufi music and has a more pronounced devotional or spiritual color. See Regula Burckhardt Qureshi, *Sufi Music of India*

and Pakistan: Sound, Context, and Meaning in Qawwali (Cambridge: Cambridge University Press, 1986). Ethnomusicologist Peter Manuel, in "Thumri, Ghazal, and Modernity in Hindustani Music Culture," in *Hindustani Music: Thirteenth to Twentieth Centuries*, ed. Joep Bor et al. (New Delhi: Manohar Publishers, 2010, 239–252), suggests that the genres developed different trajectories: thumri (and I would add, the dadra and the hori too) eventually became part of the classical music concert repertoire in the twentieth century, while the ghazal turned into a "commercial pop phenomenon."

33 Ashish Rajadhyaksha, email message to author, April 17, 2014.
34 A comprehensive picture of Bhatkhande's life and work is to be found in Sobhana Nayar, *Bhatkhande's Contribution to Music* (Bombay: Popular Prakashan, 1989).
35 Ashok Ranade, "Music and Music Drama in Maharashtra," in *Hindustani Music: Thirteenth to Twentieth Centuries*, ed. Joep Bor et al. (New Delhi: Manohar, 2010), 363.
36 Hansen, "Parsee Theatre and the City," 47. She also lists the neighborhoods close to Grant Road from where Hindu and Muslim middle-class audiences came, and mentions that the textile mills in Tardeo to the west of the theater district ensured the presence of factory workers too (43).
37 For more details, see Aban E. Mistry, *The Parsis and Indian Classical Music: An Unsung Contribution* (Bombay: Swar Sadhna Samiti, 2004); and Jennifer Post Quinn, "Marathi and Konkani-Speaking Women in Hindustani Music, 1880–1940" (PhD diss., University of Minnesota, 1982).
38 For an elaborate list of female singers who obtained taleem from various ustads, see Quinn, "Marathi and Konkani-speaking Women in Hindustani Music, 1880–1940." Aneesh Pradhan mentions these ustads who taught Goan singers: Sher Khan (Agra) (1805–1862), Mohammed Khan (1870–1922) (son of Natthan Khan of the Agra gayaki), and Haider Khan (Sahaswan—Badayun—Gwalior), in "Changing Facets of Indian Music in a Colonial Situation, 1818–1947" (PhD Diss., University of Mumbai), 65.
39 Details in Mohan Nadkarni, "Anjanibai Malpekar," in *The Great Masters: Profiles in Hindustani Classical Vocal Music* (New Delhi: Harper Collins, 1999), 127–130.
40 N. M. Kelkar, *Bhaskarbuwa Bakhle* (Mumbai: Karnatak Prakashan Samstha, 1967).
41 Pradhan, "Changing Facets of Indian Music," 48. Pradhan, himself a well-known tabla player, is one of the first scholars to examine the place of Hindustani music in Bombay, and his work is pioneering in its pulling together of diverse material and for the research possibilities it opens up.
42 Nayan Ghosh, interview with the author in Mumbai, February 17, 2014. In this interview, Ghosh details his father Nikhil Ghosh's forays with his guru Amir Husain Khan into the houses of the tawaifs in the "forbidden areas" near Grant Road for musical evenings, which were typically held on Fridays. Famous Muslim musicians used to gather and perform at these events sponsored by tawaifs,

and listened to and corrected aspiring musicians. There were also *dangal* (challenges) resulting in serious fights between musicians over a particular aspect of musical performance or interpretation. Nayan Ghosh says that the tawaifs used the money they obtained from rich patrons to encourage musicians. "These," he quotes his father as saying, "were the real *devis* (goddesses) who saved our music and kept it alive."

43 We can only guess that in the mid-nineteenth century pupils from outside the family were still not common, and this could also be one of the reasons why tawaifs were not acknowledged as carrying forward the gayaki of a particular musical tradition. An interesting parallel development was that of men from *sarangiya* (players of the *sarangi*) families who took to vocal music and excelled at it, with two famous examples being Abdul Karim Khan (founder of the Kirana gharana) and Bade Ghulam Ali Khan.

44 Deodhar, *Thor Sangeetkaar*; Michael David Rosse, "Music Schools and Societies in Bombay, c. 1864–1937," in *Hindustani Music: Thirteenth to Twentieth Centuries*, ed. Joep Bor et al. (New Delhi: Manohar, 2010), 313–29; Kelkar, *Bhaskarbuwa Bakhle*.

45 Rosse, "Music Schools," 320–21.

46 Information about the music syllabus prepared for girls' schools run by the SLSS is to be found in Pradhan, *Hindustani Music in Colonial Bombay*, 74–75.

47 Eriko Kobayashi, "Hindustani Classical Music Reform Movement and the Writing of History, 1900s to 1940s" (PhD diss., University of Texas, 2003), 174.

48 Rao, *Sajan Piya*, 67.

49 Kobayashi, "Hindustani Classical Music"; Rosse, "Music Schools"; Dard Neuman, "Pedagogy, Practice, and Embodied Creativity in Hindustani Music," *Ethnomusicology* 56, no. 3 (2012): 426–49.

50 To use a popular distinction, one of the main objectives of such schools was to train listeners (*kaan-sens*), who were likely to be more numerous than those who went on to become concert-level performers (*tan-sens*). In 1884, the Bombay branch of the Poona Gayan Samaj had more than thirty male students (Rosse, "Music Schools," 320). In 1912, the GUM had ninety-five members; in 1911, the Lahore GMV school, the original one founded by Vishnu Digambar Paluskar, had eighty-one students who took exams. By contrast, the Bombay branch had 792 students on its roster, of whom eighty-eight were women (Bakhle, *Two Men and Music*, 161). Figures are not available for all the other music schools that mushroomed in Bombay in the early twentieth century. If we jump forward a hundred years and look at the situation in 2014, the big music schools accounted for at least 3,000 students in Bombay. This figure does not include those studying with individual teachers, which would add up to nearly twenty students per teacher. All in all, it is estimated that around 10,000 people are studying Hindustani music in a variety of pedagogical settings in Bombay today (figure suggested by Amarendra Dhaneshwar, singer and music critic, in personal conversation with the author, April 12, 2014). Hindustani

music was introduced in the University of Bombay as a subject of study at the postgraduate level in 1969. This kind of pedagogical setting, prevalent all over India, has often attracted criticism from performing musicians for not producing accomplished performers.

51 Rosse, "Music Schools and Societies in Bombay," 313–14.
52 Rosse, "Music Schools and Societies in Bombay," 313–14.
53 Kobayashi, "Hindustani Classical Music," 168.
54 Kobayashi, "Hindustani Classical Music," 169 (emphasis added).
55 H. V. Mote, ed., *Vishrabdha sharada*, vol. 2 (Theater and music), in Marathi, with notes by Vasant S. Desai and Arvind Mangrulkar (Mumbai: H. V. Mote Prakashan, 1975).
56 Hansen, "Languages on Stage," 394.
57 Meera Kosambi, "British Bombay and Marathi Mumbai," in *Bombay: Mosaic of Modern Culture*, ed. S. Patel and A. Thorner (New Delhi: Oxford University Press, 1995), 7–8.
58 Hansen, "Languages on Stage," 402.
59 Advertisements in the *Times of India*, accessed through the ProQuest database, April 3–5, 2014.
60 Hansen, "Languages on Stage," 396.
61 Hansen, "Languages on Stage," 383.
62 Eminent Gwalior gharana musician Neela Bhagwat, personal communication with the author, January 20, 2014.
63 Fieldwork observations, January 2017.
64 Ranade, "Dhrupad Represents the Precomposed Tendency in Hindustani Music." Interview with Deepak Raja, August 19, 1998.
65 For an extensive discussion of the background of Mumbai's female entertainers, see Morcom, *Courtesans, Bar Girls and Dancing Boys*, especially chapters 1 and 2.
66 The dayan tabla is usually played by the right hand when the accompanist is using two instruments, as in the customary setting for Hindustani music concerts.
67 Translation by Sohnee Harshey.
68 Thanks to Sohnee Harshey for this description: Ruby had a few kathak influences in her dancing—the *chakkars,* or whirling, being most prominent. Her dress (anarkali kurta) was also important in enhancing the effect of the chakkars. While she did not exactly move her feet as one would during *tatkaar* (4 + 4 + 4 + 4 = 16 beats for *teentaal*), she was able to catch the rhythm (1 + 1 + 1 + 1 + 1 + 1 + 1 + 1 + 1 + 1 + 1 + 1 + 1 + 1 + 1 + 1 = 16) and thus gave the appearance of actually doing tatkaar. Her hand movements (right hand extended in front with palm facing down) during these times also imitated the kathak hand movements as seen during the *tihai* or even *gat* (types of walking). She was also able to switch between the standing stance and the gliding movement on the floor toward the audience quite smoothly. I could not find out whether Ruby had had formal dance training, like earlier tawaifs did, and if so, where and by whom

she would have been trained. Raghunathji, in "Bombay's Dancing Girls," writes that women who became performers were trained in both singing and dancing. Singing was learned from sarangi-playing accompanists. Naikins from Goa usually employed a *vastadji* to teach them dancing. Vastadjis were brothers or sons of Muslim or Hindu women performers. Dancing girls were also taught by *mirasi*s or kathaks.

69 Ethnographitis is my term for the anxiety experienced by those in the role of anthropologist or tourist who do not want to seem too curious about the lives of those they are meeting for the first time, lest it be construed as prying by a socially privileged observer.

Chapter 2

1 Doreen Massey, *For Space* (London: Sage, 2005).
2 The map can be accessed at Google Maps, https://www.google.com/maps/d/u/0/edit?mid=1U8MedN7BujG3Vkvui2KVr_m7gE0&hl=en_US&ll=18.9536198210448
4%2C72.82069150000007&z=15.
3 *Times of India*, April 7, 1929, 13.
4 Details in Taras Grescoe, *Shanghai Grand* (Toronto: HarperCollins, 2016).
5 See among others Janaki Bakhle, *Two Men and Music* (New York: Oxford University Press, 2005). These details of Hirabai's genealogy are to be found in multiple sources in Marathi, Hindi, and English, too numerous to be listed here.
6 S. M. Edwardes, *The Gazetteer of Bombay City and Island* (Bombay: Times Press, 1909), 191–92. Also cited in Aneesh Pradhan, *Hindustani Music in Colonial Bombay* (Gurgaon: Three Essays Collective, 2014).
7 Anna Morcom, *Courtesans, Bar Girls and Dancing Boys: The Illicit Worlds of Indian Dance* (Gurgaon: Hachette India, 2014).
8 Nitin Shirodkar, interview by the author, June 23, 2013.
9 Rudolf Steiner, *Spiritualism, Madame Blavatsky, and Theosophy: An Eyewitness View of Occult History* (Great Barrington, MA: Anthroposophic Press, 2002).
10 For a discussion of Besant's astonishing political career, see Catherine Wessinger, *Annie Besant and Progressive Messianism, 1847–1933* (Lewiston, NY: Edwin Mellen, 1988).
11 Lakshmi Subramanian, in *From the Tanjore Court to the Madras Music Academy: A Social History of Music in South India* (New Delhi: Oxford University Press, 2011), has an extensive discussion of Annie Besant's presence in Chennai (then Madras), where Theosophy had a significant influence on the middle and upper classes who were getting involved in the nationalist movement. These were the same groups who led the initiative to reform music pedagogy for Carnatic or South Indian music. Theosophy does not seem to have had the same impact on the aficionados of Hindustani music.
12 "Deodhar School of Indian Music," My City 4 Kids, accessed on June 20, 2019,

https://www.mycity4kids.com/Mumbai/Hobbies/Deodhar-School-Of-Indian-Music_Girgaon/8786_bd.

13 Vamanrao H. Deshpande, *Between Two Tanpuras*, trans. Ram Deshmukh and B. R. Dhekney (Bombay: Popular Prakashan, 1989), 168.

14 Deshpande, *Between Two Tanpuras*, 166.

15 Sangeeta Gogate talks about some of the musicians she remembers hearing at the School: "I remember Prabha Atre. She had come here and performed here, with her famous Kalavati and Maru Bihag. We had told her to perform, and it was lovely. Really lovely to listen to. She is performing there and we are sitting here. There are so many I can tell you . . . like Prabha Atre, then Vasundhara Komkali-ji, Kumar-ji, Ashwini Bhide, Aarti Ankalikar, then Pandit Jitendra Abhishekhi, so many people have performed here, Devaki Pandit in the young generation, then Shahid Parvez, Pandit D. K. Datar, then Pandit Jog, whoever has learnt here also have performed here, and many big artistes also have." Interview by Tejaswini Niranjana and Surabhi Sharma, June 24, 2013.

16 Arvind Parikh, *The Raga of My Life* (Mumbai: International Foundation for Fine Arts, 2002), 25.

17 Nitin Shirodkar, in a discussion with the author on June 23, 2013, spoke about an event that took place in 1950 or so: "Now Deodhar's class at Opera House was, you know, like a meeting place for everybody. Now Dattaram Parvatkar sarangi, his son Ajit Parvatkar is a dear friend of mine, and he tells me that on his first birthday—now Ajit would be about sixty-three, sixty-four—and on his first birthday it seems Ravi Shankar performed in Deodhar's classes with Ustad Ahmed Jan Thirakwa on the tabla."

18 Mallikarjun Mansur, *Rasa Yatra: My Journey in Music*, trans. Rajshekhar Mansur (New Delhi: Roli, 2005).

19 Mansur, *Rasa Yatra*, 41.

20 Raghavwadi is part of another aspect of musical history in Mumbai. In 1952, B. V. Keskar became director-general of All India Radio and set up an audition system in which artists were heard by judges who asked them questions about their musical knowledge. Depending on their ability to impress the judges, the musicians were graded A, B, or C. Arvind Parikh describes how a Kalakar Mandal or Artists' Association was formed by classical musicians who were upset by this auditioning system, which threatened to eliminate precisely the *khandani* or hereditary musicians who did not have "book knowledge." The Mandal picketed AIR and boycotted the radio station. After the personal intervention of the then chief minister of Bombay, Morarji Desai, the strike was eventually ended. All the meetings of the Mandal took place at the Raghavwadi residence of Kausalya and Dinkar Manjeshwar, who were involved in music. See Parikh, *The Raga of My Life*, 26–27.

21 Shirodkar, interview, June 23, 2014.

22 Deshpande, *Between Two Tanpuras*, 83.

23 Deshpande, *Between Two Tanpuras*, 83.

24 Deshpande, *Between Two Tanpuras*, 87.

25 Deshpande, *Between Two Tanpuras*, 83.
26 Kumar Gandharva, "Kumar Gandharva in His Childhood Performance," YouTube, July 7, 2012, https://www.youtube.com/watch?v=jJL_bohxEdU.
27 Pradhan, *Hindustani Music in Colonial Bombay*; Geeta Thatra, "Contentious (Socio-spatial) Relations: Tawaifs and Congress House in Contemporary Bombay/Mumbai," *Indian Journal of Gender Studies* 23, no. 2 (2016): 197–217.
28 Thatra, "Contentious (Socio-spatial) Relations"; Dayalsingh Thakur, interview by Surabhi Sharma, September 14, 2016.
29 Batuk Diwanji, "Anjanibai Malpekar," in *Sangeetkaro Ane Sangeetagno* (Mumbai: N. M. Thakkar, n.d.), 36. Passage translated by Sohnee Harshey.
30 Chandrakant (Chandu) Ramjibhai Mewada, interview by Surabhi Sharma and Tejaswini Niranjana, June 22, 2013.
31 Thakur, interview, September 14, 2016.
32 Around 1906, he was forced to move to this mixed neighborhood where Christians and *kalavantins* or performers lived when his Brahmin neighbors in Shastri Hall, Tardeo, objected to Muslim singers visiting his house. From N. M. Kelkar, *Bhaskarbuwa Bakhle* (Mumbai: Karnatak Prakashan Samsthan, 1967), 147. Passage translated by Rutuja Lad.
33 Kaiwan Mehta, "The Terrain of Home and Within Urban Neighbourhoods: Case of the Bombay Chawls," in *The Chawls of Mumbai: Galleries of Life*, ed. Neera Adarkar (Delhi: ImprintOne, 2011), 81–88.
34 Arvind Adarkar, "Marathi Manus in Girgaon," in *The Chawls of Mumbai: Galleries of Life*, ed. Neera Adarkar (Delhi: ImprintOne, 2011), 145–51.
35 Mehta, "Terrain of Home," 81.
36 Oral sources for the year in which Trinity Club was established seem to clash with a number of written sources cited by Aneesh Pradhan, who mentions 1904–5 as the likely date in *Hindustani Music in Colonial Bombay*, 70.
37 Balasaheb Tikekar, trustee of the Trinity Club, interview by Tejaswini Niranjana and Surabhi Sharma, June 24, 2013.
38 Balasaheb Tikekar, interview by Tejaswini Niranjana and Surabhi Sharma, June 24, 2013.
39 Chandrakant Ramjibhai Mewada, interview by Surabhi Sharma and Tejaswini Niranjana, June 22, 2013.
40 Chandubhai passed away late in 2014. The shop is now closed, since his children have moved on to other professions.
41 Satchit Dabholkar, interview by the author, February 25, 2015.
42 Nitin Shirodkar, interview by the author, June 23, 2013.
43 Parikh, *The Raga of My Life*, 23.
44 Parikh, *The Raga of My Life*, 24.
45 Nitin Shirodkar, interview by Surabhi Sharma, June 23, 2013. Shirodkar was quoting his teacher Firoz Dastur's anecdote about the runners.
46 Shirodkar, interview, June 23, 2013.
47 Kalyani Puranik, interview by Surabhi Sharma, July 25, 2014.
48 Keshavji Naik Chawl in Girgaum is where the first public Ganeshotsav or cele-

bration was organized in 1893 by nationalist leader Balgangadhar Tilak. As political scientist Bhikhu Parekh puts it, "Tilak and his colleagues reinterpreted and collectivized the worship of Ganesh" (a household god for some centuries), and Ganesh celebrations were partly inspired by a desire to find an equivalent to the Muslim tazia. See Bhikhu C. Parekh, *Colonialism, Tradition, and Reform: An Analysis of Gandhi's Political Discourse* (Delhi: Sage, 1999), 166.

49 Vaman Nadkarni, Chunam Lane resident, quoted in Reema Gehi, "One Beat at a Time," *Mumbai Mirror*, June 7, 2015, https://mumbaimirror.indiatimes.com/others/sunday-read/One-beat-at-a-time/articleshow/47569659.cms.

50 Kaiwan Mehta, *Alice in Bhuleshwar: Navigating a Mumbai Neighbourhood* (New Delhi: Yoda, 2009), 131; Paroma Sadhana, "Compilation of Information on 'Bombay Movie Theatres,'" in *Project Cinema City*, ed. K. Bhaumik, M. Dutta, and R. Shivkumar (New Delhi: Leftword, 2014), 150–51; Virchand Dharamsey, historian of cultural practice in Mumbai, interview by the author, October 18, 2012.

51 Several tanks were filled up after Vihar Lake in 1860 and Tulsi Lake in 1897 began supplying water to Mumbai.

52 Agra gharana singer Lalith Rao suggested in an email message to the author on November 12, 2016, that Nand would have been a likely option, and also provided the translation of the composition.

53 Satchit Dabholkar, interview by Surabhi Sharma, February 25, 2015.

54 "Anjanibai Malpekar," *Women on Record*, Centre for Media and Alternative Communication, accessed August 15, 2018, http://www.womenonrecord.com/music-makers/artists/anjanibai-malpekar. Vidya Shah's invaluable project includes an interview with Geeta Sarabhai, who studied with Anjanibai.

Chapter 3

1 An influential account of rasa theory in relation to Hindustani music is presented by Deepak Raja, *The Raga-ness of Ragas: Ragas beyond the Grammar* (New Delhi: DK Printworld, 2016).

2 See Raja, *The Raga-ness of Ragas*, 56–57, for an elaboration of the nine sthayi bhavas and corresponding rasas as outlined by Abhinavagupta (c. 950–1016 CE), including love, anger, disgust, wonder, fear, and so on.

3 Durga Khote, *I, Durga Khote*, trans. Shanta Gokhale (New Delhi: Oxford University Press, 2006), 42.

4 Khote, *I, Durga Khote*, 47.

5 Vamanrao H. Deshpande, *Between Two Tanpuras*, trans. Ram Deshmukh and B. R. Dhekney (Bombay: Popular Prakashan, 1989), 2. Deshpande says he "practised hard day and night for years" (14). He actually changed gurus, all of them famous singers, three times in search of the perfect taalim that suited his musical sensibility. But when Natthan Khan, the third guru, suggested that he undergo *gandabandhan* (tie the black thread that would make him an official

disciple), he claimed he could not afford it: "I never intended to develop into a professional singer. I had taken up music as a hobby" (19).
6   Murli Manohar Shukla, interview by the author, January 2, 2017.
7   Dayalsingh Thakur, interview by Surabhi Sharma, September 14, 2016.
8   Dargah is the tomb of a Sufi saint, venerated by both Hindus and Muslims in South Asia.
9   Arvind Parikh, interview by Tejaswini Niranjana, February 16, 2014.
10 The drut usually ends the exposition of a particular raga.
11 Girish Sanzgiri, interview by Tejaswini Niranjana and Surabhi Sharma, July 3, 2013.
12 Quoted by Janaki Bakhle, in *Two Men and Music*, from the Marathi text by Rajaram Humne, *Dhanya Janma Jaahla: Shrimati Hirabai Barodekar yaanche jeevan gane* (Poona: 1980), 28.
13 Govindrao Tembe, *My Pursuit of Music*, trans. C. R. Kuddyady (Mumbai: Bharatiya Vidya Bhavan, 2014), 71.
14 Note by S. V. Gokhale, in the English translation of Tembe, *My Pursuit of Music*, 115.
15 Gokhale, in Tembe, *My Pursuit of Music*, 139. Tarabai (1857–1918) and her sister Saraswatibai had migrated to Mumbai from Weling in Goa. They were singers and dancers patronized by prominent businessmen. Gokhale says they lived in a large bungalow surrounded by chawls, and this area in Girgaum was known as Tara Bapu's wadi.
16 Bakhle, *Two Men and Music*, 161. Bakhle points out that in the incoming GMV class of 1912, of the sixty-eight women students, thirty-five were Parsi, with the rest being Hindu (fifteen Brahmin, ten Prabhus, and eight Kshatriya by caste). She suggests that the visibility of Parsis in the GMV can be attributed to the mutually shared communal sentiment of Hindus and Parsis against Muslims. The near invisibility of Muslims in the school, says Bakhle, is because Paluskar presented his institution as a quintessentially Hindu one, thus remaking raga music as a Hindu cultural practice (Bakhle, *Two Men and Music*, 137–79).
17 Bakhle, *Two Men and Music*, 171. Bakhle draws attention to a sixteen-page pamphlet Paluskar wrote, titled "Mahila Sangeet" (Women's music), which was intended to teach women to use their musical training "for devotional purposes and for such purposes alone" (171).
18 Ramdas Bhatkal, email message to the author, April 10, 2017. Bhatkal says that the syllabus was based on Deodhar's own book, *Raaga Bodh*.
19 Sangeeta Gogate, interview by Tejaswini Niranjana and Surabhi Sharma, June 24, 2013.
20 An advertisement in the *Times of India*, dated December 12, 1925, announces that the Bombay Municipality by arrangement with the Bombay Presidency Radio Club will do an open-air wireless broadcast of a "select programme of Indian music" from 6 to 8 p.m., in the Victoria Garden.
21 Nilima Kilachand, interview by Tejaswini Niranjana, January 4, 2017.
22 Khote, *I, Durga Khote*, 37.

23 Nitin Shirodkar, interview by Tejaswini Niranjana and Surabhi Sharma, June 23, 2013.
24 Simin Patel, historian of Bombay, told me in an email message on June 21, 2017, that the "Parsi ease with shoes" has to do with their wearing *sapaats* or traditional footwear at all times, unlike other communities in India, whose members would not wear them inside the house, at least in the time frame of the Dastur story.
25 Although the first music textbook intended for women was published in Marathi as early as 1864 for the vernacular schools of the reformist Students' Scientific and Literary Society, it was not—just like similar publications with the same intended audience—meant to help women become performers. Instead, as Bakhle perceptively suggests, music was being used "as an instrument of educational reform" (Bakhle, *Two Men and Music*, 64–65).
26 Shukla, interview, January 2, 2017.
27 Ramdas Bhatkal, interview by the author, February 12, 2014.
28 Lalith Rao in a discussion with the author, January 10, 2017.
29 For a comprehensive account of the Chitrapur Saraswats, see Frank Conlon, *A Caste in a Changing World: The Chitrapur Saraswat Brahmans, 1700–1935* (Berkeley: University of California Press, 1977).
30 Nayan Ghosh added that his father "was deeply spiritual at that time, associated with Ramakrishna Mission. So he discussed this with the chief swamiji [spiritual leader] here in Khar Ramakrishna Mission. He was young, so he said, 'My ustad has taken me to this area. It is troubling me very much. What do I do?' The swamiji said, 'You have nothing to worry about, if your mind is clean and pure and you're going for this [the music]. Your ustad lives there, and he's such a great soul.' Amir Husain was a godly person. 'He himself is staying there. You should have full faith in your guru and just be with him like a shadow. Forget about anything else. It doesn't matter where you're going, you know. The real *vidya* is there. You try to bring it out from there,' he said. That's when he got some confidence."
31 Gogate, interview, June 24, 2013.
32 Chandrakant Ramjibhai Mewada, interview by Surabhi Sharma and Tejaswini Niranjana, June 22, 2013.
33 Kilachand, interview, January 4, 2017.
34 Kilachand, interview, January 4, 2017.
35 Kilachand speaks of her early musical training thus: "My maternal grandfather kept a Khan Sahib in his house. He lived in a huge *haveli*, a huge bungalow in Bombay. He had an in-house Khan Sahib. A lot of people did do that kind of thing. The Khan Sahib was a gentleman called Rashid Khan who was not a very well-known performing musician, but a good teacher.... Subsequently, when I grew up and was about fourteen–fifteen years old, he migrated to Pakistan. By then, my grandmother had passed away and all that. Theirs was a Jain household and keeping a *musulman* (Muslim). Khan Sahib ... nobody thought about such things. He is there because he has the treasure of music. He has a treasure

house of music. You don't worry about all the other things. Of course they had told him that you cannot bring nonveg in the house. He was running his own kitchen, and his wife was there [with him]. He was actually living in an outhouse (in India, the outhouse is a small structure in the yard of the main house that is sometimes rented out or given to employees to live in) in my grandfather's house. There were some preconditions. But then like the Rajwadas he would summon him at any time of the day. Or the Khan Sahib would want to sing at any time of the day or teach him. So he would summon my grandfather and say, "Come on . . . *aajao, seekho* [come, learn]." Nilima speaks of her grandfather as being "very passionate about music." "So he [the ustad] taught us—my sisters and I. My sisters slowly sort of dropped out because either they were not interested or they wanted to do other things. They dropped out and I continued because I had a reasonably good voice that was trainable. So I continued. So I learnt before I was married from Rashid Khan Sahib. When I got married, there used to be a Khan Sahib like that here [in the Kilachand mansion] also. And he was Faiyaz Khan Sahib's nephew, Khadim Husain Khan. My mother-in-law asked me, 'Would you like to learn from him because he comes to the house?' Since my Khan Sahib had migrated, I said, 'Yes, why not!' So I started learning from him."

36 Kilachand talked about the membership fees for Sajan Milap: "Our experience with Sajan Milap was that even though we were in existence for thirty years, membership, as Lalith and all may have told you, was earlier twenty rupees and then it became thirty rupees. Willy-nilly we increased it to fifty rupees. Fifty rupees and everybody was saying, '*Baap re*, fifty rupees!' Fifty rupees in a year!" I said, "This was in the '80s?" She replied, "In the '70s and '80s, shortly after we started. We started in '77. But yes, mostly in the '80s . . . by the '90s and early part of 2000. We, I think, wound up in 2007."
37 Kilachand, interview, January 4, 2017.
38 Balasaheb and Sumathi Tikekar, interview by Surabhi Sharma and Tejaswini Niranjana, June 24, 2013.
39 Kishor Merchant, interview by Tejaswini Niranjana, February 16, 2014.
40 B. R. Deodhar, *Thor Sangeetkaar* (Bombay: Popular Prakashan, 1993), 257.
41 Farida Sabnavis, interview by Tejaswini Niranjana and Surabhi Sharma, July 31, 2013.

Chapter 4

1 Jayavanth Rao, *Sajan Piya: A Biography of Ustad Khadim Husain Khan* (Mumbai: Sajan Milap, 1981), 46–47.
2 Daniel Neuman, *The Life of Music in North India: The Organization of an Artistic Tradition* (Detroit: Wayne State University Press, 1980), 21.
3 For existing writing on music school pedagogy in Mumbai, see Janaki Bakhle, *Two Men and Music* (New York: Oxford University Press, 2005); Aneesh Pradhan, *Hindustani Music in Colonial Bombay* (Gurgaon: Three Essays Col-

lective, 2014); and Michael Rosse, "Music Schools and Societies in Bombay, c. 1864–1937," in *Hindustani Music: Thirteenth to Twentieth Centuries*, ed. Joep Bor et al. (New Delhi: Manohar, 2010).

4   Lakshmi Subramanian, *New Mansions for Music: Performance, Pedagogy and Criticism* (New Delhi: Routledge, 2018). See in particular chapters 1 to 3.

5   The coexistence of these pedagogical modes from the late nineteenth century on is referred to by Aneesh Pradhan in *Hindustani Music in Colonial Bombay*. Urmila Bhirdikar makes the useful point that "the dissemination of music through music schools and the householders' interest in music produced a vast body of written documents of bandishes, sometimes with notations." Urmila Bhirdikar, "The Spread of North Indian Music in Maharashtra in the Late Nineteenth and Early Twentieth Centuries: Socio-cultural Conditions of Production and Consumption," in *Music and Modernity*, ed. Amlan Das Gupta (Kolkata: Thema, 2007), 230.

6   Rao, *Sajan Piya*, 47.

7   Writers like B. R. Deodhar and Vamanrao Deshpande in the 1960s and '70s did acknowledge that the khayal gharanas were not older than the mid-eighteenth century, when the khayal form itself began to be popular, and that by "gharana" they meant something that was about three generations old. See Deodhar's preface to Vamanrao Deshpande, *Indian Musical Traditions: An Aesthetic Study of the Gharanas in Hindustani Music* (Mumbai: Popular Prakashan, 1987).

8   Neuman, *The Life of Music in North India*, 204.

9   Tejaswini Niranjana, "Music in the Balance," *Economic and Political Weekly* 48, no. 2 (January 12, 2013), 4–48.

10 According to Deepa Ganesh, author of *A Life in Three Octaves* (Palam Vihar: Three Essays Collective, 2014), in the mid-1930s, Gangubai was paid Rs. 50 for singing on All India Radio (65).

11 Gangubai Hangal, *Nanna badukina haadu* (Hubli: Sahitya Prakashana, 2002), 9. Translation mine.

12 An amusing story is told about Kirana singer Hirabai Barodekar asking Gangubai for a recipe for her signature *rasam*, and the latter putting all the ingredients on a plate to show her, since she did not know their Hindi names. Narrated in Deepa Ganesh's biography of Gangubai (Ganesh, *A Life in Three Octaves*, 122).

13 Gangubai Hangal, *The Song of My Life* (Hubli: Sahitya Prakashana, 2003), 16–17; some sentences retranslated from the Kannada original.

14 Hangal, *The Song of My Life*, 18.

15 Hangal, *The Song of My Life*, 18, with some lines retranslated.

16 Hangal, *Nanna badukina haadu*, 16. Translation mine.

17 Hangal, *The Song of My Life*, 19.

18 Hangal, *Nanna badukina haadu*, 22–23. Translation mine.

19 Anmol Vellani, interview by the author, September 5, 2014.

20 Sheila Dhar, *The Cooking of Music and Other Essays* (New Delhi: Permanent Black, 2001), 32.

21 Gwalior belonged to the Maratha Confederacy in the eighteenth century and

then in the nineteenth century became one of the native states under indirect rule of the British. Most of the native or princely states, following in the wake of the Mughal Empire, displayed certain features of royal pomp, which included having court musicians and dancers.

22 Shankarrao's father, Vishnupant Pandit, had moved to Gwalior after the Indian Mutiny of 1857 and was employed at the Gwalior darbar to teach Sanskrit to Haddu Khan and Nathhu Khan. For more details, see Neela Bhagwat, *Krishnarao Shankar Pandit, a Doyen of Khayal* (Bombay: Popular Prakashan, 1992).

23 Sharad Sathe, interview by the author, June 24, 2014.

24 In his *Sangeet Sargam Saar*, written in Hindi and published in 1928 for the Shankar Gandharva Vidyalay of Gwalior, Krishnarao Shankar Pandit presents, in addition to sargams or note combinations in different ragas, a dialogue between guru and disciple to exemplify the basics of Hindustani music. Typical questions include: How many notes are there in a *saptak*? What are the names of the notes?

25 Bhagwat, *Krishnarao Shankar Pandit*.

26 Neuman, *The Life of Music in North India*, 22.

27 Amanda J. Weidman, *Singing the Classical, Voicing the Modern: The Postcolonial Politics of Music in South India* (Durham, NC: Duke University Press, 2006), 25–26.

28 Weidman, *Singing the Classical*, 55.

29 For a detailed and insightful discussion of how many hereditary musicians performed without naming the raga, see Dard Neuman, "Pedagogy, Practice, and Embodied Creativity in Hindustani Music," *Ethnomusicology* 56, no. 3 (2012): 426–49. However, Neuman's opposition between craft-based practice and scientific musicological knowledge is not evident in the story about Ghagge, because here it is a fellow musician asking him for a raga he is supposed to know, because he performs it.

30 By "educated person" I mean someone who has been through a modern Western-style education system, such as those that became common in India after the mid-nineteenth century. Hereditary Muslim musicians like Vilayat Khan could be seen as highly educated in their own way, as established in the ethnomusicological scholarship, but not necessarily formed in the modern system. Even supposedly illiterate musicians are educated, given that they are custodians of musical knowledge.

31 Weidman, *Singing the Classical*.

32 Niharika Seth, *Ustad Vilayat Khan: A Life Set to Music* (New Delhi: Rupa, 2004), 11.

Chapter 5

1 Adrian McNeil has a fascinating account of *guru seva* or service to the teacher among three generations of tabla players in Kolkata in his essay, "Generational Friction: An Ethnographic Perspective on *Guru Seva* within a Line-

age of Tabla Players in Kolkata," *MUSICultures* 44, no. 1 (2017): 116–33. He observes that the most intense friction was experienced in the relationship of Bengali Hindu middle-class students and Muslim hereditary musicians, but when both teacher and student happened to be Hindu, the friction, if any, was absorbed into traditional rituals of devotion. This is not an aspect I have focused on in discussing music in Mumbai, but it is certainly a topic that merits further research.

2   A very different relationship existed between Arvind Parikh and Vilayat Khan, who were close to each other in age. Parikh says, "Our relationship was threefold. One, of course I was his student and shishya; secondly, I was his secretary, looking after all his correspondence, his telephone, this, that, and the other; and thirdly, we were good friends, you see—*chalo aaj raat ko* picture *pe chalte hain*, let's go to see a film tonight. See, I was placed in a position where I had a car, driver, everything, so *ghoomne chalo*, picture *pe chalo*, so whatever he wanted we could do. And I had enough pocket money [even as a student] for all those luxuries. That is how we built up [the relationship] over a period of time. Sixty years is a long period—my association with him—until he passed away in 2004."

3   Jayavanth Rao, *Sajan Piya: A Biography of Ustad Khadim Husain Khan* (Mumbai: Sajan Milap, 1981), 25.

4   Arvind Parikh, interview by the author, February 16, 2014

5   Aneesh Pradhan, interview by the author, February 13, 2014.

6   Gangubai Hangal, interview by the author, 2006.

7   Gangubai Hangal, *The Song of My Life*, narrated by N. K. Kulkarni, trans. G. N. Hangal (Hubli: Sahitya Prakashana, 2003), 3.

8   Amarendra Dhaneshwar, interview by the author, July 1, 2013.

9   Girish Sanzgiri, interview by the author, July 3, 2013.

10 Amanda J. Weidman, *Singing the Classical, Voicing the Modern: The Postcolonial Politics of Music in South India* (Durham, NC: Duke University Press, 2006), 247.

11 Weidman, *Singing the Classical*, 247.

12 Weidman, *Singing the Classical*, 270.

13 Jeff Roy, "The Internet Guru: Online Pedagogy in Indian Classical Music Traditions," *Asian Music* 47, no. 1 (2016): 103–35. Roy's point is well taken in the context of learning an instrument, where tactile contact—of the teacher's hand on the student's—is crucial, but as my accounts show, embodiment works rather differently in vocal music instruction.

14 See Pandita Neela Bhagwat, *Treasure of Gwalior Gharana*, Wikisource, January 1, 2019, https://wikisource.org/wiki/Index:TREASURE_OF_GWALIOR_GHARANA_BOOK_1.pdf.

15 Neela Bhagwat, interview by the author on Skype, February 17, 2016.

16 The language of monetization that is today part of discussions of intellectual property worldwide is still not expressed bluntly in the relationship between student and teacher of Hindustani music. To speak of such things too obvi-

ously, even when the musician makes a living primarily from teaching, is not part of the etiquette of musical knowledge. There is no standard fee that each student pays for a session, since that is negotiated delicately in the context of the willingness and ability of the teacher to ask, and the student to pay.

17 A fascinating discussion of a hereditary musician, sarod player Sakhawat Husain Khan, engaging with Bhatkhande's idea of notation is available in Max Katz, *Lineages of Loss: Counternarratives of North Indian Music* (Middletown, CT: Wesleyan University Press, 2017). Sakhawat Husain praised Bhatkhande for rendering "a very complex thing easy, and which creates the exact picture of every movement of the throat" (120) by using the "singing camera" of notation. This has enabled everyone to receive the album of music in which pictures of old compositions are captured, says Sakhawat Husain. In Katz's argument, this "thwarts the assumption of a binary opposition between hereditary musicians and modern music theory" (121), since the former saw notation as "propagating the heritage of hereditary musicians." Indeed, Sakhawat Husain taught hundreds of students at the Bhatkhande College for nearly three decades, until his death in 1955.

Afterword

1 The first line is close to Raag Charukeshi, but subsequently the thumri moves into a mixed melody, not clearly identifiable with any one raga. I thank Omkar Havaldar for pointing this out to me.
2 Interestingly, the actor who plays the husband Hamid is Sanjeev Kumar, who appeared in chapter 3, along with his friend the tabla maker who took him to see the people mad about music in the kothas of Foras Road.
3 For more details of the complex story of the embourgeoisement of the Hindustani music performer, see for example Anna Morcom, *Courtesans, Bar Girls and Dancing Boys: The Illicit Worlds of Indian Dance* (Gurgaon: Hachette India, 2014).
4 When the project we called *Mumbai Music* was initially put together by myself and Surabhi Sharma the filmmaker, we had set out to draw on our individual competences to create, respectively, a documentary film and a research monograph. For financial support, we approached the Mumbai Metropolitan Region Development Authority, which had set up a Heritage Conservation Society to strengthen research, documentation, and policy work on the city. It took several rounds of meetings with the society's advisory board, consisting mostly of architects and conservationists, to convince them that a scholar and a filmmaker interested in music could produce fresh perspectives on urban space. Without Prasad Shetty, architect and consultant to the conservation society, who shepherded our application through the bureaucratic maze, we would never had the courage to engage with the Metropolitan Development Authority. Like most government funding in India, our reluctantly given grant would reach us in dribbles, and long after the deadlines for paying people had passed.

Inventive cross-subsidizing is the only way to support the kind of research we wanted to do. Multiple sources of support, multiple small grants, and individual generosity came together in miraculous combinations as the work proceeded over a five-year period.

5 Set up by Columbia University, Studio X was headed at the time of our exhibition by Rajeev Thakker, architect and teacher. The Studio X in Mumbai closed down in June 2016 (WhatsApp communication from Rajeev Thakker, September 19, 2017). See Studio X Global Network, Columbia GSAPP accessed September 19, 2017, https://www.arch.columbia.edu/studio-x.

6 Drawing, Sonal Sundararajan; design and execution, Farzan Dalal; concept, Tejaswini Niranjana.

7 Direction, Surabhi Sharma; camera, Ajay Noronha; sound, Suresh Rajamani; editing, Monisha Baldawa; sound design, Mohandas V. P.

8 The intricate politics of the development of Hindi and its connection to Indian nationalism is discussed in Alok Rai, *Hindi Nationalism: Tracts for the Times* (New Delhi: Sangam, 2001).

9 Design, selection, and execution, Tejaswini Niranjana and Farzan Dalal. Special thanks to Samira Sheikh for her help in obtaining the Parsi theater plays.

10 Selection and arrangement, Nishad Matange and Tejaswini Niranjana.

11 Direction and montage, Surabhi Sharma; map design, Farzan Dalal.

12 Thanks to Geeta Thatra and Anna Morcom for their help in introducing me to the NB Compound.

Selected Bibliography

Adarkar, Arvind. "Marathi Manus in Girgaon." In *The Chawls of Mumbai: Galleries of Life*, edited by Neera Adarkar, 145–51. New Delhi: ImprintOne, 2011.

Allen, Matthew Harp, and T. Viswanathan. *Music in South India: The Karnatak Concert Tradition and Beyond*. New York: Oxford University Press, 2004.

Appiah, Kwame Anthony. *In My Father's House: Africa in the Philosophy of Culture*. Oxford: Oxford University Press, 1992.

Arondekar, Anjali. "Subject to Sex: A Small History of the Gomantak Maratha Samaj." In *South Asian Feminisms*, edited by Ania Loomba and Ritty A. Lukose, 244–63. Durham, NC: Duke University Press, 2012.

Athavale, V. R. *Vishnu Digambar Paluskar*. New Delhi: National Book Trust, 1967.

Awasthy, G. C. *Broadcasting in India*. Bombay: Allied, 1965.

Bakhle, Janaki. *Two Men and Music: Nationalism in the Making of an Indian Classical Tradition*. New York: Oxford University Press, 2005.

Banga, Indu, ed. *The City in Indian History: Urban Demography, Society, and Politics*. New Delhi: Manohar and Urban History Association of India, 1991.

Baradi, Hasmukh. *A History of Gujarati Theatre*. Translated by Vinod Meghani. New Delhi: National Book Trust, 2003.

Bhagwat, Neela. *Krishnarao Shankar Pandit, a Doyen of Khayal*. Bombay: Popular Prakashan, 1992.

Bhatkhande, V. *A Short Historical Survey of the Music of Upper India*. Bombay: Bombay Samachar, 1917.

Bhirdikar, Urmila. "The Spread of North Indian Music in Maharashtra in the Late Nineteenth and Early Twentieth Centuries: Socio-cultural Conditions of Production and Consumption." In *Music and Modernity*, edited by Amlan Das Gupta, 220–38. Kolkata: Thema, 2007.

Bor, Joep, and Allyn Miner. "Hindustani Music: A Historical Overview of the Modern Period." In *Hindustani Music: Thirteenth to Twentieth Centuries*, edited by Joep Bor, Francoise Nalini Delvoye, Jane Harvey, and Emmie Te Nijenhuis, 197–220. New Delhi: Manohar, 2010.

Bourdieu, Pierre. *The Logic of Practice*. Translated by Richard Nice. Stanford, CA: Stanford University Press, 1990.

Cashman, R. I. *The Myth of the Lokmanya: Tilak and Mass Politics in Maharashtra*. Berkeley: University of California Press, 1975.

Chakravarty, Uma. *Rewriting History: The Life and Times of Pandita Ramabai*. New Delhi: Zubaan, 2006.

Chandavarkar, Rajnarayan. *History, Culture and the Indian City.* Cambridge: Cambridge University Press, 2009.
Chandavarkar, Rajnarayan. *Imperial Power and Popular Politics: Class, Resistance, and the State in India.* Cambridge: Cambridge University Press, 1998.
Chandavarkar, Rajnarayan. *The Origins of Industrial Capitalism in India: Business Strategies and the Working Classes in Bombay.* Cambridge: Cambridge University Press, 1994.
Chandavarkar, Rajnarayan. "Peasants and Proletarians in Bombay City in the Late Nineteenth and Early Twentieth Centuries." In *History, Culture and the Indian City,* 59–82. Cambridge: Cambridge University Press, 2009.
Chatterjee, Partha. "Our Modernity." South-South Exchange Programme for Research on the History of Development (SEPHIS) and the Council for the Development of Social Science Research in Africa (CODESRIA) Lecture No. 1, 1996. Rotterdam/Dakar: SEPHIS CODESRIA, 1997.
Clements, Ernest. *The Ragas of Hindustan.* 2 vols. Sangli: 1918, 1919.
Darukhanawala, H. D. *Parsi Lustre on Indian Soil.* Vol. 1. Bombay: G. Claridge, 1939.
Darukhanawala, H. D. *Parsi Lustre on Indian Soil.* Vol. 2. Bombay: G. Claridge, 1963.
Das Gupta, Amlan, ed. *Music and Modernity.* Kolkata: Thema, 2007.
Das Gupta, Amlan. "Rhythm and Rivalry." Review of *Two Men and Music: Nationalism in the Making of an Indian Classical Tradition,* by Janaki Bakhle. *Economic and Political Weekly* 41, no. 36 (September 9, 2006): 3861–63.
Deodhar, B. R. *Thor Sangeetkaar.* Bombay: Popular Prakashan, 1993.
Deshpande, Vamanrao H. *Between Two Tanpuras.* Translated by Ram Deshmukh and B. R. Dhekney. Bombay: Popular Prakashan, 1989.
Deshpande, Vamanrao H. *Indian Musical Traditions: An Aesthetic Study of the Gharanas in Hindustani Music.* Mumbai: Popular Prakashan, 1987.
Deshpande, Vamanrao H. *Maharashtra's Contribution to Music.* Bombay: Popular Prakashan, 1972.
Devidayal, Namita. *The Music Room.* New Delhi: Random House India, 2007.
Dhar, Sheila. *The Cooking of Music.* New Delhi: Permanent Black, 2001.
Dhar, Sheila. *"Here's Someone I'd Like You to Meet": Tales of Innocents, Musicians and Bureaucrats.* New Delhi: Oxford University Press, 1995.
Dobbin, Christine. *Urban Leadership in Western India: Politics and Communities in Bombay City, 1840–1885.* London: Oxford University Press, 1972.
Dossal, Mariam. *Imperial Designs and Indian Realities: The Planning of Bombay City, 1845–1875.* New York: Oxford University Press, 1991.
Douglas, James. *Bombay and Western India: A Series of Stray Papers.* 2 vols. London: Sampson Low, Marston, 1893.
Dwivedi, Sharada, and Rahul Mehrotra. *Bombay: The Cities Within.* Bombay: India Book House, 1995.
Edwardes, S. M. *By-ways of Bombay.* Bombay: D. B. Taraporevala, 1912.
Edwardes, S. M. *The Gazetteer of Bombay City and Island.* Bombay: Times Press, 1909.
Erdman, Joan, ed. *Arts Patronage in India: Methods, Motives and Markets.* New Delhi: Manohar, 1992.

Farooqui, Amar. *Opium City: The Making of Early Victorian Bombay*. Gurgaon: Three Essays Collective, 2006.
Farrell, Gerry. *Indian Music and the West*. Oxford: Oxford University Press, 1997.
Fisher, Michael. *Indirect Rule in India: Residents and the Residency System, 1764–1858*. Oxford: Oxford University Press, 1991.
Gaisberg, Fredrick. *The Music Goes Round*. New York: Macmillan, 1942.
Gazetteer of Bombay City and Island. 3 vols. Bombay: Times Press, 1909–10.
Gazetteer of the Bombay Presidency. Vol. 26, *Materials towards a Statistical Account of the Town and Island of Bombay*. 3 parts. Bombay: 1893–94.
Gokhale, Sharatchandra Vishnu. "Indian Music among the Parsis." In *The Parsis in Western India 1818–1920*, edited by Nawaz B. Mody, 235–47. Bombay: Allied, 1998.
Gordon, A. D. D. *Businessmen and Politics: Rising Nationalism and a Modernising Economy in Bombay, 1918–1933*. New Delhi: Manohar, 1978.
Grossberg, Lawrence. *Cultural Studies in the Future Tense*. Durham, NC: Duke University Press, 2010.
Gumperz, Ellen McDonald. "City-Hinterland Relations and the Development of a Regional Elite in Nineteenth Century Bombay." *Journal of Asian Studies* 33, no. 4 (1974): 581–604.
Gupt, Somnath. *The Parsi Theatre: Its Origins and Development*. Translated and edited by Kathryn Hansen. Calcutta: Seagull, 2005.
Hangal, Gangubai. *The Song of My Life*. Narrated by N. K. Kulkarni. Translated by G. N. Hangal. Hubli: Sahitya Prakashana, 2003.
Hansen, Kathryn. "Languages on Stage: Linguistic Pluralism and Community Formation in the Nineteenth-Century Parsi Theatre." *Modern Asian Studies* 37, no. 2 (2003): 381–405.
Hansen, Kathryn. "Parsi Theatre and the City: Locations, Patrons, Audiences." In *Sarai Reader 02: The Cities of Everyday Life*, edited by Ravi Sundaram et al., 40–49. New Delhi: Sarai, 2002.
Hansen, Kathryn. "Stri Bhumika: Female Impersonators and Actresses on the Parsi Stage." *Economic and Political Weekly* 33, no. 35 (August 29, 1998): 2291–2300.
Hansen, Thomas Blom. *Violence in Urban India: Identity Politics, "Mumbai," and the Postcolonial City*. New Delhi: Permanent Black, 2001.
Herlekar, V. M., and Purshottam Ganesh Gharpure. *Studies in Indian Music*. Bombay: 1889.
Houston, John, ed. *Representative Men of the Bombay Presidency*. Bombay: C. B. Burrows, Care William Watson, 1897.
Jalbhoy, R. H. *The Portrait Gallery of Western India*. Bombay: Education Society's Press, 1886.
Johnson, William. *The Oriental Races and Tribes, Residents and Visitors of Bombay: A Series of Photographs, with Letter-Press Descriptions*. 2 vols. London: 1863–66.
Joshi, G. N. "Music in Maharashtra." *Journal of the Indian Musicological Society* 1, no. 3 (1972): 5–12.
Kapileshwari, Balkrishnabuwa. *Abdul Karim Khan: The Man of the Times*. Self-published, 1973.

Karkaria, R. P., ed. *The Charm of Bombay: An Anthology of Writings in Praise of the First City in India*. Bombay: D. B. Taraporevala, 1915.

Karkaria, R. P. *India, Forty Years of Progress and Reform: A Sketch of the Life and Times of Behramji M. Malabari*. London: Henry Frowde, 1896.

Katz, Max. *Lineages of Loss: Counternarratives of North Indian Music*. Middletown, CT: Wesleyan University Press, 2017.

Kelkar, N. M. *Bhaskarbuwa Bakhle*. Mumbai: Karnatak Prakashan Samstha, 1967.

Keskar, B. V. *Indian Music: Problems and Prospects*. Bombay: Popular Prakashan, 1967.

Khan, Alladiya. *Sangeet Samrat Khansahab Alladiya Khan: My Life—As Told to His Grandson Azizuddin Khan*. Translated and introduced by Amlan Dasgupta and Urmila Bhirdikar. Calcutta: Thema, 2000.

Khan, Mobarak Hossain. *Islamic Contribution to South Asia's Classical Music*. New Delhi: Sterling, 1992.

Kinnear, Michael. *The Gramophone Company's First Indian Recordings 1899–1908*. Bombay: Popular Prakashan, 1994.

Kinnear, Michael. *Sangeet Ratna, the Jewel of Music: Khan Sahib Abdul Karim Khan, a Bio-discography*. Self-published, 2003.

Kobayashi, Eriko. "Hindustani Classical Music Reform Movement and the Writing of History, 1900s to 1940s." PhD diss., University of Texas, 2003.

Kosambi, Meera. *Bombay in Transition: The Growth and Social Ecology of a Colonial City 1880–1980*. Stockholm: Almqvist and Wiksell, 1986.

Kosambi, Meera. "British Bombay and Marathi Mumbai." In *Bombay: Mosaic of Modern Culture*, edited by S. Patel and A. Thorner, 3–24. New Delhi: Oxford University Press, 1995.

Kumar, Ravindra. *Western India in the Nineteenth Century: A Study in the Social History of Maharashtra*. London: Routledge, 1968.

Lakshmi, C. S. *The Singer and the Song*. New Delhi: Kali for Women, 2000.

Lobo, Antsher. *Three Monographs on Music*. Bombay: Indian Musicological Society, 1980.

Mahmood, Saba. *Politics of Piety: The Islamic Revival and the Feminist Subject*. Princeton, NJ: Princeton University Press, 2005.

Malabari, P. B. M. *Bombay in the Making: Being Mainly a History of the Origin and Growth of Judicial Institutions in the Western Presidency, 1661–1726*. London: T. Fisher Unwin, 1910.

Mansur, Mallikarjun. *Rasa Yatra: My Journey in Music*. Translated by Rajshekhar Mansur. New Delhi: Roli, 2005.

Masselos, Jim. "Appropriating Urban Space: Social Constructs of Bombay in the Time of the Raj." *South Asia: Journal of South Asian Studies* 14, no. 1 (1991): 33–63.

Masselos, Jim. *City in Action: Bombay Struggles for Power*. New Delhi: Oxford University Press, 2007.

Masselos, Jim. *Towards Nationalism: Group Affiliations and the Politics of Public Associations in Nineteenth Century Western India*. Bombay: Popular Prakashan, 1974.

Massey, Doreen. *For Space*. London: Sage, 2005.
McNeil, Adrian. "Generational Friction: An Ethnographic Perspective on *Guru Seva* within a Lineage of Tabla Players in Kolkata." *MUSICultures* 44, no. 1 (2017): 116–33.
Meer, Wim van der. "The Influence of Social Change in Indian Music." *World of Music* 20, no. 2 (1978): 123–34.
Mehrotra, Rahul, and Sharada Dwivedi. *Bombay: The Cities Within*. Mumbai: Eminence Designs, 2001.
Mehta, Kaiwan. *Alice in Bhuleshwar: Navigating a Mumbai Neighbourhood*. New Delhi: Yoda, 2009.
Mehta, Kaiwan. "The Terrain of Home and Within Urban Neighbourhoods: Case of the Bombay Chawls." In *The Chawls of Mumbai: Galleries of Life*, edited by Neera Adarkar, 81–88. New Delhi: ImprintOne, 2011.
Mishra, Amar. *Some Musical Memories*. New Delhi: Rupa, 2004.
Misra, Susheela. *Great Masters of Hindusthani Music*. New Delhi: HEM, 1981.
Misra, Susheela. *Music Makers of the Bhatkhande College of Hindusthani Music*. Calcutta: Sangeet Research Academy, 1985.
Misra, Susheela. *Music Profiles*. Lucknow: Bhatkhande Music College, 1960.
Mistry, Aban E. *The Parsis and Indian Classical Music: An Unsung Contribution*. Bombay: Swar Sadhna Samiti, 2004.
Mitter, Partha. "Architectural Planning and Other Building Activities of the British in Madras, Bombay and Calcutta c.1630–1757." In *The Rise and Growth of Colonial Port Cities in Asia*, edited by Dilip Basu. Berkeley: University of California Press, 1985.
Mitter, Partha. *Art and Nationalism in Colonial India, 1850–1922: Occidental Orientations*. Cambridge: Cambridge University Press, 1994.
Mody, J. R. P. *Jamsetjee Jeejeebhoy: The First Indian Knight and Baronet (1783–1859)*. Bombay: Mody, 1959.
Mody, Nawaz B., ed. *The Parsis in Western India: 1818–1920*. Bombay: Allied, 1998.
Morcom, Anna. *Courtesans, Bar Girls and Dancing Boys: The Illicit Worlds of Indian Dance*. Gurgaon: Hachette India, 2014.
Mote, H. V., ed. *Vishrabdha Sharada*. Vol. 2 (Theater and Music), in Marathi, with notes by Vasant S. Desai and Arvind Mangrulkar. Mumbai: H. V. Mote Prakashan, 1975.
Nadkarni, Mohan. *The Great Masters: Profiles in Hindustani Classical Vocal Music*. New Delhi: Harper Collins, 1999.
Nag, Dipali. *Ustad Faiyaaz Khan*. New Delhi: Sangeet Natak Akademi, 1985.
Narayan, Govind. *Govind Narayan's Mumbai: An Urban Biography from 1863*. Edited and translated by Murali Ranganathan. London: Anthem, 2012.
Naregal,Veena. *Language Politics, Elites, and the Public Sphere: Western India under Colonialism*. New Delhi: Permanent Black, 2001.
Natarajan, Srividya. "Another Stage in the Life of the Nation: Sadir, Bharatanatyam, Feminist Theory." PhD diss., University of Hyderabad, 1997.
Natesan, G. A. *Famous Parsis: Biographical and Critical Sketches*. Madras: 1930.

Natesan, G. A. *Old and New Bombay: A Historical and Descriptive Account of Bombay and Its Environs*. Bombay: G. Claridge, 1911.

Nayar, Sobhana. *Bhatkhande's Contribution to Music*. Bombay: Popular Prakashan, 1989.

Neuman, Daniel. "A *Khandani* Perspective: Room for a (Long) View." *MUSICultures* 44, no. 1 (2017): 210–34.

Neuman, Daniel. *The Life of Music in North India: The Organization of an Artistic Tradition*. Detroit: Wayne State University Press, 1980.

Neuman, Dard. "A House of Music: The Hindustani Musician and the Crafting of Traditions." PhD diss., Columbia University, 2004.

Neuman, Dard. "Pedagogy, Practice, and Embodied Creativity in Hindustani Music." *Ethnomusicology* 56, no. 3 (2012): 426–49.

Nightingale, Pamela. *Trade and Empire in Western India, 1784–1806*. Cambridge: Cambridge University Press, 1970.

Niranjana, Tejaswini. *Mobilizing India: Women, Music and Migration between India and Trinidad*. Durham, NC: Duke University Press, 2006.

Nowrozjee, Furdoonjee. *On the Civil Administration of the Bombay Presidency*. Bombay: Education Society's Press, 1853.

Owen, David Edward. *British Opium Policy in China and India*. New Haven, CT: Yale University Press, 1934.

Parikh, Arvind. *The Raga of My Life*. Mumbai: International Foundation for Fine Arts, 2002.

Parulekar, R. V., ed. *Selections from Education Records (Bombay) Part II: 1815–1840*. Bombay: Asia Publishing House, 1955.

Patel, Sujata, and Jim Masselos, eds. *Bombay and Mumbai: The City in Transition*. New Delhi: Oxford University Press, 2003.

Patel, Sujata, and Alice Thorner, eds. *Bombay: Metaphor for Modern India*. Bombay: Oxford University Press, 1995.

Patel, Sujata, and Alice Thorner, eds. *Bombay: Mosaic of Modern Culture*. New Delhi: Oxford University Press, 1995.

Pradhan, Aneesh. "Cultural Interaction and Social Change: The Contribution of the Parsi Gayan Uttejak Mandali to the Musical Life of Bombay." In *State Intervention and Popular Response: Western India in the Nineteenth Century*, edited by Mariam Dossal and Ruby Maloni, 63–76. Bombay: Popular Prakashan, 1999.

Pradhan, Aneesh. *Hindustani Music in Colonial Bombay*. Gurgaon: Three Essays Collective, 2014.

Prasad, M. Madhava. "Public Modernity: Some Issues." Review of *Consuming Modernity: Public Culture in a South Asian World*, edited by Carol Breckenridge. *Economic and Political Weekly* 33, no. 18 (May 2, 1998): 1020–23.

Purohit, Vinayak. *Arts of Transitional India*. 2 vols. Bombay: Popular Prakashan, 1988.

Quinn, Jennifer Post. "Marathi and Konkani-Speaking Women in Hindustani Music, 1880–1940." PhD diss., University of Minnesota, 1982.

Raghunathji, K. "Bombay's Dancing Girls." *Indian Antiquary* 13 (June 1884): 165–78.

Rahaim, Matthew. *Musicking Bodies: Gesture and Voice in Hindustani Music*. Middletown, CT: Wesleyan University Press, 2012.
Rai, Alok. *Hindi Nationalism: Tracts for the Times*. New Delhi: Sangam, 2001.
Raja, Deepak S. *The Raga-ness of Ragas: Ragas beyond the Grammar*. New Delhi: DK Printworld, 2016.
Ranade, Ashok D. *Hindustani Music*. New Delhi: National Book Trust, 1997.
Ranade, Ashok D. *Maharashtra's Art Music*. New Delhi: Maharashtra Information Centre, 1989.
Ranade, Ashok D. *Music and Drama*. New Delhi: Shriram Centre, 1992.
Ranade, Ashok D. "Music and Music Drama in Maharashtra." In *Hindustani Music: Thirteenth to Twentieth Centuries*, edited by Joep Bor, Francoise Nalini Delvoye, Jane Harvey, and Emmie Te Nijenhuis, 357–69. New Delhi: Manohar, 2010.
Ranade, Ashok D. *Stage Music of Maharashtra*. New Delhi: Sangeet Natak Akademi, 1986.
Ranade, G. H. *Maharashtra's Contribution to Music*. Bombay: 1965.
Rao, Jayavanth. *Sajan Piya: A Biography of Ustad Khadim Husain Khan*. Mumbai: Sajan Milap, 1981.
Rao, Subba. *Studies in Indian Music*. Bombay: Asia Publishing House, 1962.
Rosse, Michael David. "The Movement for the Revitalization of 'Hindu' Music in Northern India, 1860–1930: The Role of Associations and Institutions." PhD diss., University of Pennsylvania, 1995.
Rosse, Michael David. "Music Schools and Societies in Bombay, c. 1864–1937." In *Hindustani Music: Thirteenth to Twentieth Centuries*, edited by Joep Bor, Francoise Nalini Delvoye, Jane Harvey, and Emmie Te Nijenhuis, 313–29. New Delhi: Manohar, 2010.
Rothenberg, Molly Anne. *The Excessive Subject: A New Theory of Social Change*. Cambridge: Polity, 2010.
Sacks, Oliver. *Musicophilia: Tales of Music and the Brain*. New York: Knopf, 2007.
Sadhana, Paroma. "Compilation of Information on 'Bombay Movie Theatres.'" In *Project Cinema City*, edited by K. Bhaumik, M. Dutta, and R. Shivkumar, 150–51. New Delhi: Leftword, 2014.
Sahasrabuddhe, Balwant Trimbuck. *Hindu Music and the Gayan Samaj*. Poona: 1887.
Schultz, Anna. *Singing a Hindu Nation: Marathi Devotional Performance and Nationalism*. Oxford: Oxford University Press, 2012.
Shankar, Ravi. *My Music, My Life*. New Delhi: Vikas, 1968.
Sharma, Amal Das. *Musicians of India: Past and Present*. Calcutta: Naya Prakash, 1993.
Shastri, Gopal. "The Contributions Made by the Parsis to Gujarati Theatre." In *The Parsis in Western India: 1818–1920*, edited by Nawaz B. Mody, 221–34. Bombay: Allied, 1998.
Sheppard, Samuel T. *Bombay Place-Names and Street-Names: An Excursion into the By-ways of the History of Bombay City*. Bombay: Times Press, 1917.
Siddiqi, Asiya. "The Business World of Jamsetjee Jeejeebhoy." *Indian Economic and Social History Review* 19, nos. 3–4 (July 1982): 301–24.

Slawek, Stephen. Review of *Two Men and Music: Nationalism in the Making of an Indian Classical Tradition*, by Janaki Bakhle. *Ethnomusicology* 51, no. 3 (fall 2007): 506–12.

Soneji, Davesh. *Unfinished Gestures: Devadāsīs, Memory, and Modernity in South India*. Chicago: University of Chicago Press, 2012.

Stocqueler, J. H. *Memoirs of a Journalist*. Bombay: Times of India, 1873.

Stoler-Miller, Barbara, ed. *The Powers of Art: Patronage in Indian Culture*. New Delhi: Oxford University Press, 1992.

Subramanian, Lakshmi. *From the Tanjore Court to the Madras Music Academy: A Social History of Music in South India*. New Delhi: Oxford University Press, 2011.

Subramanian, Lakshmi. *New Mansions for Music: Performance, Pedagogy and Criticism*. Abingdon: Routledge and Social Science Press, 2018.

Subramanian, Lakshmi. *Three Merchants of Bombay: Doing Business in Times of Change*. New Delhi: Allen Lane, 2012.

Thatra, Geeta. "Contentious (Socio-spatial) Relations: Tawaifs and Congress House in Contemporary Bombay/Mumbai." *Indian Journal of Gender Studies* 23, no. 2 (2016): 197–217.

Tikekar, Aroon. "Dr. George Buist of the *Bombay Times*: A Study of the Self-Proclaimed Messianism of an Anglo-Indian Editor, 1840–57." In *Writers, Editors and Reformers*, edited by N. K. Wagle, 98–113. New Delhi: Manohar, 1999.

Tindall, Gillian. *City of Gold: The Biography of Bombay*. London: Penguin, 1982.

Trivedi, Madhu. "Music Patronage in the Indo-Persian Context: A Historical Overview." In *Hindustani Music: Thirteenth to Twentieth Centuries*, edited by Joep Bor, Francoise Nalini Delvoye, Jane Harvey, and Emmie Te Nijenhuis, 65–93. New Delhi: Manohar, 2010.

Urban Design Research Institute. *Mumbai Reader 07*. Mumbai: UDRI, 2008.

Vedak, G. S. *A Life Sketch of the Hon. Mr. Jagannath Shankerseth*. Bombay: 1937.

Wacha, D. E. *Shells from the Sands of Bombay*. Bombay: 1920.

Wade, Bonnie. *Khayal: Creativity within North India's Music Tradition*. Cambridge: Cambridge University Press, 1984.

Wade, Bonnie. *Music in India: The Classical Traditions*. Cambridge: Cambridge University Press, 1979.

Wagle, N. K., ed. *Writers, Editors and Reformers: Social and Political Transformations of Maharashtra, 1830–1930*. New Delhi: Manohar, 1999.

Weidman, Amanda J. *Singing the Classical, Voicing the Modern: The Postcolonial Politics of Music in South India*. Durham, NC: Duke University Press, 2006.

Index

Abhinavagupta, 87
Adarkar, Arvind, 65, 217n34
Allen, Matthew Harp, and T. Viswanathan, 205n1
Amonkar, Kishori, 38, 79, 84, 115
Appiah, Kwame Anthony, 8
Arolkar, Sharadchandra, 139, 141–43, 162–69, 180
Arondekar, Anjali, x, 11, 21, 208n4

Bakhle, Bhaskarbuwa, 17, 25, 30, 63, 65, 88, 110, 129
Bakhle, Janaki, 14, 26, 35, 94, 207n30, 213n50, 215n5, 219n16, 219n17, 220n25, 221n3
Balaporia, Jal, 122, 164, 165–67, 180
Bal Gandharva, 30, 48, 88, 89, 172
bar dancing, bar dancer, 40, 42, 43, 44, 45
Barodekar, Hirabai, 38, 48, 49–50, 60, 79, 91, 92, 208n6, 222n12
Bhagwat, Neela, ix, 7, 16, 139, 141–44, 161, 162–69, 170–73, 177–78, 180, 214n62, 223n22
Bhangwadi, 49, 67, 80–81, 83, 192
Bhat, S. C. R., 121, 180
Bhatkal, Ramdas, x, 94, 98–99, 120–22, 169, 180, 219n18, 220n27
Bhatkhande, V. N., 27, 33, 34, 35, 96, 130, 135, 137, 212n34, 225n17
Bhave, Vishnudas, 31
Bhirdikar, Urmila, x, 206n16, 208n6, 222n5
Blavatsky Lodge, 52–54
B. Merwan and Co. (Irani restaurant), 49, 83, 92
bodies in affect, 10, 88
Bombay Sangeet Kalakar Sangh, 49. *See also* NB Compound
Bor, Joep, 210n17

Bourdieu, Pierre, 11–12
Brahman Sabha, 20, 72, 74–76, 88, 90, 92, 188

Census of India, 1891, 209n10
Chatterjee, Partha, 8, 206n13
Chhatre, V. M., 28–29
Clements, Ernest, 4
Congress House, 32, 43, 48–49, 51–52, 59–60, 62, 63, 67, 88, 90, 94, 99, 188
Conlon, Frank, 220n29
Copland, Ian, 25
cultural vernacular, 38
cyber teaching, 174–78

Dabholkar, Satchit, x, 74
Dalal, Farzan, ix
Das Gupta, Amlan, x, 28, 208n6, 209n15, 211n26
Dastak [The Knock] (film), 181–84
Dastur, Firoz, 27, 52, 75, 76, 91, 96–77, 115–16, 136, 172, 180, 220n24
Deodhar, B. R., 27–28, 34, 52, 54–56, 59–60, 63, 94–95, 102, 114–15, 140–41, 180, 211n27, 211n28, 222n7
Deodhar School, 48, 50, 57, 91, 94, 102, 120, 121. *See also* School of Indian Music
Deshpande, Ashwini Bhide, x, 149, 180
Deshpande, Pu La, 67, 91, 93
Deshpande, Vamanrao, 89, 218n5, 222n7
Dhaneshwar, Amarendra, ix, 171, 213n50
Dhar, Sheila, 138–39, 222n20
Dharamsey, Virchand, 218n50
Diwanji, Batuk, 62
Dobbin, Christine, 208n7

Edwardes, S. M., 215n5
excessive subject, 6, 13, 17, 206n17

Farooqui, Amar, 209n9
Fernandes, Remo, 4
Framjee Cowasiee Institute, 49, 81–82, 83
Furber, Holden, 209n9

Gandharva Mahavidyalaya (GMV), 27, 54, 94, 130, 140–41, 195
Ganesh, Deepa, 222n10, 222n12
Ganesh Utsav, 49, 50, 52, 75, 80, 81, 88, 91, 93, 95, 98, 211n26, 217n48
Gangabai, 32, 62, 63, 67, 90, 94, 99, 102, 197
gayaki (singing style), 34, 156, 157, 169, 213n43
Gayan Uttejak Mandali (GUM), 30, 81, 94, 195
gharana, 16, 25, 34, 67, 106, 108, 132, 133, 146, 148, 149, 210n16, 222n7
Ghosh, Nayan, x, 62, 100–102, 180, 211n29, 212n42, 220n30
Ghosh, Nikhil, 28, 34, 62, 100–102, 176, 180, 212n42
Gogate, Sangeeta, x, 55, 57, 94, 210, 216n15
Gokhale, Shanta, 206n15
Gordon, A. D. D., 209n7
Grescoe, Taras, 215n4
Grossberg, Lawrence, 8
guru-shishya (ustad-shagird) (guru-disciple social relationship), 129, 130, 141, 161–64, 175

habitus (Bourdieu), 11–12
Haldankar, Babanrao, x, 17, 109, 180
Hangal, Gangubai, 7, 25, 79, 80, 91, 92, 133–38, 170, 180, 190
Hansen, Kathryn, 31, 36, 37, 211n31, 211n32, 212n36
Havaldar, Omkar, x, 7, 225n1

Ichalkaranjikar, Balakrishnabuwa, 33

Jairazbhoy, Nazir, 14
Joshi, Bhimsen, 30, 67, 80, 91, 107, 108, 113–17, 134, 137

Kabraji, K. N., 30, 33, 81, 82, 94
Katz, Max, 225n17
Kaikini, Dinkar, 34, 106, 152

Kaikini, Jayant, 206n15
Kapileshwari, Balkrishnabuwa, 77, 172
Kathak, 42, 55–56, 214n68
Kelkar, N. K., 211n30, 217n32
Kerkar, Kesarbai, 32, 115, 128, 129, 137, 145–48, 149, 150, 162, 180, 188, 208n6
Khan, Abdul Karim, 17, 25, 27, 33, 34, 38, 49, 52, 60, 77–80, 89, 91, 132, 134, 172, 188, 190, 195, 213n43
Khan, Alladiya, 30, 32, 38, 57, 88–89, 128, 129, 145–48, 149, 180, 209n15, 211n26
Khan, Amir, 32, 63, 90, 91, 99–100, 120, 172
Khan, Amir Hussain, 62, 63, 100, 212n42
Khan, Bade Ghulam Ali, 28, 32, 56–57, 62–63, 75, 91, 99, 102, 114, 211n27, 213n43
Khan, Bhurji, 145, 180
Khan, Faiyaz, 99, 120, 121, 152, 169, 170
Khan, Haddu, 29, 139, 223n22
Khan, Hassu, 139
Khan, Khadim Husain, 17, 56, 100, 109–10, 129, 132, 152–56, 170, 180, 208n2, 221n1, 221n35, 221n3
Khan, Manji, 57, 64
Khan, Natthan, 30, 32, 82, 83, 129, 212n38, 218n5
Khan, Nazir, 25, 83
Khan, Niyaz Ahmed, 138–39
Khan, Rahimat, 29, 211n28
Khan, Vilayat, 28, 74, 137, 157–61, 169–70, 180, 223n30, 224n2
Khan, Vilayat Hussain, 56, 75, 108
Khote, Durga, 30, 88–89, 96
Khudabuksh, Ghagge, 154–55, 223n29
Kilachand, Nilima, 88, 95, 106, 107–10, 220n35, 221n36
Kobayashi, Eriko, 35
Kulkarni, Dhondutai, x, 7, 16, 128, 129, 145–51, 162, 180, 188
Kumar Gandharva, 57, 59, 60, 80, 84, 114, 134, 217n26
Kurdikar, Mogubai, 32, 38, 79, 137, 180

Lad, Rutuja, ix, 149–52, 174, 180, 188, 211n27, 217n32
Laxmi Baug, x, 20, 49, 56, 73, 74–76, 84, 88, 90, 93, 119, 120, 188
lingua musica, 36–38, 87

Making Music Making Space (exhibition), 17, 21, 208n5
Malpekar, Anjanibai, 32, 83–85, 94, 218n54
Mansur, Mallikarjun, 25, 30, 57, 58, 64, 91, 107, 113, 134, 180
Manuel, Peter, 212n32
Masselos, Jim, 209n12
Massey, Doreen, 47, 215n1
Master Krishnarao, 30, 31, 92
McNeil, Adrian, 223n1
mehfil, 15, 28, 34, 46, 56, 59, 62, 63, 79, 81, 84, 89, 90, 93, 99, 101, 107, 108, 140, 184
Mehta, Kaiwan, ix, 64, 80, 185, 217n33, 217n35, 218n50
Merchant, Kishor, x, 112–14
metropolitan unconscious, 10–12, 17, 21, 26, 29, 37, 48, 67, 128, 130, 131, 133, 179, 184, 186, 188
Mewada, Chandrakant Ramjibhai (Chandubhai), x, 63, 67–72, 86, 102–6, 217n40
Miner, Allyn, 210n17
Mistry, Aban E., 122, 212n37
Morcom, Anna, 208n6, 214n65, 225n3, 226n12
Mote, H. V., 214n55
mujra, 39, 40–44
mujra hall, 38, 40, 41, 43, 51, 52, 59, 183, 197, 202
musical archive, 12, 27, 39, 67, 131
musical interiority, 6, 8, 16, 86, 93, 131
musical persistence, 27
musical precinct, 75–76
musicophilia, 6, 7–11, 13–15, 20–21, 24, 30, 35, 39, 45–46, 47, 72, 114, 137, 154, 161, 183–86, 192; and lingua musica, 36–38; and modernity, 26; social subject of, 26, 163, 188, 197; and social transgression, 102, 183; and space, 185, 188
music pedagogy, 15–16, 34–35, 47, 128–61, 215n11, 221n3, 223n29, 224n13
music school, 13, 20, 34, 37, 38, 47, 52, 97, 98, 130, 141, 143, 153, 161, 179, 183, 192, 213n50, 214n52, 221n3, 222n5
Muzaffarabad Hall, 20, 83–84

Nadkarni, Mohan, 212n39
Nag, Dipali, 210n17
Nagarkar, Kiran, 206n15
Naik, Ramrao, 152, 180
Narayan, Govind, 209n9
Natarajan, Srividya, 205n1
national modern, 12
Nayar, Sobhana, 212n34
NB Compound, 43, 44, 59–63, 88, 90, 94, 99, 100, 102, 183, 196–97, 226n12
Neuman, Daniel, 14, 129, 133, 144, 205n2
Neuman, Dard, 159, 213n49, 223n29
notation, 33–34, 81, 96, 134, 135, 137–38, 141, 143, 150, 156–57, 166, 177–79, 225n17; in Carnatic music, 143, 150; tensions around, 143

Opera House (Royal Opera House), 48–50, 51, 52, 58, 60

Paluskar, D. V., 117, 139–41, 180
Paluskar, Vishnu Digambar, 27, 33, 49, 54, 56, 91, 94, 114, 130, 139, 140, 213n50, 219n16, 219n17
Pandit, Krishnarao Shankar, 139, 141–43, 223n22, 223n24, 223n25
Parekh, Bhikhu, 218n48
Parikh, Arvind, 28, 56, 74, 90–91, 93, 137, 157–61, 169–70, 171, 180, 210n18, 216n20, 224n2, 224n4
Patel, Simin, 220n24
Pathak, Saroj, 206n15
performance, 15, 20, 28, 29, 34, 35, 44, 46, 47, 48, 59, 60, 67, 69, 83, 93, 130–31, 140, 143, 162, 190; of modernity, 7, 12–13, 20, 30, 184; spaces of, 19, 52, 59, 65, 74, 87
Phir se Samm pe Aana (*Returning to the First Beat*) (film), 188, 207n32
pradarshan (exhibition), 13, 184
Pradhan, Aneesh, x, 14, 128, 170, 172, 173–74, 176–77, 180, 208n6, 212n38, 212n41, 213n46, 217n36, 221n3, 222n5
Prarthana Samaj, 55, 94–95, 192
Prasad, M. Madhava, 8, 9, 182–83
Puranik, Kalyani, x, 77, 79, 188

Quinn, Jennifer Post, 212n38
Qureshi, Regula Burckhardt, 211n32

Raghunathji, K., 208n6, 215n68
Rai, Alok, 225n8
Raja, Deepak, x, 207n28, 210n19, 218n1, 218n2
Rajadhyaksha, Ashish, 29–30
Ranade, Ashok, 30–31, 34, 207n28, 210n19
Ratanjankar, Srikrishna, 34
Rao, Jayavanth, x, 109, 129, 152, 153, 169
Rao, Lalith, x, 100, 108–10, 117, 152–57, 175–76, 179, 180, 218n52, 221n36
riyaaz, 7, 17, 28, 34, 64, 129, 149, 152, 162, 179, 188
Rosse, Michael, 33, 35, 213n50
Rothenberg, Molly Anne, 12, 206n17
Roy, Jeff, 175, 224n13

Sabnavis, Farida, x, 122–26, 221n41
Sacks, Oliver, 205n6
Sadhana, Paroma, 218n50
Sanjeev Kumar (Haribhai), 102, 181, 225n2
Sanzgiri, Girish, x, 75, 171
Saraswati Sangeet Vidyalay, 72, 78, 188, 195
Sathe, Sharad, x, 106, 139–41, 170–71, 180
Sawai Gandharva, 27, 30, 75, 76, 91, 92, 97, 115, 134, 135–37, 138, 172, 180
School of Indian Music, 33, 49, 52, 54–57, 94, 97, 114, 140–41, 215n12. *See also* Deodhar School
Schultz, Anna, 210n17
Seth, Niharika, 223n32
Shah, Vidya, 218n54
Shankar, Ravi, 1, 2, 57, 67, 158, 216n17
Sharma, Surabhi, ix, 46, 185–86, 197, 216n15, 225n4
Sheikh, Samira, 226n9
Shirodkar, Nitin, x, 74–75, 96, 97, 115–17, 188, 216n17, 217n45
Shukla, Murli Manohar, x, 89, 98, 99–100, 102, 116–20

sina-basina teaching, ix, 130, 161, 174, 179
Slawek, Stephen, 28, 210n23, 210n24
social subject, 10, 12, 13, 17, 26, 29, 36, 39, 67, 86, 92, 127, 129, 163, 184, 188, 197, 206n17, 206n18
Soneji, Davesh, 205n1
sonic materiality, 131
Steiner, Rudolf, 215n9
Subramanian, Lakshmi, 14, 130, 205n1, 207n29, 208n7, 215n11
Sukthankar, Dhaklibai, 96
Sultana, Rehana, 181
Sundar, Pushpa, 209n14
Sundararajan, Sonal, ix, 185, 192, 225n6

Tagore, Rabindranath, 39
taleem, 7, 16, 28, 30, 34, 57, 64, 97, 106, 128–38, 140–41, 145, 147, 149–50, 152–53, 160, 169, 170, 177–78, 179, 183, 184, 212n38
Talmakiwadi, 76, 118
Tembe, Govindrao, 17, 88, 93, 190, 219n15
Thakur, Dayalsingh, 88, 90, 93, 197
Thatra, Geeta, 217n28, 225n12
Tikekar, Balasaheb, x, 65, 66, 110–12, 217n37
Trinity Club, 56, 63–64, 65–68, 72, 75, 95, 110–12, 185, 188, 195, 217n36, 217n38
Trivedi, Madhu, 208n1

Vellani, Anmol, x, 138, 222n19
Vishrabdha Sharada (Mote), 214n55

Wade, Bonnie C., 207n27
Weidman, Amanda, 14, 143, 150, 159, 174, 175
Wessinger, Catherine, 215n10
Williams, Raymond, 20, 208n3
Willmer, David, 21

www.ingramcontent.com/pod-product-compliance
Lightning Source LLC
Chambersburg PA
CBHW070759230426
43665CB00017B/2418